The Chinese Armed Forces Today

The Chinese Armed Forces Today

The U.S. Defense
Intelligence Agency Handbook
of China's Army, Navy
and Air Force

PRENTICE-HALL, INC.,
Englewood Cliffs, N.J.

First American edition published by
Prentice-Hall, 1979.

ISBN 0-13-132902-2
Library of Congress Catalog Card Number
79-84841

The Chinese Armed Forces Today is reproduced
from Handbook on the Chinese Armed Forces
(DD1-2680-32-76) produced by the U.S. Defense
Intelligence Agency, Washington, 1976.

Printed in Great Britain.

TABLE OF CONTENTS

CHAPTER 1–THE PEOPLES LIBERATION ARMY AND GROUND FORCES ORDER OF BATTLE

Section I–Roles, Composition, Historical Development, Doctrine, and Nature of Combat

Section II–Ground Forces Order of Battle

CHAPTER 2–ORGANIZATION AND EQUIPMENT

Section I–Organization

Section II–Equipment

CHAPTER 3–THE BASIS OF CHINESE TACTICS

CHAPTER 4–PHASES OF WAR AND SPECIALIZED WARFARE

Section II—River Crossing

Section III—Defensive Operations

Section IV—Retrograde Operations

Section V—Airborne Operations

Section VI—Warfare under Special Conditions

CHAPTER 5—LOGISTICS AND PERSONNEL

Section I—Logistics

CHAPTER 8–CHINESE MISSILE SYSTEMS

CHAPTER 9–THE POLITICAL STRUCTURE OF THE PEOPLES LIBERATION ARMY

CHAPTER 10–UNIFORMS AND INSIGNIA–AWARDS AND DECORATIONS

Section I–Uniforms and Insignia

Section II–Awards and Decorations

ANNEXES

CHAPTER 1
THE PEOPLES LIBERATION ARMY AND GROUND FORCES ORDER OF BATTLE

SECTION I–ROLES, COMPOSITION, HISTORICAL DEVELOPMENT, DOCTRINE, AND NATURE OF COMBAT

Chinese Armed Forces

1-1. The Peoples Liberation Army (PLA)–the collective name for the armed forces of the Peoples Republic of China (PRC)–is the world's largest military force. The PLA, which encompasses the army, the navy, and the air force, has a total strength of about 4 million men. The ground forces total some 3.5 million men or about 85 percent of the PLA's total manpower. The navy and air force, though significantly smaller, are the largest in Asia and the third largest in the world.

Roles

1-2. The deployment, composition and size of Chinese armed forces are dictated by their roles which are:

   a. To defend the Chinese Communist Party.
   b. To defend the territory of the PRC.
   c. To deter attack by any nation and, should deterrence fail, to bring any war to a conclusion favorable to the PRC.
   d. To assist in the maintenance of internal security.
   e. To engage in production and construction work and aid in the national development of the PRC.
   f. To support the foreign policy objectives of the PRC.

Composition

1-3. The Chinese armed forces consist of the Peoples Liberation Army and the Paramilitary.

   a. The Peoples Liberation Army includes:
      (1) The Army–PRCA.
      (2) The Navy–PRCN.
      (3) The Air Force–PRCAF.
   b. The Paramilitary includes:
      (1) The Militia.
      (2) The Production and Construction Corps–PCC.[1]

1-4. The PLA is controlled by the Military Commission (MC) of the Chinese Communist Party through General Departments and consists of the following services:

   a. Ground forces.
   b. Air forces (includes air defense).

---

[1] The PCC, although a paramilitary force, is officially part of the PLA.

    c. Naval forces (includes naval air force).
    d. Missile forces.

Historical Development

1-5. The birthplace of the Peoples Liberation Army is Nanchang where on 1 August 1927 some 30,000 Communists and dissidents of Chiang Kai-shek's National Revolutionary Army revolted against the central government in Nanking. While the insurrection was unsuccessful, it marked the beginning of the armed struggle for political power between the Chinese Communists and the Kuomintang (KMT).[2]

1-6. During the period 1930-34, the Nationalists undertook five major "annihilation campaigns" against the Communist forces in Kiangsi Province. They finally succeeded in encircling the Communists but in October 1934 Mao Tsetung and the First Front Army broke through the encirclement and, together with forces from other areas, began the epic 6,000-mile "Long March," which ended one year later in Yenan, Shensi Province.

1-7. The political struggle between the Nationalists and the Communists continued in a desultory manner despite efforts by Mao to bring the fighting to an end and unite with the Nationalists in an attempt to halt Japanese aggression in China which had begun in 1931. It was not until 1937 that the Nationalists agreed to join the Communists in a "united front." Ostensibly integrated with the Nationalist Army to fight the Japanese, the Communists concentrated on winning over the people, integrating military and civilian activities, and setting up base areas from which to mount guerrilla operations. Mao's policy essentially was to conserve the strength of his army and avoid decisive engagements while consolidating his political power. It has been described as 70 percent expansion, 20 percent skirmishing with the Nationalists, and 10 percent fighting the Japanese.

1-8. The Japanese surrender in August 1945 precipitated a race between the Nationalists and Communists for control of the mainland. The Communists, under Lin Piao, moved an estimated 100,000 troops into the prized area of Manchuria where they made contact with the Soviet forces which had accepted the surrender of the Japanese Kwantung Army. Following the Soviet withdrawal in 1946, large stocks of Japanese arms and equipment, including heavy artillery, armor and some aircraft, were allowed to fall into the hands of the Communist forces, by then renamed the Chinese Peoples Liberation Army (PLA).

1-9. Civil war was renewed in July 1946 after negotiations failed to produce a political settlement. The general situation at that time was one in which the Nationalists secured the cities and main lines of communication, while the Communists controlled the countryside and waged a war of attrition. The strength of the Communist forces had grown to over one million men, with a militia of about 2 million. During the summer of 1947, the PLA embarked upon large-scale offensive operations against the Nationalists destroying their forces

---

[2] The Kuomintang (or Nationalist Party) was founded in 1912 following the collapse of the Ching Dynasty in 1911. Chiang Kai-shek had assumed leadership of the Kuomintang upon the death of Sun Yat-sen, one of its founders, in 1925.

piecemeal through a combination of guerrilla and conventional warfare. Following the fall of Peking in January 1949, Nationalist resistance virtually collapsed. In March of that year, the PLA crossed the Yangtze River and captured Nanking; a month later Shanghai fell. In August, the Nationalist government withdrew to Taiwan (Formosa). On 1 October 1949 the Peoples Republic of China (PRC) was founded.

1-10. The Chinese Communist Army of 1949 was basically a peasant-infantry force organized and trained mainly for guerrilla-type operations in which conventional military science and technology played a lesser role. Its firepower, mobility, communications, and logistics were limited and for the most part archaic. The PRC clearly recognized the need to modernize its military establishment. This modernization process was initiated with the signing of the 1950 Treaty of Friendship, Alliance, and Mutual Assistance between China and the Soviet Union. Additional impetus to the PLA's modernization process was provided by its experiences in the Korean War, which the PLA entered in October 1950 under the aegis of the Chinese Peoples Volunteers. In Korea, initial successes aside, the Chinese quickly learned that in the offensive, unsupported massed infantry attacks ("human wave tactics") against vastly superior firepower were not only unavailing but in most cases led to disastrously high losses in personnel and equipment. Furthermore, to avoid the possibility of United Nations forces entering the PRC proper, the Chinese found themselves in a situation in which they were unable to employ the *Peoples War* doctrine of strategic retreat (see paragraph 1-18). They were no longer able to trade space for time as they had done in the past in the vast heartland of China. For the first time, they were forced to assume a form of defense previously abhorrent to them—a linear, positional defense.

1-11. Taking advantage of the provisions of the 1950 Sino-Soviet Treaty and of the Soviet advice and assistance furnished during the Korean War, the Chinese leadership decided to modernize the PLA generally along the lines of the Soviet model, utilizing Soviet tables of organization and equipment (TOE) and the combined-arms concept of armor- and artillery-heavy mobile forces. It should be pointed out that these "foreign" concepts were accepted and implemented in the light of the *Thoughts of Mao Tsetung* and as they pertained to the peculiar circumstances and conditions in China. However, the deepening of the Sino-Soviet dispute, followed by the total withdrawal of Soviet aid and technicians in 1960, forced the Chinese to chart a course of military self-reliance—which continues today.

1-12. During the mid and late 1950's, Chinese relations with India slowly deteriorated due in part to conflicting claims over nearly 40,000 square miles of territory that India regarded as its own. This territory included virtually the whole North East Frontier Agency (NEFA) of Assam and parts of Ladakh, particularly the area of Aksai Chin through which China had constructed a highway in 1957 linking Tibet and Sinkiang. In October 1962, following mutual allegations of frontier intrusions, the Chinese launched large-scale attacks in the NEFA and Ladakh. While Chinese forces penetrated as far down as the foothills of the Himalayas in the western sector of NEFA, they made only limited penetrations into the eastern sector and refrained from entering the plains of India, remaining within the territory claimed by China. On 21 November 1962,

Peking announced a unilateral cease-fire and began withdrawing its troops back to the original line of actual control which prevailed before they launched their attacks. (See map, figure 1).

1-13. During the Great Proletarian Cultural Revolution (1966-69) the PLA emerged as the dominant and most stable political power group in China. The PLA assumed a major role as leader and administrator in both party and governmental affairs, as well as in economic matters. This preeminence passed with the demise of Lin Piao in late 1971, although military influence in China's sociopolitical life remains extensive.

1-14. The signing of the 1966 Soviet-Mongolian Treaty of Friendship, Cooperation and Mutual Assistance, the extensive buildup of Soviet forces along the Sino-Soviet border, the enunciation of the Brezhnev Doctrine in 1968, coupled with border tensions which resulted in a series of clashes in the Amur-Ussuri border areas in 1969, brought home to the Chinese the real dangers of the Soviet threat. A concentrated effort followed to strengthen defenses at home together with a worldwide political campaign to counter Soviet influence abroad.

1-15. In January 1974 the PRC occupied the Crescent Group of the Paracel Islands following naval engagements between Chinese and South Vietnamese forces. This was only the second successful joint amphibious operation undertaken by the PLA, the first being against Nationalist-held I Ching Shan Island off Chekiang Province in January 1955.

Doctrine

1-16. China's current official military doctrine is founded on the *Military Thoughts of Mao Tsetung*. It is the product of nearly 50 years of military experience under the most varied conditions. It incorporates the concepts of numerous military strategists—from Sun Tzu (*The Art of War*, circa 350 B.C.) through Napoleon and Clausewitz to those of modern times—as well as the lessons learned from the peasant revolutions of 18th and 19th century China. In addition, Mao's military doctrine has assimilated some innovations derived from the conventional and nuclear technology of the present era.

1-17. The Peoples Republic of China maintains two major military doctrines:

    a. Peoples War
    b. Wars of National Liberation.

1-18. *Peoples War.* Peoples War is the doctrine for the defense of China against various types of warfare ranging from a surprise long-range nuclear strike combined with a massive ground invasion to a conventional ground attack with limited objectives. In peoples war, the army and paramilitary forces, supported by the populace, would conduct a protracted war against an invader. Initially the Chinese main forces, using conventional tactics, would carry out a strategic withdrawal supported by guerrilla-type operations until the invading forces were overextended and dispersed. When this occurred, overwhelming Chinese forces would be concentrated to annihilate the enemy forces in detail.

1-19. In recent years, there have been changes in Chinese training and organization which are indicative of a swing away from the guerrilla-type concept of peoples war towards improving their existing capability for

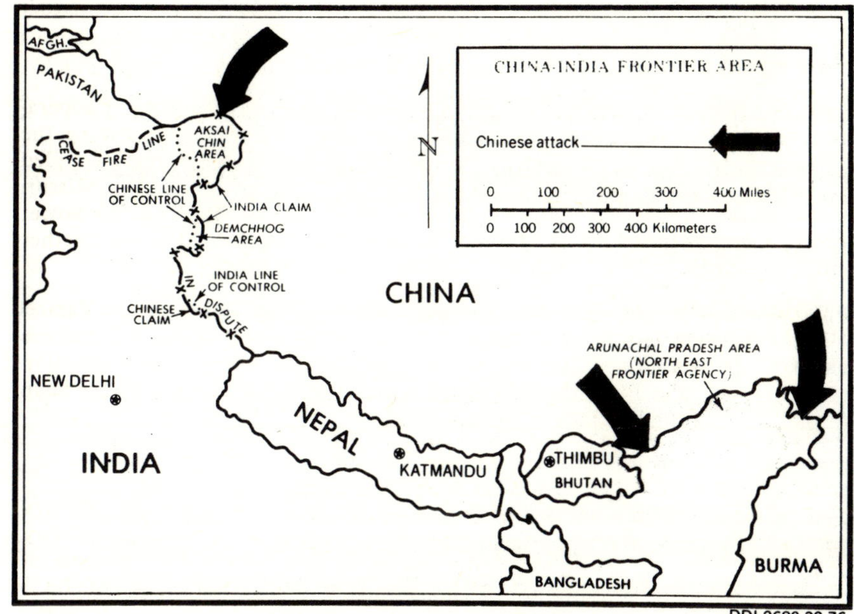

Figure 1. China-India Frontier Area.

conventional operations. It appears that while the strategic doctrine for the defense of China remains based generally on peoples war, the concept of conventional positional-type defense, as recognized by the Western nations, has been accepted as essential for the protection of the political and industrialized areas. Nevertheless, this does not negate the central thesis which is: *territory has no relevance. The enemy will be permitted to enter so that all forces, military and paramilitary, and the ordinary people can participate in the defense of their country and the ultimate destruction of the enemy.*

1-20. *Wars of National Liberation.* This is a revolutionary doctrine which is exported to indigenous, insurgent movements outside of China. It is essentially an offensive doctrine aimed at the seizure and maintenance of political power. In their support of "wars of national liberation," the Chinese do not necessarily promise or provide direct military aid. While political and ideological encouragement is given, the emphasis is on self-reliance as the only way to victory.

Nature of Combat

1-21. Chinese ground forces have the capability, although limited in some cases due to lack of technical knowledge and equipment, to carry out all forms of conventional operations from guerrilla-type warfare to combined operations using massed armor.

1-22. *Nuclear Operations.* Though there is no confirmed doctrine on nuclear warfare, the Chinese are well aware that the advent of nuclear weapons has generated many new features in warfare, and they appear to have the necessary training and knowledge to lessen the effects of nuclear weapons employed against them. Chinese nuclear weapons apparently are intended to serve as a deterrent to any would-be aggressor: that China has them, it is hoped, will keep any conflict at a conventional level. If faced with defeat, however, China possibly would decide to use its nuclear weapons.

1-23. *Chemical Operations.* There is no confirmed Chinese doctrine on the offensive use of chemical weapons. However, as China has the technical knowledge to develop modern chemical agents and to add to supplies of older toxic and nontoxic agents, an offensive capability undoubtedly exists. The current organization of antichemical warfare units and training against chemical attack conducted by both the military and the civilian populace would indicate the existence of a defensive doctrine against chemical warfare.

1-24. *Biological Operations.* Although little is known about PRC's *state of the art* concerning biological warfare (BW), it is probable that its BW doctrine is similar to that of chemical warfare. There are reports of BW defensive preparations and of installations which are engaged in research and development of biological agents.

1-25. *Radiological Operations.* Since nuclear reactors are available which can produce large quantities of radioactive waste, the PRC probably has contingency plans for spreading such waste along major avenues of approach into China to slow invading forces. However, there is little specific information on employment doctrine.

1-26–1-30. *Reserved.*

PARADE DRESS
UNIFORM

WINTER PARADE
DRESS UNIFORM

SERVICE DRESS
UNIFORM

SUMMER FIELD
DRESS UNIFORM

CAP INSIGNIA

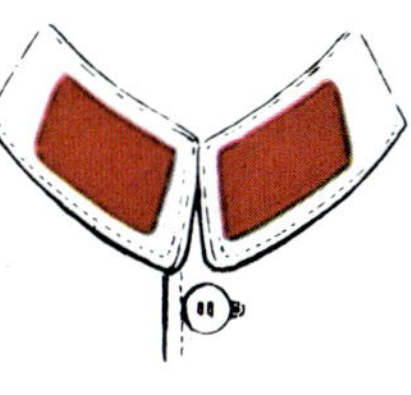

COLLAR TABS

WINTER FIELD
DRESS UNIFORM
(COMBAT)

WINTER FIELD
DRESS UNIFORM

ARMY OFFICERS UNIFORMS AND INSIGNIA.

PARADE DRESS
UNIFORM

WINTER PARADE
DRESS UNIFORM

SERVICE DRESS
UNIFORM

CAP INSIGNIA

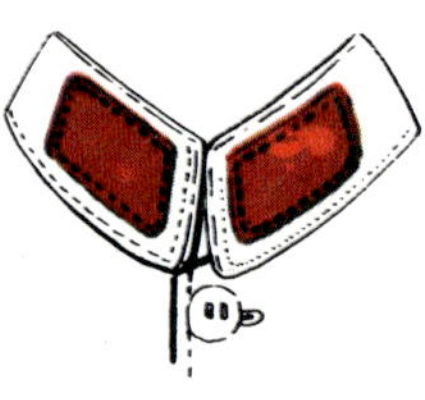

COLLAR TABS

SERVICE DRESS
UNIFORM

ARMY ENLISTED UNIFORMS AND INSIGNIA.

SUMMER FIELD
DRESS UNIFORM

SUMMER FIELD
DRESS UNIFORM
(COMBAT)

WINTER FIELD
DRESS UNIFORM

WINTER FIELD
DRESS UNIFORM

CAP INSIGNIA

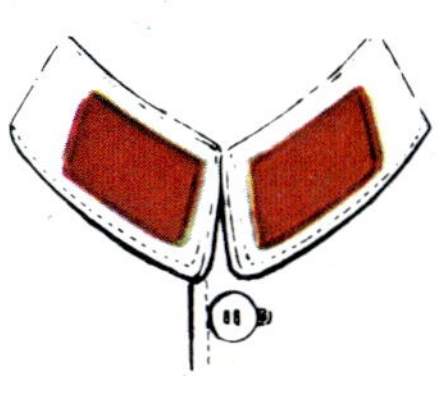

COLLAR TABS

CHEMICAL
PROTECTIVE UNIFORM

ARMY ENLISTED UNIFORMS AND INSIGNIA.

PARADE DRESS
UNIFORM
AFLOAT

CAP INSIGNIA

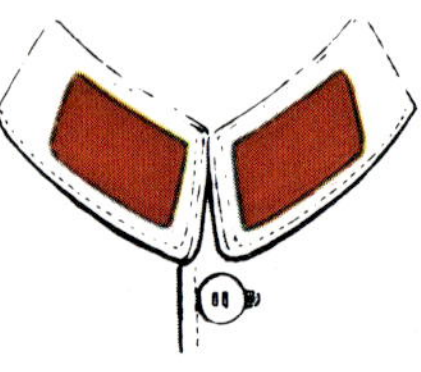

COLLAR TABS

WINTER PARADE
DRESS UNIFORM
AFLOAT

SERVICE DRESS
UNIFORM
AFLOAT

SUMMER SERVICE
DRESS UNIFORM
AFLOAT

SUMMER FIELD
DRESS UNIFORM
SHORE-BASED

WINTER FIELD
DRESS UNIFORM
SHORE-BASED

NAVAL OFFICERS UNIFORMS AND INSIGNIA.

WINTER SERVICE
DRESS UNIFORM
AFLOAT

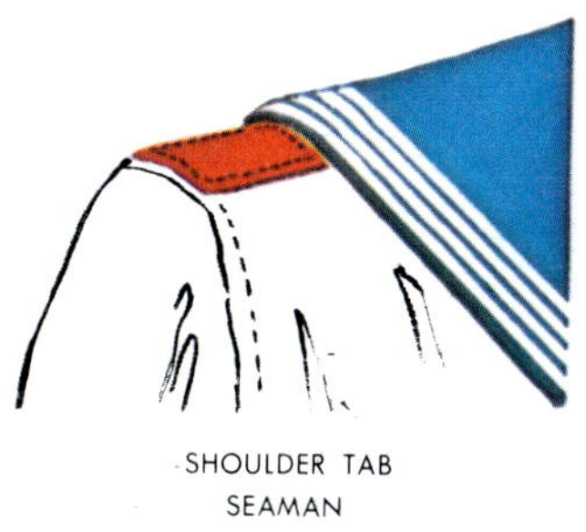

SHOULDER TAB
SEAMAN

SUMMER SERVICE
DRESS UNIFORM
AFLOAT

CAP INSIGNIA

CAP BAND INSIGNIA SEAMAN
CHINESE PEOPLE'S LIBERATION ARMY   NAVY

WORK UNIFORM
AFLOAT

NAVAL ENLISTED UNIFORMS AND INSIGNIA.

PARADE DRESS
UNIFORM
SHORE-BASED

WINTER PARADE
DRESS UNIFORM
SHORE-BASED

SERVICE DRESS
UNIFORM
SHORE-BASED

SUMMER SERVICE
DRESS UNIFORM
SHORE-BASED AND AVIATION

WINTER SERVICE
DRESS UNIFORM
SHORE-BASED AND AVIATION

SUMMER SERVICE
DRESS UNIFORM

NAVAL ENLISTED UNIFORMS.

**SUMMER SERVICE
DRESS UNIFORM**
OFFICER

**SUMMER FIELD
DRESS UNIFORM**
OFFICER

**SUMMER SERVICE
DRESS UNIFORM**
OFFICER AND ENLISTED

**SUMMER SERVICE
DRESS UNIFORM**
ENLISTED

WORK UNIFORM
ENLISTED

**PILOT
UNIFORM**
MALE

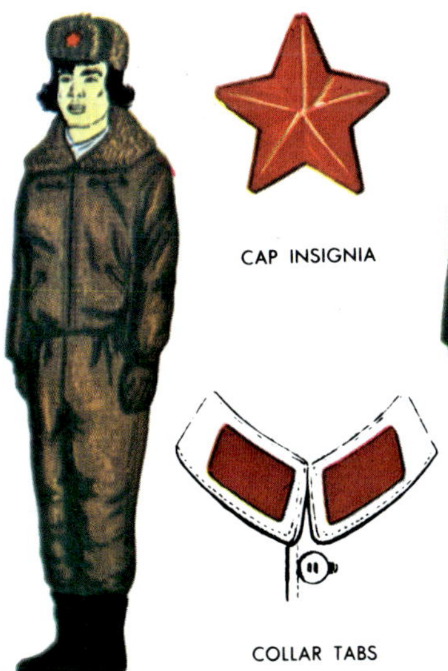

CAP INSIGNIA

COLLAR TABS

**WINTER FLIGHT
UNIFORM**
FEMALE

**SERVICE
UNIFORM**

**PARATROOPER
UNIFORM**

AIR FORCE UNIFORMS AND INSIGNIA.

CAP INSIGNIA
(ARTIST'S CONCEPTION)

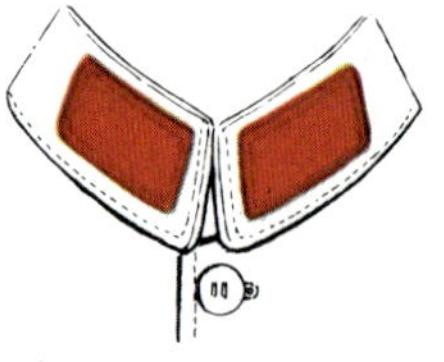

COLLAR TABS

SUMMER SERVICE
DRESS UNIFORM

TRAFFIC CONTROL POLICE

SUMMER/WINTER
SERVICE DRESS UNIFORM

BORDER POLICE, FORESTRY POLICE,
RAILWAY TRANSPORTATION POLICE,
AND FIRE FIGHTER POLICE.

SUMMER SERVICE
DRESS UNIFORM

PUBLIC SECURITY BUREAU UNIFORMS AND INSIGNIA. (PEOPLE'S POLICE)

"GOOD-IN-FIVE" SOLDIER
(OVAL DESIGN)

"GOOD-IN-FIVE" SOLDIER
(PENTAGONAL DESIGN)

REENLISTMENT BADGE

PEACE MEDAL

MODEL SOLDIER

MAO TSE-TUNG BADGE
(PENTAGONAL DESIGN)

MAO TSE-TUNG BADGE
(ROUND DESIGN)

CHINESE PEOPLE'S LIBERATION ARMY BADGES

SECTION II–GROUND FORCES[3] ORDER OF BATTLE

Chinese Ground Forces

1-31. The present structure of the ground forces reflects operational concepts adopted some years ago which envision large numbers of divisions being employed in conjunction with vast paramilitary forces in the defense of the PRC against an all-out attack. The PRCA is predominantly an infantry force; it does, however, possess a number of armored, artillery, antitank, antiaircraft and railway engineer divisions.

1-32. The ground forces consist of combat, combat support, and combat service support units in 250+ divisions and 200+ independent regiments of all types. The main combat power is found in the 130-140 regular main force divisions (118-125 infantry, 9-12 armor, 3 airborne-air transportable) and in the 70-odd smaller sized border defense, garrison and internal defense divisions. The 35+ artillery divisions (field artillery, antitank and antiaircraft) together with engineer, signal, and antichemical regiments and smaller units provide combat support. The combat service support railway engineer divisions, motor transport regiments and other logistical-type units balance out the ground forces.

Subordination to Military Regions

1-33. Territorially, the PRC is divided into 11 military regions (see map, figure 2).

1-34. The military regions are responsible for the command and control operations of most ground forces in their geographical areas.

Strength and Mobilization

1-35. Despite the costly development of Chinese strategic attack and defense forces, the Chinese ground forces remain the largest element of the military establishment.

1-36. The Chinese ground forces consist of some 3,500,000 men. This total does not include the paramilitary forces.

1-37. While no specific plans are known, it appears that Chinese mobilization is based on the militia which has as one of its roles the provision of a reserve of trained manpower for the PRCA. The militia also maintains a pool of labor for logistic purposes.

Foreign Military Agreements

1-38. The 30-year Sino-Soviet Treaty of Friendship, Alliance and Mutual Assistance, signed in 1950, no longer appears to be in force. The Chinese have a mutual defense agreement with North Korea, signed in 1961, which provides for military aid to the Koreans.

1-39. The PRC has nonaggression pacts with Afghanistan, Burma and Cambodia.

---

[3] Navy and air force are discussed in chapters 6 and 7.

1-40. The PRC has given military equipment and logistic support to an increasing number of countries, particularly in Africa. Major recipients of arms in recent years have been Albania, Pakistan and Tanzania.

1-41. Road construction and supporting troops, totaling 10,000 to 20,000 men, are deployed in Laos. In addition there is evidence of Chinese troops supporting the insurgency in Burma. There are also some Chinese railway engineers employed in Tanzania.

1-42—1-50. *Reserved.*

Figure 2. Military Regions.

DDI-2680-32-76

CHAPTER 2
ORGANIZATION AND EQUIPMENT

SECTION I–ORGANIZATION

The Chinese High Command

2-1.   Command and control of the PLA is exercised by the Military Commission (MC) of the Chinese Communist Party. The Ministry of National Defense (MND) provides administrative support to the PLA. There are three General Departments.

>   a. General Staff Department. The General Staff Department performs staff and operational functions for the PLA. This department in effect serves as the army general staff headquarters in addition to discharging staff duties for the navy and the air force.
>   b. General Rear Services Department. The General Rear Services Department provides logistical support and services to the PLA as a whole.
>   c. General Political Department. The General Political Department is the agency within the PLA responsible for matters relating to political affairs.

2-2.   Specific operational functions are carried out, as directed by the General Staff Department, by the headquarters of the various arms and services. These include the navy, the air force, the armored force, the artillery force, the engineer corps, the railway engineer corps, the second artillery (strategic missile) corps, the capital construction engineer corps, and the antichemical warfare corps. There is no ground force or infantry headquarters as such.

2-3.   The military organization of the PRC is depicted in annex A.

Organization of a Front

2-4.   In response to real or perceived threats to its national security or in the event of war, the PRC may form up forces into "fronts." A Chinese front would probably be organized along structural lines with the size and composition of forces, including paramilitary forces and their supporting elements, drawn up according to the military situation and the geographic area and military regions concerned.

2-5.   A possible arrangement of Chinese fronts is shown below:

FRONT	MILITARY REGIONS	ORIENTATION
Northeastern (Shenyang) Front	Shenyang	USSR
Northern (Peking) Front	Peking, Lanchou	USSR, Mongolia
Western (Sinkiang) Front	Sinkiang	USSR, Mongolia
Southwestern Front	Chengtu	India
Southern Front	Kunming, Kuangchou	Indochina
Eastern (Fukien) Front	Nanching, Fuchou, Tsinan, Wuhan	Taiwan (Formosa)

Army

2-6.   The largest current PRCA tactical formation is the army. The standard army has three infantry divisions, one artillery regiment, and other supporting troops totaling about 43,000 men. A Chinese army equates approximately to a U.S. corps.

2-7.   The organizational structure of an army is depicted in annex B.

2-8.   The regular ground forces of the PRCA are divided into two general categories: main forces and local forces.

Main Forces

2-9.   Main forces are those regular army troops under the strategic command of the PLA Headquarters. Main force units are intended to be available whenever necessary for operations anywhere in China. They consist of combat units, combat support units, and combat service support units.

2-10. *Combat Units.* Combat units in the PRCA consist of infantry, airborne, (under PRCAF), armor, cavalry, border defense, internal defense, and garrison units.

2-11. Organizational structures of combat units are depicted as follows:

Infantry Division	Annex C
Infantry Regiment	Annex D
Tank/Assault Gun Regiment	Annex E
Infantry Battalion	Annex F
Airborne Division	Annex G
Armored Division	Annex H
Armored Regiment	Annex I
Mechanized Infantry Regiment	Annex J

2-12. *Cavalry.* Although the Chinese consider cavalry, i.e., horse cavalry, a combat arm, its employment is restricted to reconnaissance and screening missions over terrain that precludes the use of vehicles. In addition, cavalry units provide flank security during tactical operations as well as conduct border patrols.

2-13. *Combat Support Units.* Combat support units are of the following type: artillery, engineer, signal, and antichemical warfare.

2-14. *Artillery.* The term artillery, as used by the Chinese, includes field artillery (FA), antiaircraft artillery (AAA), and antitank artillery (AT), as well as rocket launchers (RL) and mortars.

2-15. Organizational structures of artillery units are depicted as follows:

Artillery Division	Annex K
Antiaircraft Artillery Division	Annex L
Antitank Artillery Division	Annex M

2-16. *Engineer.* Engineer units in the PRCA are basically of two types: independent and organic. Independent engineer regiments are controlled at army and/or military region level. Engineer battalions are organic to armies and to both infantry and armored divisions. Companies are organic to airborne divisions and infantry regiments.

2-17. The organizational structure of an engineer regiment is depicted in annex N.

2-18. *Ponton Bridge Regiment.* The ponton bridge regiment is an independent engineer unit attached to an army or higher level unit which is engaged in river-crossing operations. It is one of several types of independent engineer units which perform specialized roles, such as tunneling, road building or mine warfare.

2-19. The organizational structure of a ponton bridge regiment is depicted in annex O.

2-20. *Signal.* The organizational structure of a signal regiment is depicted in annex P.

2-21. *Antichemical Warfare.* Antichemical warfare units are organic to units from armies down to regiments. Some independent antichemical warfare units do exist. As their name implies, their primary orientation is defense against chemical, biological and radiological (CBR) attack. Their limited offensive capability includes procurement, storage, and distribution of CBR agents; the dissemination of smoke, riot control, incapacitating and lethal agents by various means; and the tactical use of flamethrowers.

2-22. *Combat Service Support Units.* Combat service support units in the PRCA are of the following types: motor transport and railway engineer.

2-23. *Motor Transport.* Motor transport units in the PRCA are subordinate to the Rear Services Department of army and division headquarters and the Rear Services Office at regiment. There are also several independent motor transport regiments.

2-24. The organizational structure of a motor transport regiment is depicted in annex Q.

2-25. *Railway Engineer.* Railway engineer units are organized into independent divisions and regiments for the purpose of railway construction and development of the national rail network. Because of their special skills, they are also employed in the construction of large projects, e.g., bridges and highways.

2-26. The organizational structure of a railway engineer division is depicted in annex R.

2-27. There is a Capital Construction Engineer Corps but little information is available on its organization.

Local Forces

2-28. Local forces, also known as regional forces or local defense forces, are those regular troops of the PRCA stationed in and assigned the task of defending a particular locale or geographic area of China. They are responsible for the immediate defense of China's coastal areas and land frontiers and, in addition, share responsibility for the internal defense and security of the PRC. Local forces are normally under the command of the headquarters of the military region in which they are stationed.

2-29. There are three distinct types of local force units in the PRC: border defense (BD) units, internal defense (ID) units, and garrison units.

2-30. *Border Defense.* Border defense units, as the name implies, are those local forces stationed along and responsible for the defense of China's border areas. Essentially a lightly armed infantry force, border defense troops would provide early warning of border violations and constitute the first line of defense in the event of a border incursion. The largest organized unit of the border defense forces is the division. It is somewhat smaller than the standard Chinese infantry division.

2-31. The organizational structure of a border defense division is depicted in annex S.

2-32. *Internal Defense.* Internal defense units are lightly armed infantry forces. In peacetime their primary responsibility is the maintenance of law and order in the localities to which they are assigned. In the event of war they are believed to be capable of conducting limited defensive and guerrilla-type operations.

2-33. The organizational structure of an internal defense division is depicted in annex T.

2-34. *Garrison.* Garrison units are those local forces tasked with the defense of China's coastal area. They are deployed in static, reinforced, artillery-heavy positions along the coast and on many of the offshore islands. Tailored to suit the mission and the topography, they have few infantry troops and possess minimal mobility.

2-35. The organizational structure of a garrison division is depicted in annex U.

Paramilitary Forces

2-36. The PRC's principal paramilitary forces consist of the Peoples Militia and the Production and Construction Corps. While these forces are capable of providing significant guerrilla and/or logistic support to the PRC's regular armed forces in the defense of the Chinese mainland, neither of these groups could make a substantial contribution to the offensive ground capability of the regular forces.

2-37. *The Militia.* The Peoples Militia is a part-time, quasi-military organization which is controlled politically by the Chinese Communist Party but trained and directed militarily by the PLA. Traditionally, the militia has been an important component of Mao's thinking on people's war. In the event of war, the militia would use guerrilla-type tactics to harass the enemy, assist in the defense of urban centers, gather intelligence, help maintain production levels, provide direct logistical support, and provide manpower reserves for the regular forces. In time of peace, the militia serves to reinforce the production effort in agriculture and industry, and to increase security through support of regular forces, especially in border and coastal areas.

2-38. The militia is found in both rural and urban areas and is usually divided into three categories: ordinary, basic, and armed. Most, approximately 60 million, of the militia force are in the ordinary category. These receive little if any military training and, as a category, are considered to have little military significance. The basic or "backbone" militia, approximately 15 million strong, is composed primarily of ex-servicemen and politically reliable elements in the 18-to-35 age group. Basic militiamen receive most of their military training from retired PLA officers, although once or twice a year they take part in training supervised by active duty PLA personnel. The approximately 5 million men and women in the armed militia are selected from the backbone militia and are considered the best trained. Their duties include mounting of armed security patrols and assisting in the training of basic and ordinary militiamen.

2-39. Overall responsibility for militia training rests with the provincial military district and is carried out through subordinate military subdistricts and the Peoples Armed Forces Departments (PAFD). Armament for the militia consists primarily of small arms but some units, especially in the urban areas, are equipped with antitank and antiaircraft artillery.

2-40. The probable militia organization is depicted in annex V.

2-41. *The Production and Construction Corps (PCC).* The Production and Construction Corps is a full-time, quasi-military organization with its primary mission being the economic development of the more remote and unproductive areas of China. Its secondary mission is one of border defense and surveillance. Formerly supervised by the Ministry of State Farms and Land Reclamation, the PCC came under military control during the Cultural Revolution. Stimulated by the "down to the countryside movement" over the past several years, the PCC has undergone rapid expansion and is now estimated to have a strength of over 3 million. There are indications that some PCC units are again being civilianized and reverting to supervision by that Ministry.

2-42. The PCC is organized administratively into agricultural production and engineering divisions with subordinate regiments, battalions and companies found in most, if not all, military regions. Although probably less than 15 percent of its members are armed, the PCC does provide local border guard detachments and offers a good mobilization potential during a national emergency. Armament of the PCC includes light machineguns, mortars and rifles. The bulk of the PCC would require substantial training before its individuals or units could reasonably be considered combat effective in a conventional sense.

2-43. The organizational structure of the PCC in a military region is depicted in annex W.

2-44—2-50. *Reserved.*

2-51. Chinese equipment, the bulk of which is of Soviet design and/or manufacture, is intended to satisfy operational concepts which differ from those of the West. Thus, no attempt at comparison will be made between Chinese equipment and that of the West; when deemed appropriate, a comparison between Chinese and Russian equipment of similar design will be made.

Operational Concept

2-52. As a result of the weaknesses exposed during the Korean War, the PRC decided to modernize its army generally along the lines of the Soviet Army, using Soviet TOE's and the combined-arms concept of armor- and artillery-heavy mobile forces. Currently, however, the PRCA remains essentially an infantry force, and the tactics employed, dictated by the relative lack of armored vehicles and the geographical restraints in certain areas, are geared to exploit foot-soldier capabilities.

Operational Requirements

2-53. *Simplicity*. The Chinese require that their equipment be relatively simple to operate, maintain and repair. This requirement results partly from a scarcity of skilled, technical personnel and, in some instances, of spare parts. To overcome these deficiencies in the PLA's maintenance and repair capabilities, commanders often rely on the individual soldier's skill and ability to improvise with available material and resources. Local fabrication, cannibalization and patching are widely practiced in an effort to keep equipment, particularly vehicles, in service.

2-54. *Quantity*. Despite China's effort to modernize its forces, the amount of equipment produced domestically and imported from abroad is believed to be insufficient to equip all its units according to standard TOE's. There remains a variance among units particularly in the areas of heavy weapons and support equipment. In addition, some equipment and spare parts, especially armor and motor transport equipment, still are in short supply. However, it is assumed that the PLA is provided with sufficient arms and equipment to conduct large-scale, conventional warfare within its own borders or against neighboring small countries who are not supported by one of the superpowers. Its capability to conduct large-scale operations against the USSR and India is limited.

2-55. *Equipment Development*. In a world preoccupied with the development of more highly sophisticated and technical equipment and weapons, the Chinese are remodeling and reequipping their forces with sufficient equipment to enable them to confront any adversary on more equal technological terms. Besides producing equipment of Soviet and other foreign design, the Chinese have developed and produced various types of domestically designed equipment. Major weapons of Chinese design, for example, include an armored personnel carrier, the Type 62 light and Type 63 amphibious tanks and the F-9 fighter aircraft.

2-56. *Reequipment*. The size of the PLA, its dispersal throughout China, and the PLA's limited logistic capability require the Chinese to expend considerable time and manpower in reequipping its armed forces. The Chinese, therefore, normally utilize their equipment for as long as it is operationally functional before replacement. In addition, recovery of equipment from the battlefield is stressed. These practices, however, do not negate China's continuing emphasis on standardizing, modernizing, and replacing obsolescent equipment when required.

Mobility

2-57. Due to the lack of land, sea and air transport capable of moving large numbers of forces, the PLA has comparatively little strategic mobility outside its own borders. But it is capable of decisive tactical mobility, especially over terrain which precludes or limits the use of mechanized vehicles. As the number of APC's and tanks increase, however, and trends toward mechanization are actualized, the PLA will be able to conduct warfare on a broader scale than at present. In a similar manner, an increased inventory of suitable air and water transport craft may result in an increased emphasis on air portability and amphibious operations, thus enhancing the PLA's overall mobility.

Details

2-58. Technical details, illustrations, and quantities of common Chinese ground forces equipment are given in annex X.

2-59—2-62. *Reserved.*

CHAPTER 3
THE BASIS OF CHINESE TACTICS

SECTION I—COMMAND AND CONTROL

Organization of Headquarters

3-1. The highest known current Chinese headquarters in the field is the army (equivalent to a U.S. Army Corps). However, it is probable that in wartime, for span-of-control purposes, these armies will be controlled and coordinated by a senior headquarters called the Army Group. Army Groups in turn would be controlled by the Front Armies.

3-2. The main sections of a Chinese army headquarters are:

a. *Operations Department.* The Operations Department is controlled by a chief of staff who is responsible for the operational direction of subordinate units in accordance with the commander's plan. This department includes subordinate sections responsible for operations and training, personnel, security, artillery, armor, engineers, chemical warfare, communications and reconnaissance.

b. *Political Department.* The Political Department deals with all political as well as security and propaganda matters. This department is also responsible for all aspects of the soldier's welfare. In addition, it is responsible, together with the Operations Department, for the interrogation of prisoners of war. All matters related to civilians, including the Youth Corps, are dealt with by this department.

c. *Rear Services Department.* The Rear Services Department is responsible for all aspects of logistic support. This department is divided into ordnance, quartermaster, finance and services sections and is supported by a medical and a transportation battalion.

d. *Party Committee.* See chapter 9.

3-3. The organization of the division headquarters is similar to that of the army headquarters but about one-third the size.

Formation Commanders

3-4. *Military Commander and Political Commissar.* At each level, the military commander and the political commissar share joint responsibility for combat operations, for all administration and for the general military and political training of all assigned troops.

3-5. *Army Group Commander.* The Army Group Commander is concerned with the conduct of the entire operation in which his group is involved and with the long-term strategic plan.

3-6. *Army Commander.* The Army Commander receives his tasks from the Army Group. His main concern is the conduct of operations in his area over a short-term period.

3-7. *Division Commander.* The Division Commander is concerned primarily with the day-to-day situation as it affects his division.

Location and Movement of Headquarters

3-8.   Each headquarters is divided basically into a forward and a rear command post to insure continuous staff activity by the three staff departments.

3-9.   The *forward command post* is organized into combat, signal and service[1] groups. The commander and political commissar and most of the Operations Department comprise the combat group of the forward command post.

3-10. The *rear command post* is commanded by the chief of the Rear Services Department and includes most of the staff of the Political and Rear Services Departments.

3-11. The commander will decide where the command posts are to be established and the axes on which they will move. The location of the headquarters will depend on the level of headquarters and the tactical situation. Army headquarters will generally be sited in depth in order to maintain control over its entire area. Division and regimental headquarters will be located well forward in order to maintain control of the battle.

Orders and Instructions

3-12. The means by which a commander controls his forces will inevitably depend to a certain degree on his own personality and methods. Normally detailed planning for tactical operations is carried out at army level. These plans direct the specific actions of units two or three echelons below the planning headquarters. Specific reactions to possible enemy actions are preplanned, and deviations from the plan may be made only within prescribed limits.

3-13. Planning during operations takes the form of continuous refinements of the tactical plans made before the initiation of the operation. This is done at planning conferences by the commander and his staff on a daily basis prior to each day's operation.

3-14. Following the daily staff planning conference, the army Operations Department prepares and disseminates combat orders and instructions to subordinate units. These instructions are limited to those which implement decisions that change the existing plan. They are dispatched several hours before the operation is to be resumed to afford subordinate commanders ample time to put them into effect.

3-15. Based on the army orders and instructions, the division commander formulates his general plan and issues detailed orders often including specific locations of key points within designated regiment and battalion areas.

3-16—3-22. *Reserved.*

---

[1] Includes administrative, mess and medical personnel from Rear Services Department.

3-23. In chapter 1 it was explained that the PRC's strategic military doctrine is defensive in nature. There is no known offensive doctrine for the employment of the PRCA outside Chinese borders. The overall objective in Chinese tactics is the destruction of enemy forces, not the capture and retention of terrain.

3-24. The Chinese are capable of undertaking any type of conventional operation. They are also capable of fighting in a nuclear environment and of employing their own limited nuclear weapons in a tactical role.

3-25. While conventional operations are constantly conditioned by the threat of the imminent use of nuclear weapons, Chinese tactics at the lower level vary little in either case. The major differences are that in conventional conditions unit frontages are narrower, objectives are closer, units fight for longer periods, and planned rates of movement are reduced.

General Principles

3-26. Mao Tsetung's writings, particularly his military writings, form the basis for present-day Chinese military doctrine. Most of Mao's military writings are directed to the broad issue of the strategic defense with heavy emphasis on the political aspects. These writings, known as the *Military Thoughts of Mao Tsetung*, are summarized below and are rigidly observed in both planning and execution.

- *The aim of war*. War aims at destroying the effective strength of the enemy rather than at holding areas or cities.
- *Security*. The conservation of the strength of one's own forces is essential to any military operation.
- *Mobility*. Withdraw before the enemy's advance; pursue the enemy's withdrawal; disperse or concentrate one's own forces swiftly on a wide and flexible battlefield.
- *Local superiority*. Concentrate overwhelming strength against the enemy's weaker points; accept a decisive engagement only with two to six times the enemy's strength.
- *Offensive action*. Attack is the vital method of destroying the enemy; surround the enemy and attack from at least two directions.
- *Singleness of direction*. Strategically, there must be only one main direction at a time; tactically, there must be a single objective.
- *Flexibility*. Tactics must be ingenious and flexible, suited to the time, the place and the situation.
- *Surprise*. One's own forces must be assembled in secrecy and must attack at the time and place which the enemy least expects.
- *Initiative*. Always seize the initiative, preserve one's own freedom of action, and force the enemy to retreat.
- *Unity of command*. Unified command is essential to success, particularly in the coordination of guerrilla and regular forces.
- *Preparation*. Combat requires meticulous preparation to avoid entry into battle without assurance of success.
- *Confidence*. Victory is determined by the confidence of commanders and troops in the inevitable triumph of their cause.

3-27. In addition to these principles, the Chinese place great emphasis on the maintenance of morale. Apart from the normal concerns for morale common to all armies, political officers are found at all levels down to and including companies. They are responsible for the morale, motivation and political education of all personnel. Chapter 9 deals with this subject in more detail.

3-28. It has already been stated that Chinese strategic doctrine is concerned with the defense of the mainland against various scales of warfare. This doctrine is based on the *peoples-war* concept in which the PRCA, in concert with the various paramilitary forces, would conduct a strategic withdrawal through successive defensive belts until the enemy is tactically and logistically over-extended. By this method of trading space for time, the Chinese hope to concentrate sufficient forces to assume the offensive and destroy the enemy. However, it is believed that in the defense of certain key political and industrial areas the Chinese would probably defend in the more conventional positional-type defense.

3-29. It must be realized that the PRCA, being essentially an infantry force, has tailored its tactics to maximize these capabilities. The Chinese endeavor to get as close as possible to the enemy—"to embrace the enemy"—believing that in close combat they are superior to all other armies. They are also convinced, from their years of guerrilla warfare, that infiltration is most important and should be reflected in all their tactics. In addition, all movement and the majority of operations should occur at night.

3-30. Also, Chinese doctrine insists that offensive operations are the only way to victory and that the defense is assumed only in the face of a superior enemy force in order to gain time to concentrate forces before resuming the offensive. The Chinese believe that defensive operations must be active; they reject passive defense and consider it the quickest way to defeat and disaster. All operations are aimed at the destruction of the enemy forces rather than at the capture and retention of terrain.

Echelons

3-31. All units are normally divided into a first and second echelon. The first echelon comprises the leading assault or main defense elements required for the first phase of an operation. The second echelon comprises followup or depth elements required for a subsequent phase or phases.

Special Techniques

3-32. *Electronic Warfare.* The Chinese have a limited ability to employ electronic support measures (ESM) such as intercept and direction finding (DF) and electronic countermeasures (ECM) such as jamming and deception. The Chinese have undoubtedly gained a considerable amount of practical experience in electronic warfare (EW) from the conflict in Indochina during the 1965-72 period.

3-33. *Chemical Warfare.* By Western and Soviet standards, the Chinese have comparatively limited capability to employ chemical agents. However, they have the ability to disseminate incapacitating and lethal agents by aircraft spray, bombs and shells. In addition, it may be assumed that the Chinese are developing modern agents to add to their stocks of older toxic and nontoxic agents.

3-34. The Chinese have the ability to apply normal tactical principles of firepower and maneuver in seeking to offset the likelihood and effects of a chemical strike upon them.

3-35. In addition to its lethality, chemical attack poses two further problems for friend and foe alike:

> a. The exhausting effect on those compelled to wear protective masks and full protective clothing for long periods.
> b. The considerable time necessary to decontaminate equipment before it can be used.

The Chinese are trained to minimize both of these problems.

3-36. Special chemical defense units, responsible primarily for decontamination, are organic to the army down to division level. The basic unit is the antichemical company composed of these platoons:

> a. Equipment Decontamination Platoon;
> b. Personnel Decontamination Platoon;
> c. Reconnaissance and Observation Platoon;
> d. Smoke Platoon; and
> e. Flamethrower Platoon.

3-37—3-45. *Reserved.*

SECTION III—RECONNAISSANCE

*Those who know the enemy as well as they know
themselves never suffer defeat. —Sun Tzu.*

Reconnaissance Means

3-46. The PRCA's inferiority to Western and Soviet forces in certain technological support aspects such as air, mobility, fire control and surveillance equipment, as well as its concern for obtaining overwhelming local tactical superiority, leads to its insistence on detailed reconnaissance.

3-47. The following excerpt from PRCA regulations indicates the importance placed on reconnaissance by the Chinese:

> *Every commander must organize reconnaissance within his unit's zone of activities. He must not wait for instructions from his superior, nor must he seek his superior's decision as to whether he should organize reconnaissance. The reconnaissance he organizes must be carried out without cessation to comply with the combat mission through each successive period and phase of combat. Each new mission requires immediate organization of reconnaissance. The conduct of continuous reconnaissance during combat is vitally important.*

3-48. The main Chinese means of reconnaissance are:

> a. *Air Reconnaissance.* This is one of the main sources of combat intelligence.

b. *Patrols and Raids.* Units from army down to battalion have their own specially trained reconnaissance subunits.

c. *Observation.* In both defensive and offensive operations, a system of fixed observation posts is established. At night, listening posts are set up to augment other early warning security measures.

d. *Motorized Reconnaissance.* Special units at army level and in infantry and armored divisions provide limited motorized reconnaissance.

e. *Artillery Observation*, including field radars.

f. *Electronic Intercept and Direction Finding.* It is presumed that the Chinese have a limited capability in this area, but the degree of development is not known.

Air Reconnaissance

3-49. *Method.* Reconnaissance missions will probably be effected at altitudes between 300 and 1,000 feet at speeds between 400 and 500 knots. The pilot can report targets direct by radio or relay his reports.

3-50. Modern Chinese aircraft are capable of photographic reconnaissance in addition to the normal method of visual reconnaissance by the pilot.

3-51. At night, aircraft would operate at a higher altitude and at a reduced intensity.

3-52. Search and destroy operations may be carried out by pairs of aircraft on reconnaissance missions.

3-53. *Reaction Time.*

    a. *Targets Found by Visual Reconnaissance.*
    (1) Targets engaged by ground attack aircraft: after about 60 minutes from first target.
    (2) Targets engaged by conventional artillery: 30 minutes from first report.
    (3) The Chinese are not known to have a tactical nuclear missile; however, they may be prepared to use SRBM's, MRBM's or IRBM's in a theater tactical role at predetermined targets on the main avenues of approach within the PRC. The reaction time for this employment is not known.
    b. *Targets Found by Photo Reconnaissance.* Photo processing and interpretation is probably not up to current Western and Soviet practice and reaction time may be delayed.

3-54. *Scale of Effort.* Due to the limited number of fighter and medium-bomber reconnaissance aircraft, it is not possible to estimate a daily sortie rate. However, the tactical air forces are thought to work in direct support of the ground forces.

Patrols and Raids

3-55. In all phases of war the Chinese patrol energetically and skillfully. These patrols are always specially equipped for their tasks and a high proportion of automatic weapons are carried.

3-56. In addition, the Chinese have no scruples about employing soldiers in civilian clothes or enemy uniforms for reconnaissance purposes.

3-57. Reconnaissance activities by day or night are often increased prior to an offensive. Patrolling is directed to every part of the front in order to discover avenues of approach, enemy positions (in particular, enemy headquarters), and any weak points. These activities may include:

    a. Feints to induce the enemy to disclose his positions.
    b. Raids in strength to test enemy reactions and to secure prisoners.
    c. Strong, limited attacks, particularly when the enemy's strength is undetermined.

Motorized Reconnaissance

3-58. *Scale and Employment.* The army, infantry, and armored divisions have special reconnaissance units equipped with light amphibious tanks, armored cars, and motorcycles with sidecars which may operate from 8 to 20 kilometers ahead of the main body. Local civilian transport may be impressed for use in reconnaissance should it be necessary.

3-59. There are also special reconnaissance elements from engineer, artillery, and chemical units.

Artillery Observation

3-60. Army and division artillery observation units contain:

    a. Surveillance and weapon-locating radars;
    b. Radar intercept/direction-finding sets;
    c. Sound-ranging devices; and
    d. Flash-spotting observation posts.

3-61. Figure 3 summarizes the ranges at which the various reconnaissance elements operate.

3-62—3-70. *Reserved.*

SECTION IV—FIREPOWER

Nuclear Fire Support

3-71. There is no confirmed doctrine for nuclear fire support.

3-72. Available evidence indicates that China's nuclear weapons will serve as a deterrent in the hope of confining any further war within limits bearable for the PRC. China professes that it will never be the first to use nuclear weapons. In this respect, as the Chinese do not possess tactical nuclear weapons at this time, they may use portions of their strategic missiles and bombs in support of their own ground forces. Nuclear mines (atomic demolitions or ADM's) may also be used.

3-73. Chinese planning for the employment of nuclear strikes is not known, but it is presumed that contingency plans for their use in the defense of the PRC have been drawn up by the General Staff Department in consultation with army or higher headquarters.

3-74. *Scale of Warheads.* Not known.

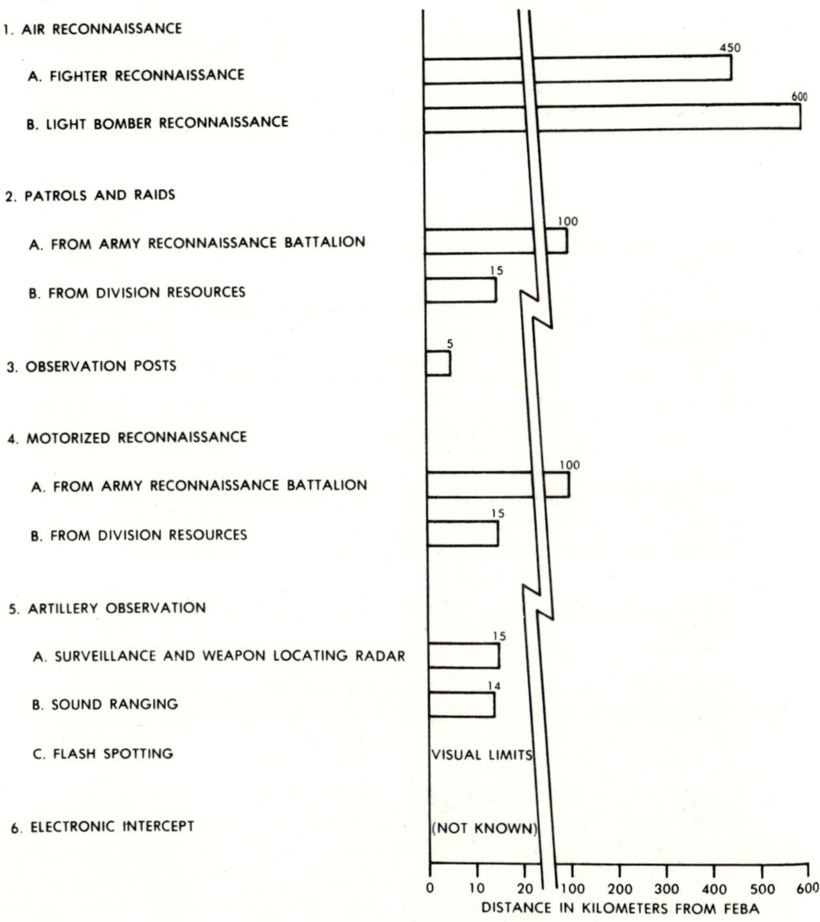

Figure 3. Effective Range of Chinese Reconnaissance Means.

3-75. *Nuclear Targets.* The following are held to be some of the more likely nuclear targets:

    a. Enemy nuclear delivery means.
    b. Headquarters.
    c. Troop concentrations and reserves.
    d. Major avenues of approach.
    e. Communications centers.
    f. Population centers.
    g. Supply areas.

3-76. *Method of Use.* Not known.

3-77. Nuclear missiles are discussed in chapter 8.

Chemical Fire Support

3-78. The Chinese possess a variety of means for chemical warhead delivery such as surface-to-surface missiles, multibarrel rocket launchers and guns of or above 122-millimeter caliber. It may therefore be presumed that chemical warheads are found in their inventory. Information on the employment of chemical weapons, however, is limited.

3-79. Chemical weapons are particularly suitable for targets where casualties to personnel are required but where damage to the terrain should be minimized. Likely targets and the type of chemical agents are:

    a. *Nonpersistent agents.*
        (1) Defiles, river crossings and communication centers on main axes of attack.
        (2) Airfields and potential dropping or loading zones.
        (3) Enemy positions close to own troops.
    b. *Persistent agents.*
        (1) To restrict the use of ground.
        (2) Airfields which are not in use.
        (3) Ports, bases and other rear area installations.
    c. *Nonpersistent or persistent agents.*
        (1) Nuclear weapon systems and artillery.
        (2) Well dug-in enemy positions.
        (3) Headquarters, reserves and assembly areas.

Conventional Surface-to-Surface Artillery

3-80. *Allocation.*

    a. In the event of hostilities, it is presumed that independent artillery divisions will normally be allocated to armies by Army Group headquarters.
    b. Army normally allocates its own and allotted conventional artillery to first echelon divisions, although an army may on occasion retain some artillery for its own requirements.
    c. A division in turn will allocate some of its organic and allotted artillery to its regiments.

d. A regiment normally places the artillery received from division in direct support of its first echelon battalions.

e. Second echelon divisions, regiments and battalions may not be allotted direct artillery support until they are committed.

3-81. *Control.*

a. Formal fire plans are detailed and meticulous, and the control of guns is retained at the highest practical headquarters.

b. On completion of a formal fire plan (some firings may last some 60 minutes), the control of artillery units is decentralized to divisions, regiments and battalions at whatever scale is required for the operation.

c. Artillery can be organized into temporary tactical groups to provide the fire support required by the tactical situation. These groups, which are made up of organic and nondivisional artillery, are of the following types:

(1) *Support groups* consisting of artillery placed in direct support of infantry regiments. Weapons used normally exceed 122 millimeters in caliber.

(2) *Long-range groups* composed of the heavier artillery. Some groups may be allotted in direct support of divisions while others will remain under army control.

(3) *Destruction groups* composed of heavy and high-powered artillery formed for the destruction of obstacles and defenses.

d. While artillery communications are adequate, a radio link is seldom established with the supporting unit and the Chinese depend instead on the collocation of the artillery commander with the supported commander.

e. Forward observers are deployed well forward with the front line battalions.

3-82. *Deployment.* Chinese field and antitank guns, towed by wheeled and tracked prime movers, have a good long-range performance. The gun and howitzer are also considered to be principal antitank weapons. If the tank threat warrants it, organic artillery will at times be employed in the antitank role. At least 5 percent of all ammunition holdings are antitank. High velocity guns are equipped with armor-piercing ammunition; lower velocity weapons, with hollow charge.

Tank and Antitank Fire

3-83. *Indirect Fire from Tanks.* It is common Chinese practice to use indirect tank fire to augment the fire plan in offensive or defensive operations.

3-84. *Antitank Fire Plan.* Antitank fire planning is detailed and is coordinated at the highest possible level. Antitank weapons are held by infantry regiments and divisions; armored divisions and independent armored regiments rely on their tanks for antitank fire. Flanks and tank approaches are covered by mutually supporting antitank weapons sited in depth.

3-85. *Antitank Reserves.* As the Chinese have incorporated a considerable amount of Soviet doctrine into their tactics, it may be assumed that regimental and divisional antitank reserves are formed in both the attack and the defense.

These reserves are probably made up of both guns and tanks and will generally include an engineer subunit to lay minefields in threatened areas. The role of an antitank reserve is to deploy rapidly to meet tank threats.

3-86. *Equipment.* In addition to the battalion weapons (40-mm antitank grenade launchers, 57/75-mm recoilless rifles), regiments have a 75/82-mm recoilless rifle company, and divisions have a 107-mm rocket launcher company. The Chinese are not known at present to have antitank guided weapons (ATGW).

Offensive Air Support

3-87. Chinese tactical air support to ground forces, compared with Western and Soviet armies, is limited in quantity and quality but has received increased emphasis in maneuvers during recent years.

3-88. *Ground Attack Tactics.* At present, Chinese ground attack pilots must see their targets visually; therefore, they require at least 2 nautical miles' visibility for the mission to be undertaken.

3-89. Ground attack aircraft normally operate in pairs or in multiples of pairs. Attacks can be made by nuclear and conventional bombs, napalm, cannon, rockets or chemical warheads. They approach the target at high, subsonic speeds. At a readily recognized identification point, the aircraft will normally pull-up to allow the pilot to identify the target. The aircraft will then execute a dive, which can be steep, medium or shallow, to weapon release.

3-90. Although a pull-up at a recognized point is normal procedure, a rocket attack at low level (150 meters) with no pull-up cannot be discounted. These methods could well be adopted if the target is large or conspicuous enough to be easily identified.

3-91. Chinese nuclear weapons may be delivered by medium-range bombers, probably in straight flight and from a medium altitude.

3-92. If more than one pair of aircraft are attacking a target and if the size of the target allows, the various pairs are likely to attack from several directions. This forces air defense weapons to change azimuth and elevation constantly.

3-93. At night, attacks could be made with the assistance of flares dropped by supporting aircraft. Approaches to the target and weapon release would then be made at much higher altitude than during daylight.

3-94. There is insufficient information to estimate the number of daily ground attack sorties.

3-95. *Control.* It is assumed that the Army Group Headquarters would normally retain control of tactical air support aircraft, allocating sorties to armies as necessary. Air liaison officers and forward air controllers are deployed with divisions to coordinate the air support of ground operations.

3-96. *Targets.* The majority of offensive air support is assigned to targets of opportunity; in particular, enemy nuclear delivery means.

Air Defense

3-97. The basis of the air defense is to provide:

    a. Cover for the Army Group through antiaircraft artillery divisions, surface-to-air missile divisions, and organic army antiaircraft resources in coordination with air defense fighters of the PRCAF.

    b. Point protection by division and regiment air defense weapons.

    c. A competent and efficient target acquisition and warning system which provides air defense units with targets and combat units with warnings of attack. The system, however, consists primarily of older Soviet radars which would have a limited effectiveness against a modern air force.

3-98. Targets will be protected in the following priorities:

    a. Nuclear delivery means.

    b. Headquarters.

    c. Assembly areas.

3-99—3-104. *Reserved.*

SECTION V—MANEUVER

3-105. The PRCA is predominantly an infantry army and its tactics of necessity are designed to exploit the capabilities of the infantry. This factor, together with its historic guerrilla warfare background, has made it capable of great tactical mobility, especially in terrain which is difficult for highly mechanized forces. Movement on foot is fast, and a rate of 40 kilometers a day can be maintained by large forces over great distances in open terrain when unopposed.

3-106. The Chinese tactics, as in other armies, are based on fire and movement. In addition, the Chinese endeavor to retain freedom of maneuver sufficient to envelop enemy positions as well as to attack them frontally. However, it is most unlikely that "human wave tactics" of the Korean War pattern will be employed without considerable refinement.

3-107. The Chinese emphasize depth in the attack and are quick to take advantage of a penetration of their opponent's forward defenses and to develop it by seizing objectives behind his main position.

3-108. Long experience in guerrilla warfare has made the Chinese masters of the art of infiltration. Teaching emphasizes the importance of substantial forces infiltrating the opponent's flanks and rear before an assault. These forces establish themselves astride their opponent's supply routes to prevent reinforcement or withdrawal of the defending force and to prevent employment of reserves.

In the Attack

3-109. *Objectives.* Units are given the following objectives:

    a. An initial objective, which must be taken by the first echelon.

    b. A subsequent objective, which may require committal of the second echelon and which normally coincides with the initial objective of the next higher headquarters.

3-110. Commanders choose tactical objectives which will help destroy the opposing forces. These objectives will normally be enemy positions, particularly on vital ground, whose seizure would facilitate future operations or offer the greatest opportunity to destroy the defenders.

3-111. *Rate of Advance.* Despite increases of motorized transport throughout the PRCA, Chinese infantry moves primarily on foot; other elements move by organic transport regiments. The rate of advance on foot can be surprisingly rapid: about 5 kilometers an hour or 40 kilometers a day. In addition, forced marches will be carried out if the Chinese think they can thereby outflank the enemy and either cut his lines of communication or attack him from the flank or rear. To achieve this, the Chinese do very detailed planning with emphasis on:

    a. Rapid and bold offensive action.
    b. Quick attacks, accepting open flanks.
    c. Maintaining the momentum of the advance by night and day.
    d. Traffic discipline and strict control of movement.
    e. Organization of forces to permit rapid deployment and commitment.

3-112. *Night Operations.* PRCA doctrine stresses the importance of night operations. The Chinese are expert in both combat and administrative operations under cover of darkness. In fact, virtually all movement and the majority of operations occur at night. They do this to avoid sustaining heavy casualties from enemy air action and to achieve tactical surprise. By marching only at night and concealing all troops and equipment during the day, they have demonstrated the capability to shift large forces without detection. During the later stages of the Korean War and in the Sino-Indian campaign of 1962, night movement became the general rule.

In the Defense

3-113. In Chinese tactical doctrine all defensive operations are planned and conducted with the aim of changing over to the offensive as quickly as possible. The defense is undertaken as an interim measure during which preparations are made and more favorable conditions are developed for resuming the offensive.

3-114. The Chinese employ two basic forms of defense. First, there is the mobile defense, developed from their long experience in guerrilla warfare. It is a hit-and-run type of defense based on a war of movement and conducted as a series of defensive actions followed by withdrawals with the aim of inflicting casualties on the enemy without undue loss to themselves.

3-115. The second type is the positional defense. It is organized in great depth and designed to deny vital areas to the enemy or to halt his attack and inflict significant losses on his men and material. Forward units engage the enemy decisively and hold at all costs with no thought of withdrawal to successive defensive positions.

Movements

3-116. The Chinese employ two categories of march: advance and withdrawal.

3-117. *The advance march* is a tactical movement made to engage the enemy, to shift troops from one part of the line to another, and to exploit and pursue the enemy.

3-118. *Withdrawal marches* are conducted to avoid combat rather than fighting a delaying operation, and are made by breaking contact and moving quickly to the rear.

3-119. There are two methods of movement:

    a. *March Efficiency Method.* When contact is not anticipated and when terrain or conditions of poor visibility afford protection against enemy air attack, units are allowed to move at their own speed to arrive at the prescribed place and time. Minimal security measures, consistent with safety, are taken during movement, and commanders seek to conserve troop energy.

    b. *Combat Readiness Method.* When contact is anticipated, commanders insure the combat readiness of their forces by:

        (1) Organizing combined arms groups capable of quick deployment and independent action.

        (2) Designating tactical bounds and boundaries to suit the terrain and general scheme of deployment. Normally, columns on secondary axes are given broader frontages.

        (3) Emphasizing combat security.

3-120. *Speed.* Normal speeds in kilometers per hour are:

		Average Speed	
Trafficability	Condition	Motor March	Foot March
Good	Day (dry)	32 km/hr	5.0 km/hr
Good	Night (lights; dry)	24 km/hr	3.0 km/hr
Good	Night (no lights; dry)	16 km/hr	3.0 km/hr
Fair	Day (dry)	24 km/hr	3.5 km/hr
Fair	Night (lights; dry)	24 km/hr	2.5 km/hr

3-121. *Halts.* Rest areas along the route of march are located in sheltered areas which afford maximum cover and concealment. Normal tactical march procedure calls for 10-minute halts each hour and a 20-minute rest period every 4 hours.

3-122. Due to the lack of air cover, the Chinese restrict vehicular movement to periods of darkness or poor visibility. Vehicles move singly or in convoys of up to 25 vehicles. Halts occur normally as follows:

    a. Short halt of 20 minutes after every 2 or 3 hours.

    b. Long halts of 2 to 4 hours after 12 hours in a move taking more than 24 hours.

3-123. *Control.* Commanders control tactical marches by timing the movement and activity of subordinate units, by personally supervising march conduct, and by making effective use of signal communications. To assist the commander, all units have personnel trained in traffic control duties.

3-124. The Movement Plan will normally include:

    a. Detailed timings and march objectives.

    b. Phase lines and routes for march columns.

    c. Detailed signal instructions including audible or visual means.

3-125. *Route Opening.* Engineer reconnaissance parties and specialized equipment move well forward on every route. Dozer blades may also be fitted to some tanks and other nonengineer prime movers.

Obstacle Crossing

3-126. Both infantry and engineers are trained in improvised methods of obstacle crossing. The Chinese make the most of locally available material. A common technique is the use of submerged bridges or fords built below water level at a safe vehicle wading depth. They are difficult to detect even by close observation. The Chinese capability for crossing obstacles is described under the phase of war in which it is generally employed. Minefield breaching is described in paragraphs 4-35—4-37; water and gap crossing is described in paragraph 4-71 ff.

3-127—3-134. *Reserved.*

Night fire practice.

CHAPTER 4
PHASES OF WAR AND SPECIALIZED WARFARE

SECTION I–OFFENSIVE OPERATIONS

Doctrine

4-1.   The fundamental Chinese military doctrine is that victory can be won only by attacking. The purpose of offensive operations is to destroy the opposing forces rather than to capture or retain ground. This doctrine applies at all levels.

4-2.   Moreover, the Chinese believe that victory can be achieved only by striking in selected areas with overwhelming numerical superiority. A ratio of 3:1 is considered the minimum, but much higher ratios of even 10:1 are preferred. This concentration of force occurs only in the area of the proposed assault and the Chinese are quite prepared to weaken other sectors to achieve this imbalance.

Application

4-3.   *Basic Tactical Maneuvers.* The Chinese Army, as with all conventional armies, employs two distinct offensive tactical maneuvers:

   a. Envelopment in its various forms.
   b. Frontal attack.

4-4.   *Envelopment.* This maneuver can take either of the following forms:

   a. *Double Envelopment.* Elements of the attacking force engage the enemy in the main defensive position to neutralize their small-arms fire and force them to disclose their mortar and artillery defensive fire tasks. The remainder of the assaulting force divides and simultaneously attacks around both flanks to cut off the enemy force and thereby prevent reinforcement or withdrawal. The encircled force is then destroyed.
   b. *Simple Envelopment.* The main assault is on one flank only; otherwise, the aim and the method of execution are the same as for the double envelopment.

4-5.   *Frontal Attack.* The frontal attack is employed only when reconnaissance has failed to find a gap in the enemy defenses and maneuvering along the FEBA has failed to develop one. The assault is launched on a narrow front with the aim of breaking through the enemy FEBA, thereby permitting successive assault waves to pass through and fan out within and behind the defensive positions.

4-6.   A frontal attack combined with an encircling movement is called a penetration-envelopment maneuver. See figure 4.

4-7.   *Tactical Techniques.* The Chinese use simple catch phrases to describe various tactical actions. Examples are "one point, two sides" and "divide and destroy."[1]

---

[1] These two Lin Piao-named tactics were criticized during the campaign against Lin, but it is believed that the tactics themselves are still valid.

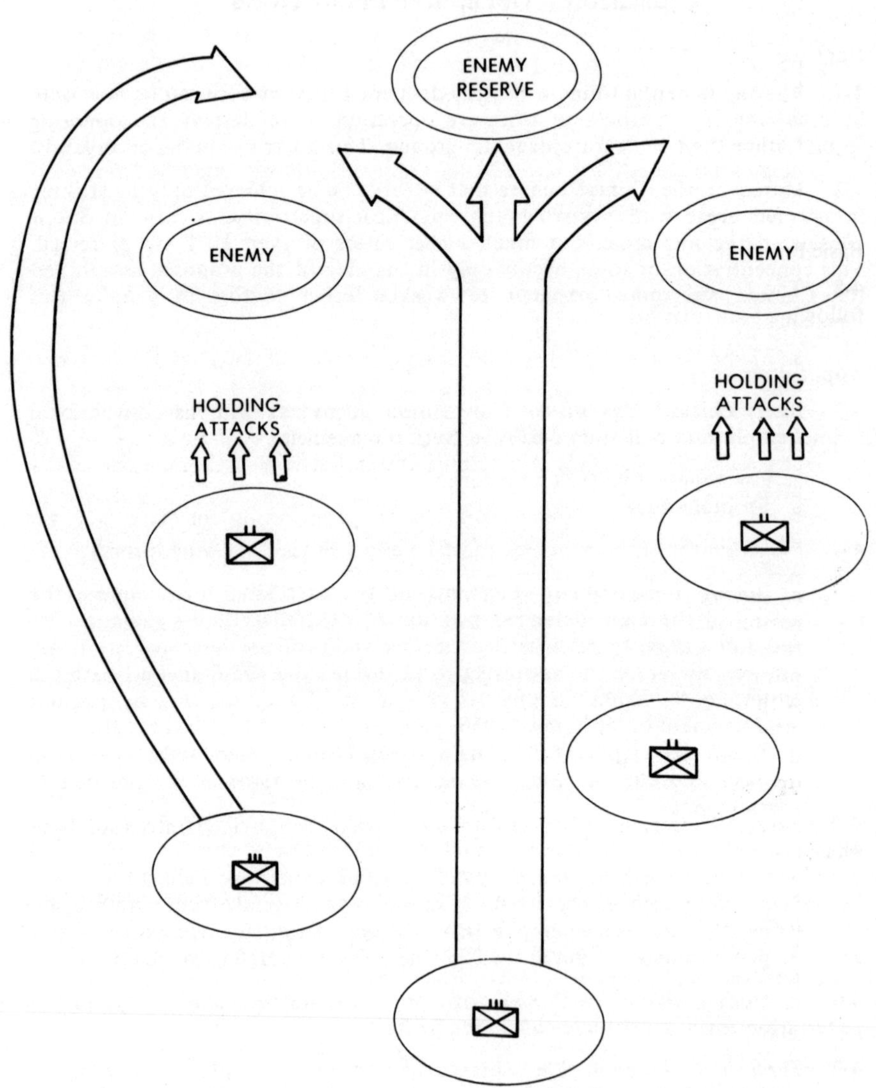

Figure 4. Penetration - Envelopment Attack.

a. *One point, two sides* is a variant of the envelopment in which the enemy's weak spot is attacked simultaneously with feints and enveloping movements. "One point" means the concentration of overwhelmingly superior strength and attack at a selected weak point. "Two sides" means the launching of an attack where two or more supporting attacks are necessary to insure that the enemy can be enveloped and annihilated. This does not mean that the attack is limited to only two sides. When strength permits, attacks on three or more sides may be launched. See figure 5.
b. *Divide and destroy* is a principle applicable at all levels and is an alternative to the "one point, two sides" tactic. As the words imply, the Chinese attempt to penetrate the enemy position and to split the defenders successively into smaller groups; then they assault to annihilate by overwhelming forces. See figure 6.

Basic Principles

4-8. The Chinese, in all their tactics, make the maximum feasible use of the following basic principles:

a. *Speed.* In the offensive, the continuous development of the attack at high speed is mandatory. The division usually is assigned an initial, an intermediate, and a subsequent mission, all to be accomplished within the first 24 hours of the operation. Successive echelons follow up and exploit any successes, thereby maintaining the initiative and momentum of the attack.
b. *Secrecy.* Secrecy is maintained in the preparation for the attack and every effort is made to surprise the enemy as to the time and place of the attack.
c. *Infiltration.* Long experience in guerrilla warfare has made the Chinese masters of the art of infiltration. Their teaching emphasizes the importance of infiltrating substantial forces around the enemy's flanks and rear prior to an assault. These forces endeavor to prevent reinforcements to or withdrawal of the defending forces prior to their destruction by the main attack.
d. *Night Operations.* Virtually all movement and the majority of operations occur at night.

4-9. *Attack Phases.* All Chinese offensive actions are divided into four basic phases (see figure 7).

a. *The Approach March.* The move from the assembly area to the attack positions.
b. *The Attack.* The move from the attack positions to the assault positions.
c. *The Assault.* The move from the assault position until the initial objectives have been secured.
d. *Combat in Depth.* This phase begins as soon as the initial objectives are secure. It may be started by the first (or assault) echelons when it is still an effective force or by the second (or support) echelon.

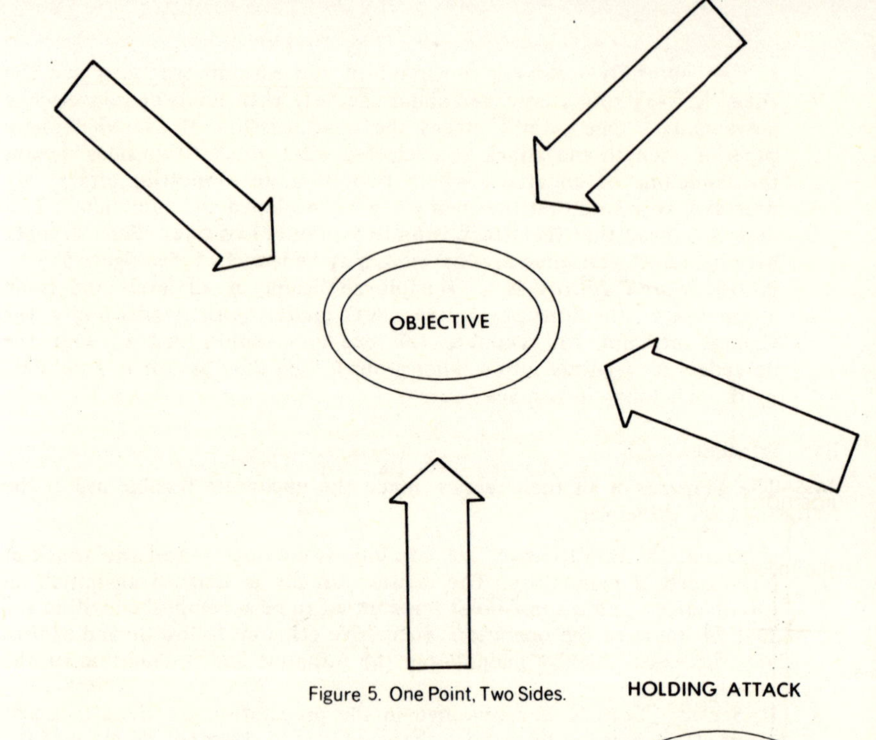

Figure 5. One Point, Two Sides.

Figure 6. Divide and Destroy.

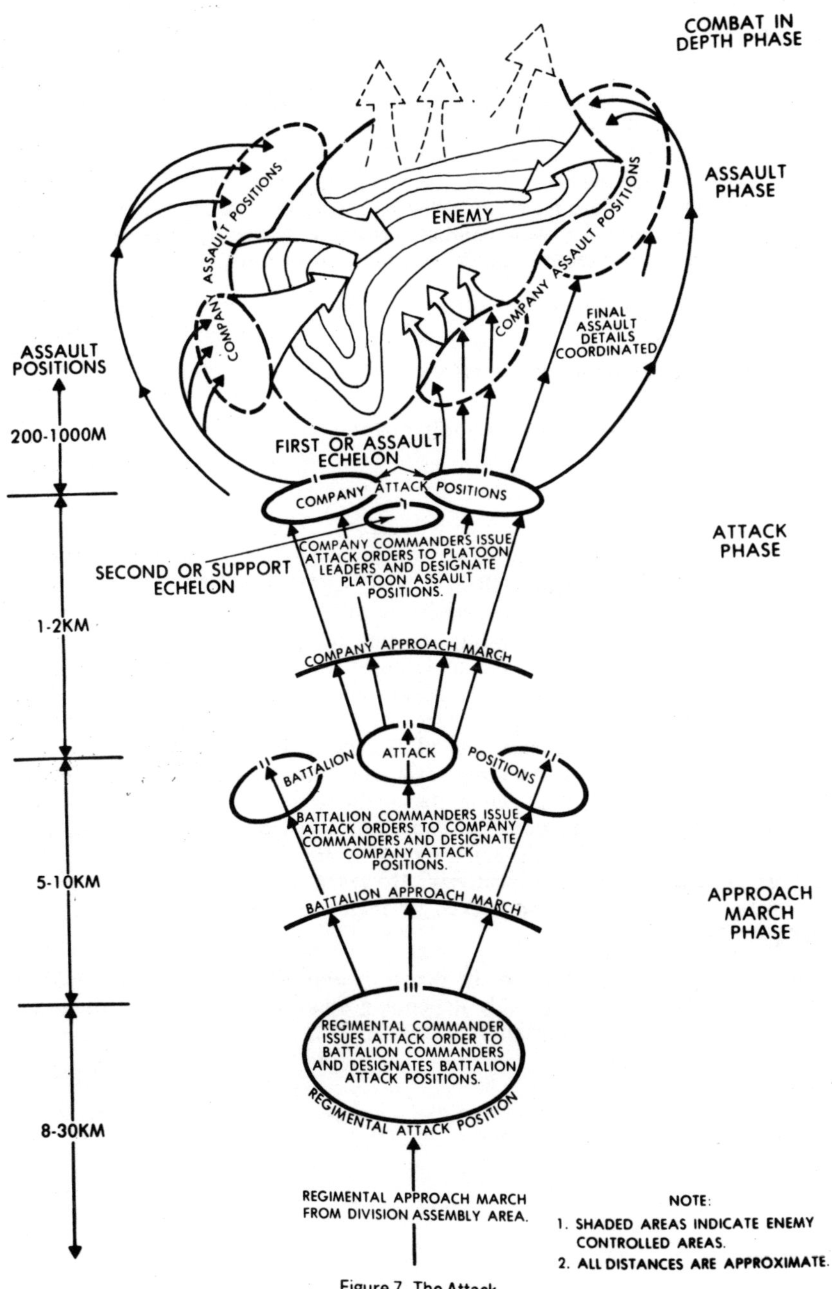

Figure 7. The Attack.

45

4-10. *Echelons.* One or more of the following echelons are employed to carry out and add weight and depth to the attack:

    a. First or assault.
    b. Second or support.
    c. Third (usually only when attack is on narrow front).

4-11. *Reserve.* The Chinese do not categorize the reserve as an echelon in the offense. The second or support echelon is tasked to follow and support the assault echelon in the attack and is therefore committed. This echelon is not a proper reserve although it may be assigned missions such as repelling counterattacks which are normally given to a reserve. The reserve proper varies in strength according to each combat situation. Normally, the reserve is an infantry-heavy, motorized if possible, combined-arms force.

4-12. A guide to the size of the reserve is as follows:

Division—Battalion in reserve
Regiment—Company in reserve
Battalion   )
Company   ) Normally do not have a reserve
Platoon   )

FRONT,[2] ARMY GROUP, AND ARMY OFFENSIVE

4-13. The aim of front, army group or army offensive is to break through the various echelons of the enemy's main defenses. The offensive will employ one or more forms of the envelopment to isolate and destroy the main body of the enemy and, whenever possible, engage his reserve. If the situation precludes envelopment, multiple penetrations of the defensive position will be made, followed by envelopment. At army level, the Chinese are capable of reaching objectives as far as 20 to 25 kilometers behind the enemy FEBA in a single night. Attacks at these levels are normally carried out in three echelons consisting of forces of roughly equal strengths; the echelons are assigned attack, support and reserve roles, respectively. However, in practice an army may be committed in its entirety and backed by reserve armies available to the higher headquarters.

4-14. The size of the sector and the depth of objectives allocated to a front or army group will vary considerably depending upon its strength, role, the terrain and whether or not the campaign is nuclear.

---

[2] A front is a geographical entity which comprises an indeterminate number of army groups or armies depending on the assigned mission.

4-15. Typical yardsticks for the army and subordinate units in offensive operations are as shown in the following table:

Frontages and Depths in Offensive Nonnuclear Operations[1]						
	Army[2]	Division	Regiment	Battalion	Company	Platoon
Frontages Sector Attack Frontage	16-40 km 4-8 km	8-12 km 2-4 km	3-4 km 1-2 km	1-2 km 500-750 m	300-500 m 250-350 m	-- 100-150 m
Depth of Objective Initial Subsequent	10-15 km 30 km	3-5 km 10-15 km	2-3 km 3-5 km	1-2 km 2-3 km	-- --	-- --
Depth of Operations	35-40 km	20-25 km	--	--	--	--
Rear Boundaries From FEBA	30 km	15 km	6 km	3 km	--	--

[1] In nuclear operations all distances would be modified.

[2] An Army Group is thought to consist of three armies.

4-16. *Airborne Operations.* A front may be allocated an airborne division although its operations will normally be of regimental or battalion group size. Airborne operations are described in section V of this chapter 4.

4-17. The Chinese have conducted a few small exercises employing helicopters in an assault landing role.

DIVISIONS, REGIMENTS AND BATTALIONS

The Advance

4-18. A division in a movement to contact (see figure 8) will deploy in the following components and will be encountered by an enemy in this order:

    a. Motorized reconnaissance elements.
    b. The advance guard consisting of:
        (1) Point,
        (2) Advance party, and
        (3) Advance guard proper.
    c. The main body.

Flank and rear protection is discussed in paragraph 4-22.

4-19. Motorized reconnaissance elements will be employed on the divisional routes from the division and regiment reconnaissance company and platoon, respectively. (See paragraphs 3-58 and 3-59.)

4-20. The advance guard or first echelon of the division is normally a combined-arms force whose size and composition will vary. The following may be used as a guide:

    a. When a division moves in a column, the advance guard is based on an infantry regiment.

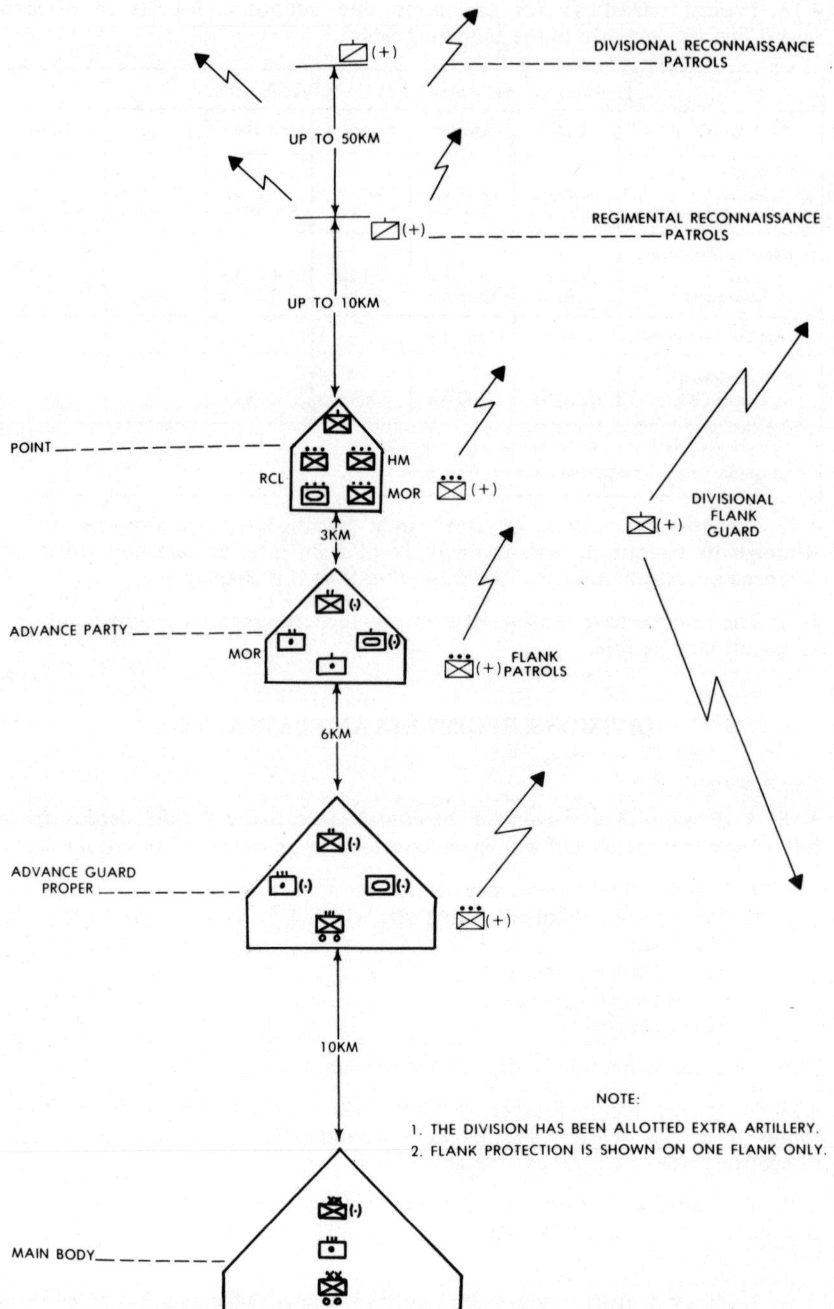

Figure 8. The Movement to Contact and Meeting Engagement by An Infantry Division.

In October 1950 the PLA entered the Korean War under the name of the Chinese Peoples Volunteers.

Peoples War-regular and paramilitary forces unite in protracted war against the invader.

Chinese chemical warfare doctrine is essentially defensive in nature. Here the crew of a 37-mm antiaircraft gun type 55 wear standard protective equipment.

Infantry forces constitute the bulk of the PRCA

Type 59 Medium Tank

Type 62 Light Tank

Type 63 Amphibious Tank

Examples of tanks found in the PRCA inventory.

Cavalry on patrol.

152-mm Gun-Howitzer Type 56

107-mm Multiple Rocket Launcher

122-mm Field Gun Type 60

85-mm Antitank Gun Type 56

130-mm Field Gun Type 59-1

Examples of artillery weapons found in the PRCA inventory.

Artist's sketch of a signal regiment member doing heroic repair work during a storm.

Trucks of a motor transport unit halted along a road in a remote area.

Railway engineer troops.

Members of a garrison unit and local militia conduct artillery training using a 130-mm field gun type 59.

Peoples Militia training with PLA regular forces.

58

These women of the Peoples Militia are practice-firing the type 69 grenade launcher, a modified copy of the Soviet RPG-7

Members of the Production and Construction Corps assist in rural construction projects.

Although basically an infantry force, the PRCA employs the combined-arms concept of armor-and artillery-heavy mobile forces. The spectacular limestone (karst) topography in the background is found in parts of Kwangsi and Kweichow Provinces and has inspired poets and painters down through the centuries.

The PRCA's concept of tactical mobility is well suited to the varied and difficult terrain environments in which its forces would most likely operate.

The commander and political officer share joint responsibility for all unit activities.

Forward command post of an infantry regiment. The 'bulletin board' contains posters on the *Criticize Lin Piao/Confucius Campaign.* **The use of the 14.5-mm** antiaircraft machine gun to provide protection against air attack at forward command posts is a common practice.

b. When a division moves in parallel columns, each leading regiment is responsible for its own security. In such a situation, the division advance guard is, in effect, a reinforced infantry battalion along each route.

4-21. *Main Body.* The main body or second echelon will advance with the headquarters, artillery and air defense elements well forward.

4-22. Flank and Rear Guards. These are established by the division as a whole, and by each march echelon on a small scale. They are composed of all arms and their size and composition will depend on the possible enemy threat. They are normally mounted and move along parallel routes, some 10 kilometers from the main body, to give early warning of enemy intentions, to prevent direct fire on the main force, and to give the commander freedom of movement. These guards, like the advance guard, deploy with:

a. A point,
b. A flank (or rear) party, and
c. A flank (or rear) guard proper.

4-23. *Antitank Defense.* The Chinese disperse their organic antitank resources, including artillery, throughout the various march echelons to blunt and stall an enemy armored attack until other elements of the division are able to mount a counterattack. In addition, armor and artillery are allocated to the advance guard whenever possible and usually travel well forward in the main body as well. Each echelon commander is responsible for his own antitank defense within the overall force commander's plan.

4-24. *Antiaircraft Defense.* In operations against a superpower, the Chinese accept that they will not have air superiority. As a consequence, their doctrine includes specific active and passive procedures against air attack. Additional antiaircraft guns from army frequently augment organic antiaircraft units which are deployed under divisional control throughout the echelons to achieve a limited defense against air attack. Also, medium and light machineguns from infantry units are deployed specifically throughout the columns to assist in this task.

4-25. *Summary of Leading Components.* The possible order and grouping in which leading Chinese combat vehicles may be encountered by a defending force are given below. Not exhaustive, the following is intended only as a guide:

Vehicles	Role in Attack
a. Light tank types 62 or 63, APC M-1967. Motorcycle with sidecar.	When first seen are divisional reconnaissance.
b. Motorcycle with sidecar, individual trucks and small parties of infantry.	Regimental reconnaissance.
c. Company of infantry with additional heavy weapons. Possibly three medium tanks.	Point of advance guard.

<table>
<tr><th><u>Vehicles</u></th><th><u>Role in Attack</u></th></tr>
<tr><td>d. Six to ten medium tanks,
battery of artillery,
battalion of infantry
and engineer vehicle.</td><td>Advance party and may be some
elements of the main guard.</td></tr>
</table>

4-26. *Routes.* A division is allotted up to five routes and a regiment up to three. The Chinese will sacrifice depth to gain a broad front. In fact, by moving large bodies of troops along minor tracks, the Chinese have often outflanked and outwitted their enemy.

The Attack

4-27. *Types of Attack.* The Chinese ground forces recognize three different types of attack which affect their tactics at division level and below:

a. *The Meeting Engagement*, logically following the advance, is a collision between opposing forces on the move. It usually takes place before either force is fully deployed.

b. *The Quick Attack*, whenever possible, is conducted from the march. Its purpose is to penetrate thinly occupied and hastily prepared defensive positions by rapid deep thrusts, disrupting the entire defensive system.

c. *The Deliberate Attack* requires careful planning and a relatively long period of preparation. It is mounted against a well-prepared defense.

4-28. Figure 8 is a schematic diagram of a Chinese division deployed in a movement to contact.

a. *Action by the Advance Guard.* On contact, the point, consisting of a reinforced company, engages the enemy and attempts to destroy or contain him. If the point and advance party cannot overcome the resistance, they will quickly dig in and engage the enemy while the advance guard proper (one regiment minus) attacks on one or both flanks to encircle and destroy the enemy or force his retirement.

b. The advance guard commander deploys his force on a wide front to seek the best avenues of approach to the enemy's flanks. The advance guard action is often a piecemeal operation, units being allotted tasks and launched into action as they become available. These rapid piecemeal attacks are part of the reconnaissance effort to define the enemy's FEBA, to locate weapon and gun positions, and to determine defensive fire tasks.

c. *Action by the Main Body.* The division commander, from the information gained by the advance guard, will deploy the main body as soon as possible to carry out an enveloping attack to annihilate the enemy.

d. If the enemy withdraws before encirclement is complete, he will be pursued.

4-29. Rapid and bold offensive action is considered the key to success, even against a stronger enemy, and envelopment is considered the best method of isolating and annihilating portions of the enemy column. The division commander, having allotted his commanders their tasks, places greater reliance on their initiative and judgment in the meeting engagement—and in the pursuit that may follow a quick success—than in the more deliberate phases of war.

4-30. *Tanks in the Advance.* The proposed role of armor, based upon the terrain, determines its positions in the advance. However, tanks are normally allocated to the advance guard to support the infantry in its operations.

4-31. The commander husbands his armor carefully and is unlikely to commit his tanks until the enemy tank strength has been reduced by artillery and antitank fire. Tanks will then be massed in the main attack to destroy the remaining enemy tanks and strong points and to pursue the withdrawing forces.

4-32. *Artillery in Advance.* The role of artillery is to deliver fire and pin down enemy forces as soon as they come within range, and to counter flank attacks.

4-33. Artillery units are deployed well forward in the advance to exploit the maximum range of the guns. On contact with the enemy, artillery units with the advance guard go into action as rapidly as possible. Direct fire, including tank fire, constitutes a considerable portion of the initial support until artillery with the main body is able to reinforce the fire of the advance guard.

4-34. Chinese doctrine stresses that artillery must be able to support the infantry and armor as they commence their attacks.

4-35. *Minefield Breaching.* Engineers organic to the division and regiment clear or supervise the clearing or breaching of obstacles and minefields on the scale of three lanes per attacking rifle company.

4-36. Mine detectors, probes and dogs are used for mine detection. Mines are neutralized and removed for use elsewhere, although attempts may be made to detonate antipersonnel mines on the spot using long bamboo poles with hooks. Bangalore torpedo-type devices are also used.

4-37. Minefields may also be breached by using mine ploughs or in difficult terrain by mine plough/roller combinations. Both are fitted to the front of tanks. These devices clear mines only from the area over which the tank tracks move. The undetonated mines may be destroyed by an explosives-filled hose dragged by the tank across the minefield.

The Quick Attack

4-38. The quick attack is made against an enemy occupying a hastily prepared defensive position. The Chinese consider that such a position is unlikely to have a fully coordinated defensive plan and that its fire support will be relatively poor.

4-39. The Chinese emphasize speed in the planning, preparation and execution of the attack consistent with an adequately coordinated fire plan. The "one point, two sides" tactical technique (a main attack with simultaneous diversionary attacks) is normally used. The principle of this technique is described in paragraph 4-7a.

4-40. *Infantry Division.* An attack by an infantry division with two regiments in the first echelon and one regiment in the second may be launched on a frontage of about 6-7 kilometers. At times, three regiments may be deployed in line for the attack.

4-41. *Infantry Regiment.* In this case the first echelon usually consists of two reinforced battalions and the second, of one battalion. The attack frontage is about 3 kilometers.

4-42. *Infantry Battalion.* The battalion attacks on a frontage of about 700 meters with two reinforced companies in the first echelon and one company in the second.

4-43. *Tanks in the Assault.* All available tanks are placed under command of the unit carrying out the attack. Tanks will normally be massed and deployed in the front of the first echelon.

4-44. *Fire Support.* Fire support is described in section IV, chapter 3. A quick conventional fire plan will be drawn up while the infantry moves into attack positions. This allows for the employment of divisional artillery and infantry mortars.

4-45. Minefield breaching is discussed in paragraphs 4-35—4-37.

The Deliberate Attack

4-46. The deliberate attack against a well-organized defensive position is characterized by careful planning, increased reconnaissance activities, and the deployment of numerically superior forces against specific positions. In fact, a Chinese infantry division may be employed against a battalion position or a battalion against a platoon.

4-47. *Army.* This formation may carry out an attack either independently or as part of an army group. The attack frontage is normally about 8 kilometers and its initial objectives are about 10 to 15 kilometers deep. Final objectives may be up to 30 kilometers.

4-48. *Infantry Division.* The division, usually controlled by army, attacks on a 4-kilometer front, normally in two echelons. Initial objectives are 3 or 4 kilometers behind the enemy FEBA and final objectives may be up to 10 to 15 kilometers. If the attack is on a narrow front, the Chinese may use three echelons.

4-49. *Infantry Regiment.* The division commander may use one or more of his infantry regiments to try to outflank and encircle the enemy. The regiment attacks in two echelons, the first consisting of two reinforced battalions, the second, of one battalion on a frontage of up to 2 kilometers. Objectives are allocated only to the first echelon battalions; the second echelon follows the first echelon and is usually given missions of mopping up bypassed centers of resistance. Both echelons are considered to be committed.

4-50. *Infantry Battalion.* The battalion normally attacks in two echelons in a manner similar to the regiment.

4-51. *Rifle Company.* The company is considered to be the smallest force capable of using the "one point, two sides" and "divide and destroy" techniques. It often attacks in two echelons, but it can attack in one. Orders are usually very specific and give the company commander little scope for independent action.

4-52. *Frontages.* The frontage allotted to a force depends on a number of variables. Listed below is a guide to the frontages for various units carrying out a deliberate attack.

a.	Army	6-10 kilometers
b.	Division	2-4 kilometers
c.	Regiment	1-2 kilometers
d.	Battalion	500-700 meters
e.	Company	250-350 meters
f.	Platoon	100-150 meters

4-53. *Tanks in the Assault.* Tanks, when available, are normally placed under operational control of the regiment which in turn allocates them to the leading battalions in the first echelon of the attack. Tanks are massed to assist the infantry's advance into the depths of the enemy's defense. It is unusual for tanks to be used in smaller than company strength (10 tanks).

4-54. *Fire Support.* At least one of the division's organic artillery battalions, consisting of three batteries, will normally be placed in direct support of each of the first echelon regiments.

4-55. Artillery from army resources will give additional fire support to the attacking regiments.

4-56. Artillery is usually in position at least 24 hours before an attack. Preliminary ranging may well reveal Chinese intentions.

4-57. An example of a fire plan of a deliberate attack is as follows:

Time (minutes)	Artillery Fire	Action by Assaulting Troops
H-68 to H-67	Rapid and concentrated neutralization.	Move to line of departure completed by H-15.
H-67 to H-43	Destruction.	
H-43 to H-33	Howitzers stop firing; guns and mortars continue.	
H-33 to H-8	Destruction.	
H-8 to H-1	Howitzers fire in depth; guns and mortars continue.	
H-1 to H+1	Rapid and concentrated neutralization.	Infantry assault preceded by tanks at H hours.
H+1	Neutralization barrage extended in depth. Ranging for defensive fire tasks.	Assault.

4-58. Direct fire from field and antitank guns often supplements the fire plan just prior to and during the assault. In addition, 5 minutes before the assault, known enemy positions are engaged by all other weapons within range, including small arms and recoilless rifles.

4-59. *Minefield Breaching.* See paragraphs 4-35—4-37.

4-60. *Battalion Attack.* As part of a regimental attack, the pattern of a typical deliberate attack might be as follows:

 a. Battalion in divisional assembly area approximately 8 to 30 kilometers behind the FEBA at H minus 2 days.
 b. Battalion moves to the regimental attack position under cover of darkness some 5 to 10 kilometers behind the FEBA at H minus 1 day.
 c. Battalion moves to its attack position some 1 or 2 kilometers behind the FEBA, at H minus 9 to H minus 2 hours, where it organizes into its assault formations (two companies up, one back).
 d. The assault echelon, under cover of artillery and battalion supporting weapons, then moves forward in close formation (usually arrowhead) to the company assault positions within 200 meters from the objectives.
 e. At this point the platoons, with each of their squads divided into three teams, advance in a skirmishing formation with 3 to 5 paces between individuals and 7 or 8 paces between teams. They follow their own artillery concentrations very closely and are prepared to suffer some casualties in order to take maximum advantage of their own fire.
 f. Depending on the terrain, the tanks will time their movement to get ahead of the infantry in the assault.
 g. The assault is made in a continuous rush. As soon as the squads are within range, handgrenades are thrown to cause confusion, smoke, dust and casualties. As the squads reach the enemy positions, all members fire their weapons and close with the enemy to destroy him at pointblank range.
 h. On clearing the objective, the assault force will continue its attack and exploit beyond the objective while the support echelon consolidates on or near the objective. If the assault echelon has suffered heavy casualties, exploitation will be carried out by the support echelon.
 i. The Chinese reorganize rapidly and are formidable diggers. Under reasonable conditions, a battalion can, in one night, dig in and provide overhead protection to a depth of 18 inches.

The Pursuit
4-61. The pursuit will start when the enemy either is routed or attempts to break contact in a preplanned withdrawal.

4-62. When it becomes apparent through intensified reconnaissance that the enemy is planning or has just begun to withdraw, an attack is launched immediately to confuse him and disrupt his plans. Once it is clearly determined that a withdrawal is in progress, pursuit is initiated. All available units are committed immediately, piecemeal if necessary, to insure that contact is maintained with the retreating enemy. Once initiated, pursuit cannot be terminated except on orders from a higher headquarters.

4-63. *Pursuit Tactics.* In the pursuit, close and continuous pressure on the enemy is considered necessary to prevent his regrouping or reassuming the defensive. As soon as possible, the Chinese form two or more columns, one to exert direct pressure and the other(s) to move on either flank parallel to the withdrawing enemy in an attempt to overtake, encircle and then destroy him.

4-64. The flanking columns are organized from units of the support echelon and the reserve. They are often motorized and reinforced with tanks if available. Speed is emphasized and enemy strongpoints are bypassed so that critical road junctions and defiles on the enemy withdrawal routes can be seized and defended.

4-65—4-70. *Reserved.*

SECTION II—RIVER CROSSING

4-71. The Chinese conducted river-crossing operations during both the Civil War and the Korean conflict. Most crossings were made by fording, swimming, utilizing hastily constructed rafts or bridges, or commandeering boats from the local populace. The acquisition of modern river-crossing equipment from the Soviet Union in the 1950's and 1960's and the Chinese manufacture of Soviet-designed equipment have improved the PRCA's capability to conduct river-crossing operations. However, this capability has yet to be tested under actual combat conditions.

4-72. Chinese doctrine considers the river crossing to be merely a phase of the normal advance to be conducted without any loss of momentum. Whenever possible, crossings are made at night or under conditions of poor visibility. If it is necessary to make a crossing by daylight, smoke is used to conceal both the preparations and the operation.

4-73. Frontages and objectives are similar to those for a normal attack (described in section I of this chapter 4).

4-74. *Principles.* The following principles are regarded by the Chinese as a key to a successful river crossing:

    a. Reconnaissance.
    b. Early planning and thorough organization.
    c. Destruction of the enemy in the area.
    d. Deception.
    e. Improvisation of crossing aids.
    f. Speed and surprise.
    g. Crossing on a broad front.
    h. Swift development of the attack on the far bank.
    i. Massing of forces against enemy weakpoints.
    j. Air defense.

4-75. *Types of River Crossings.* The Chinese execute two types of river crossings: the hasty crossing and the deliberate crossing.

    a. *The hasty crossing* is a swift, uninterrupted movement normally conducted from the line of march.

b. *The deliberate crossing* is undertaken only if a hasty crossing has failed or if a large, well-defended water obstacle has to be crossed and breached.

Nonengineer Water-Crossing Capability

4-76. *Infantry.* The standard Chinese infantry division possesses limited organic equipment for river crossings. However, it is thoroughly trained in improvising field expedients for crossing minor water obstacles. Ponchos make temporary floats for ferrying machineguns, recoilless rifles, and mortars. Rafts made from oil drums and bamboo are used to carry heavier weapons and supplies. The bulk of the forces swim or wade even major rivers. Ropelines from bank to bank speed up the crossing and provide safety.

4-77. *Tanks.* The PRCA T-34/85, Type 59, and Type 62 tanks can wade up to a depth of 1.2 meters. The Chinese are not known to possess snorkel equipment. The Type-63 light tank, found in the reconnaissance elements of both infantry and armored divisions, is the only amphibious tank in the Chinese inventory. It is the PRCA's primary armored reconnaissance vehicle. (See appendix 1 to annex x.)

4-78. *APC's.* The M-1967 APC, found in the mechanized infantry regiment of the armored division, is amphibious. (See appendix 1 to annex x.)

4-79. *Artillery.* Chinese guns and prime movers are not amphibious and rely on engineer crossing facilities.

Engineer Water-Crossing Equipment (see appendix 4 to annex x)

4-80. The PRCA has only a limited quantity of engineer water-crossing equipment. Most are of Soviet manufacture or design; some date back to World War II. As a result, China's ground forces rely heavily on improvisation and local resources to support any major river-crossing operation.

4-81. *Amphibians.* The Chinese are thought to possess a few Soviet-built tracked amphibians at army level. In addition, U.S.-manufactured DUKW-type wheeled amphibious trucks and LVT-type tracked amphibious carriers captured from the Nationalists (or Chinese copies thereof) are probably still in the Chinese inventory.

4-82. *Bridging.*

    a. *Tank Bridge Layer.* It is thought that the Chinese have some T-54 MTU Soviet class 50 bridge layers which span 11 meters.

    b. *Vehicle Launched Bridge.* The Soviet truck-mounted scissors bridge (KMM) is known to be in the inventory. In addition it is thought that the Chinese may have some TMM's, load class 60.

    c. *Bridges.*

        (1) Light bridge with plywood pontons, wooden superstructure similar to the obsolete Soviet DLP.

        (2) Medium bridge with steel pontons and superstructure similar to the Soviet N2P-45.

        (3) Heavy bridge with steel pontons and superstructure (Soviet TPP/TMP) imported from USSR.

(4) Improvised bridges built below water level at a safe vehicle traversing depth.

(5) TZ1 footbridge (Soviet).

(6) Unknown quantities of Bailey bridging.

4-83. *Rafts and Ferries.* Varying numbers of rafts can be constructed from the bridging mentioned above in paragraph 4-82-c. If rafts are to be built then the length of the bridges must be reduced in proportion to the number of rafts used.

4-84. *Boats.*

a. Simple, collapsible assault boats capable of carrying 10 men or 2 short tons.

b. Steel ponton boats, of 25-man or 6-short-ton capacity, normally used as the basis for ponton bridges.

c. Inflatable five-man reconnaissance boats.

d. An almost inexhaustible supply of civilian wooden boats ranging from one-man fishing boats to large junks.

Conduct of the Operation (in the hasty crossing)

4-85. A possible Chinese view of the sequence of actions by an infantry division crossing a water obstacle from the line of march is described in the paragraphs below.

4-86. *Preliminaries.* The division commander makes an outline plan for the crossing and issues orders in the rear assembly area. Division and regiment reconnaissance platoons, reinforced with elements of division's engineer battalion, are dispatched ahead of the main body to reconnoiter crossing sites, forward assembly areas, and the near bank. So far as possible, they also reconnoiter the far bank to determine terrain conditions and enemy strengths and dispositions. Concurrently, river-crossing equipment, both organic and improvised, is assembled in selected areas near assault positions and crossing sites.

4-87. *Approach.* The division adopts a formation normal for a movement to contact in its approach to the water obstacle. After the reconnaissance is completed, an advance guard or forward detachment from each first echelon regiment, normally of reinforced battalion strength, is assigned the mission of securing the near bank and, when possible, of forcing the initial crossing. If the crossing cannot be accomplished in this manner, the advance guard is employed to secure the near bank on a broad front, destroy obstacles, and establish a base of fire to support crossings by the assault elements of the regimental first echelons.

4-88. *The Assault.* The assault regiments are located in covered assembly areas some 3 to 5 kilometers from the obstacle. The first echelon battalions move from these assembly areas, cross a line of departure as near to the obstacle as possible, and begin crossing, under the cover of direct and indirect fires. The assaulting battalions initially move in column to facilitate control, but on nearing the obstacle deploy and make the crossing on a broad front. The supporting battalions normally cross in successive waves at the closest interval possible. Every effort is made to get some artillery across the river with the assaulting battalions and regiments. Usually the artillery plan employs two-thirds of the artillery engaging the enemy while one-third is crossing the river.

4-89. *Operations on the Far Bank.* Upon reaching the far shore, the assaulting troops move inland as quickly as possible to clear the crossing area of direct enemy fire and secure the flanks. Each assault battalion is expected to establish a beachhead from 1 to 2 kilometers wide and approximately 1 kilometer deep, but these dimensions will vary with the terrain. The landing area is cleared of mines and obstacles so that bridges may be constructed and ferries utilized to facilitate the crossing of tanks, supporting weapons, and second echelon forces.

The Deliberate Crossing

4-90. The deliberate crossing differs from the hasty crossing largely in the degree of preparation. A thorough reconnaissance is conducted in advance and a detailed fire plan is organized. Preliminary preparations are carried out in assembly areas well to the rear of the obstacle. Movement toward the obstacle is usually made at night, under the cover of preliminary bombardment fires and the actions of forces in contact on the obstacle. The actual assault and crossing usually take place at dusk or during other periods of poor visibility, under cover of artillery fires. The crossing and consolidation will generally then follow the lines of the hasty crossing although timings will inevitably be slower by night.

4-91—4-96. *Reserved.*

SECTION III—DEFENSIVE OPERATIONS

4-97. The Chinese define the defense as an intermediate stage in the overall, broad offensive aim. It is assumed if the offensive is terminated due to strong enemy action or if time is required to concentrate forces for the counteroffensive. Defense is regarded as a temporary expedient adopted in order to:

    a. Preserve friendly forces while weakening those of the enemy.
    b. Gain time to concentrate forces for the offensive or counteroffensive.
    c. Economize forces to allow an offensive to be mounted in another area.
    d. Consolidate captured objectives.
    e. Cover a withdrawal.

(See figure 9.)

4-98. Chinese defensive postures are based on:

    a. Firmly holding areas of tactical importance with well dug-in troops.
    b. Retaining in the second echelon mobile reserves to block penetrations and to counterattack.
    c. Using all available firepower.
    d. Making maximum use of both natural and artificial obstacles throughout the defensive area. Defensive positions are normally placed behind natural antitank obstacles which are improved or supplemented by constructing boobytrap entanglements and laying antitank and antipersonnel mines.

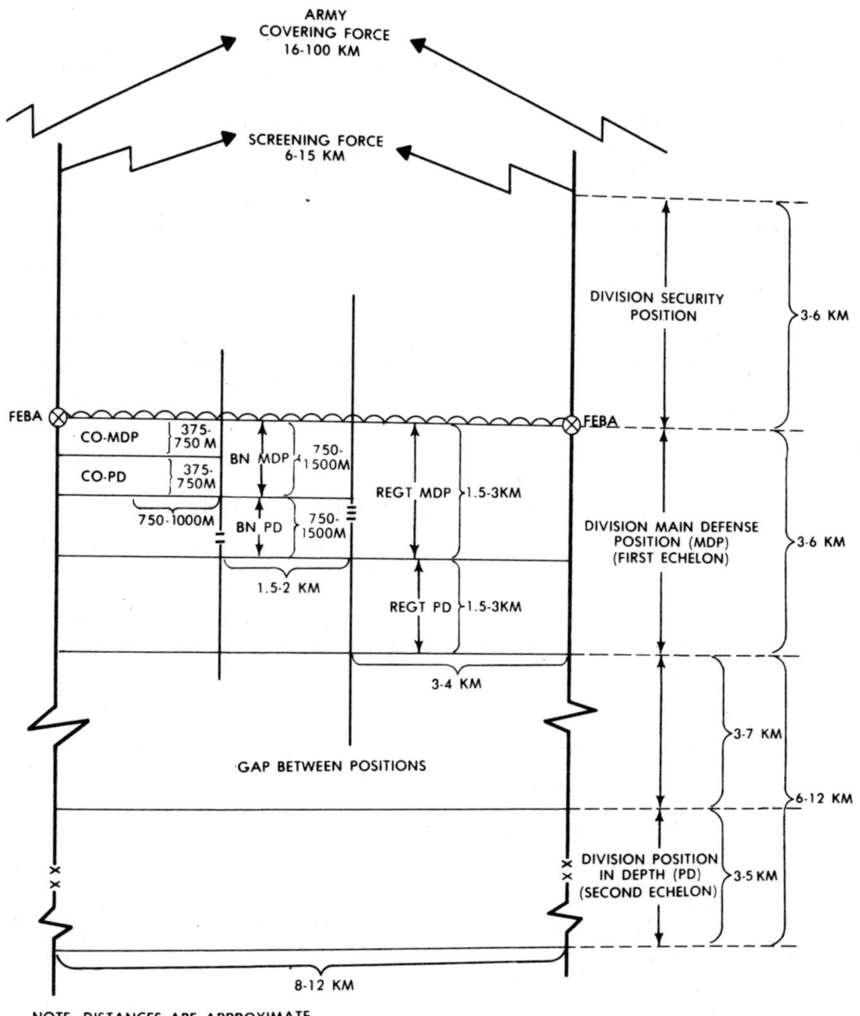

Figure 9. Division Defense Boundaries.

Forms of Defense

4-99. Broadly, the Chinese employ two types of defense: positional and mobile.

    a. *Positional Defense.* This is similar to the U.S. concept of the area defense. It is organized in depth and designed to deny vital areas to the enemy or to halt his attack while inflicting significant losses on his men and material. Forward units engage the enemy decisively and hold at all costs with no thought of withdrawal to successive positions. At the same time, this defense permits the massing of Chinese forces for the counteroffensive.

    b. *Mobile Defense.* This has developed from China's long experience in mobile revolutionary warfare. It is a "hit-and-run" type of defense based on a war of movement. It is conducted as a series of defensive actions followed by controlled movement to the rear, with the aim of inflicting maximum casualties on the enemy without undue loss to one's own forces. Retention of terrain, *per se*, has only a passing relevance or importance. Chinese forces are organized so they can break contact at will, thereby enabling them to continue their stepping-back process until the purpose of the mobile defense is achieved or until they have withdrawn back to an area where the bulk of their forces are deployed in a positional defense role.

Organization for Defense

4-100. *Echelons.* At all levels, a commander will divide his forces into two echelons for the purpose of defending a given area.

4-101. *Defensive Areas.* The area to be defended by a unit is divided into three positions:

    a. *The Security Position.* It is occupied by the unit's screening force, its reconnaissance elements, and the security force.

    b. *The Main Defensive Position (MDP).* The MDP is occupied and defended by the unit's first echelon.

    c. *The Position in Depth (PD).* The PD is occupied and defended by the unit's second echelon, also considered to be the unit reserve. It consists of the balance of the unit's organic and attached strength. At division level, it also includes the motorized counterattack force normally deployed in assembly areas between the main defense position and the position in depth.

4-102. *Frontages and Depths.* The following table sets forth frontages and depths for various formations. These figures relate to frontages and depths in defense in a main sector. Frontages in subsidiary sections are considerably greater.

Frontages and Depths in Defense in a Main Sector				
	Mobile Defense		Positional Defense	
	Frontage	Depth	Frontage	Depth
Army	32-80 km	Depth varies	16-40 km	40-60 km
Division	16-24 km	too much	8-12 km	9-18 km
Regiment	6-8 km	for average	3-4 km	3-6 km
Battalion	2-4 km	figures	1-2 km	1.5-3 km
Company	1-1.5 km	to be	500-700 m	500-700 m
Platoon	500-700 m	given	250-350 m	250-350 m

4-103. *Deployment.*

    a. *Army.* An army normally deploys with two infantry divisions in the first echelon and one infantry division in the second. However, in a wide subsidiary sector, it might deploy with three infantry divisions forward.
b. *Division.* An infantry division normally deploys with two regiments in the first echelon and one regiment in the second. In a subsidiary sector, some or all of the third regiment may be in the first echelon.

4-104. *Dispersion.* Chinese forces are always sufficiently dispersed to prevent a single tactical nuclear weapon from destroying more than one battalion-size unit.

4-105. *Covering Forces.* Elements (usually not more than a reinforced regiment) of the army's second echelon or of an armored division attached to the army will normally be employed as the covering force in front of the division defense zones. The distance that it operates in front of the FEBA varies from 16 to 100 kilometers and obviously depends on the terrain, the relative strength of opposing forces, and the overall mission of the Chinese commander.

The Division in Positional Defense (see figure 10)

4-106. The infantry division normally participates in defensive operations as part of a larger force. The army commander prescribes the area to be defended by the division and coordinates the employment of artillery and armor. He also coordinates barrier and denial operations throughout the army defense zone.

4-107. The infantry division commander is responsible for the following:

    a. Organizing and defending an assigned defensive zone.
b. Providing security for supporting arms and services within the zone.
c. Constructing fortifications to withstand artillery fire and attacks by armor and from the air.
d. Maintaining the integrity of the FEBA and inflicting maximum casualties on the enemy in front of the FEBA.
e. Should a penetration of the FEBA occur, counterattacking to restore the integrity of the FEBA or, if this is not possible, containing any penetration of the FEBA until counterattacks can be mounted by a higher headquarters.

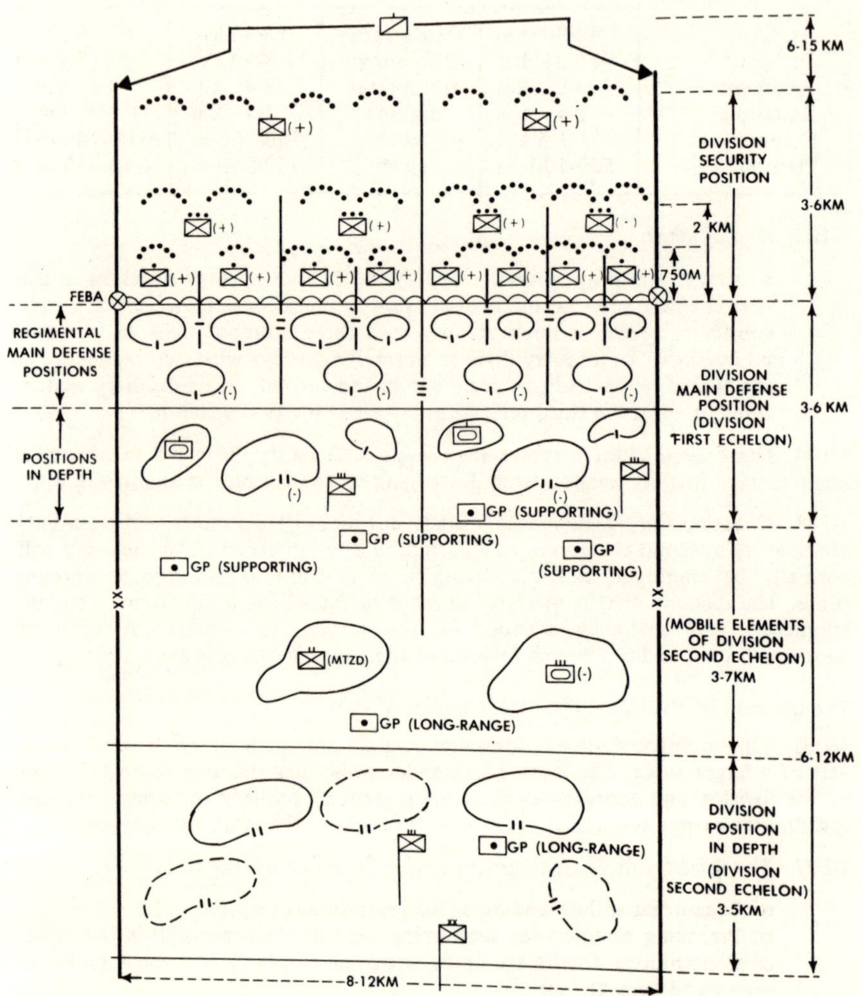

Figure 10. Positional Defense - The Division.

4-108. *Division Defense Area.*

a. *Security Position.* The security position is located forward of the main defensive position. It is lightly manned by mobile troops who provide security for forces in the main defensive position.

(1) *Screening Force.* This consists of the division reconnaissance company. It is deployed 6 to 15 kilometers forward of the main defensive position to provide early warning, to maintain liaison with the army's covering force, and to determine enemy strength and main axes of advance. It will fall back under pressure through the security forces into the main defensive position where it will be used to cover gaps, to protect flanks, and to provide rear area security, particularly against airborne attacks.

(2) *Regimental Security Force.* This force operates some 3 to 6 kilometers in front of the FEBA and is deployed in locations prescribed by the division commander. The force normally consists of one reinforced company from each of the frontline regiment's second echelons. The regiments retain operational control over their reinforced companies. The tasks of the security force are to:

(a) Defend stubbornly if the situation permits.

(b) Engage the enemy at long range in an attempt to force him to deploy prematurely and thereby slow down his advance.

(c) Deceive the enemy as to the strength, dispositions and intentions of the main defensive force.

(d) Maintain contact with the attacking force.

(e) Protect the main position from a surprise attack.

(3) *The Battalion Security Force.* Normally, each battalion is required to provide a reinforced platoon to man security positions up to some 2,000 meters in front of the FEBA. Operational control is retained by the battalion commander. Tasks are the same as for the regimental security force.

(4) *The Company Security Force.* Each frontline company usually provides a reinforced squad to man security positions up to some 750 meters in front of the FEBA. In very close terrain the battalion commander may not order the establishment of such a force. Operational control remains with the companies at all times.

(5) *Supporting Fire.* Artillery, tank and heavy weapon fires are carefully coordinated to support the security forces mentioned above.

b. *Main Defensive Position (MDP).* The bulk of the division is deployed in the division MDP. The position is organized in depth as a continuous defensive belt. This defensive belt is made up of mutually supporting strongpoints or localities employing all-round defense across the entire frontage. These strongpoints are expected to hold out even if bypassed or encircled. Gaps between companies and battalions are covered by observation, fire and minefields.

(1) *Forces:*

(a) in the division MDP—normally two reinforced regiments.

(b) in the regimental MDP—normally two reinforced battalions.

(c) in the battalion MDP—normally two reinforced companies.

(d) in the company MDP—normally two reinforced platoons.

(e) in the platoon MDP—normally two reinforced squads.

(2) *Tasks:*
>   (a) to organize and defend their assigned sectors.
>   (b) to inflict significant losses on the enemy and his equipment in front of the FEBA.
>   (c) to prevent penetration of the FEBA and, should penetration occur, to restore the integrity of the FEBA.

c. *Position in Depth (PD).* The position in depth is organized in such a way as to stop deep penetration of the defense zone, to provide a firm base to support counterattacks, and to provide rear area security. This organization applies to all units carrying out a positional defense. At division level one regiment normally mans the PD, the forward edge of which is usually located 6 to 13 kilometers behind the FEBA. The regiment normally organizes the PD with two of its three battalions. Strongpoints are often constructed on the reverse slopes of key terrain features. In addition, blocking positions are constructed. The third battalion of the regiment is usually motorized, forming part of the mobile counterattack force of the PD, and is located between the MDP and the actual PD itself.

(1) *Forces:*
>   (a) in the division PD—one infantry regiment and one tank assault gun regiment (−).
>   (b) in the regiment PD—one battalion.
>   (c) in the battalion PD—one company.
>   (d) in the company PD—one platoon.
>   (e) in the platoon PD—one squad.

(2) *Tasks:*
>   (a) to organize and defend the PD.
>   (b) to provide rear area security.
>   (c) to counterattack in order to destroy any enemy penetration and to restore the integrity of the FEBA.
>   (d) to contain enemy penetrations.
>   (e) to act as a division reserve.

4-109. *Division Antitank Force.* The Chinese may use an artillery support group (possibly battery size) in the antitank role. It will be sited to cover the most likely enemy thrusts or to cover a "killing zone" into which enemy armor has been purposely canalized.

4-110. *Division Counterattack Force.* The tank assault gun regiment (−) and one motorized infantry battalion of the division second echelon, which are located in assembly areas forward of the positions in depth, comprise the counterattack force.

4-111. *Reserve.* The regiment less one infantry battalion which mans the position in depth is also considered the reserve. If a counterattack by the division counterattack force should fail, the army commander may direct the reserve to be used as a counterattack force. The committal of the reserve may be made only on orders from the army commander.

4-112. *Division Headquarters.* A forward command post is established forward of the position in depth. Main headquarters is located behind the division second echelon regiment in the position in depth. Rear headquarters is with the rear service units up to 50 kilometers behind the FEBA.

4-113. *Fire Support.* The principles of fire support and the allocation of artillery are described in section IV, chapter 3.

    a. *Fire Plan.*

        (1) *Nuclear and Chemical.* While the Chinese are not known to possess tactical nuclear launchers, they may use strategic missiles in support of ground forces in defensive operations. In this event, preplanned nuclear and chemical strikes will be targeted against communication centers, on likely enemy deployment areas, and to cover any large gaps in the overall defensive concept.

        (2) *Conventional.* Fire planning is centralized, some of it at army level, until the enemy's main attack has begun. It is designed to fulfill three main roles:

            (a) *Counter Preparation.* An elaborate fire plan is made by the army artillery commander. It aims to engage the enemy's batteries and deployment areas as early as possible and to concentrate the fires of all weapons so that the enemy is subjected to progressively heavy bombardment as he approaches the main defensive zone.

            (b) *Defensive Fire.* Linear and area concentrations are planned and registered to cover gaps, likely areas of attack and possible areas of penetration.

            (c) *Counterattack Support.* Concentrations are preplanned to support counterattacks.

    b. *Antitank Plan.* The division plan basically implements the army antitank plan employing organic antitank units and those units allotted from army resources. It expands the army's concept to include the manner in which the battalion and sometimes the company organize their antitank defense.

        (1) Normally the antitank defense comprises four belts; three belts in front of the FEBA and a fourth in the defense-in-depth position.

            (a) The *first belt* is located in the division security position and is manned by the regimental security force. It consists of antitank minefields and obstacles covered by supporting fire. In addition, special antitank teams organized from the regimental security force are employed.

            (b) The *second belt,* also located in the division security position, is manned by the battalion security force. It is organized in a similar fashion to the first belt mentioned above.

            (c) The *third belt* generally coincides with the belt of final protective fires established by frontline units of the main defensive position. It consists of obstacles and minefields covered by small-arms fire and organic antitank weapons.

            (d) *Defense in Depth.* Antitank weapons are sited to cover the main tank approaches and areas into which tanks are hopefully being canalized. They are located principally in the MDP and the area between the MDP and the PD.

(2) In addition special antitank teams of three to five men may be formed to seek out and ambush enemy tanks in the main defensive position.

(3) A mobile division reserve of antitank weapons is collocated with the mobile elements of the second echelon in the area between the MDP and PD. Its role is to deploy rapidly to meet and contain enemy tank thrusts.

(4) Antitank guns, recoilless rifles, and artillery employed in the antitank role are usually sited in pairs. These weapons are normally moved after each firing to avoid detection.

c. *Air Defense Plan.* The air defense plan is coordinated at division level employing regiment and division antiaircraft weapons to protect:

(1) Division headquarters.

(2) Artillery positions.

(3) Mobile elements of the second echelon and the reserve.

In addition, where possible, some antiaircraft weapons are so located as to have a dual but subsidiary role of assisting in the antitank defense.

d. *Deployment of Division Artillery.* The division commander, through his artillery commander, organizes his organic and attached artillery units into the following groups:

(1) Long-range groups consisting of heavy and high-powered artillery under division control deployed 6 to 10 kilometers behind the FEBA.

(2) Direct support groups deployed 2 to 5 kilometers behind the FEBA.

(3) Roving artillery groups deployed in the division security position or in alternative positions in the MDP to support the security forces and confuse the enemy.

4-114. *Digging.* The ability and the willingness of the Chinese soldier to dig in and construct extensive, elaborate trenchwork are extraordinary. Given time, he will build weapons emplacements and troop shelters that will withstand all but direct hits by conventional weapons.

a. *Infantry.* All infantry are dug in in a series of interconnecting strongpoints which are organized for all-round defense and are mutually supportive. If time permits communication trenches and alternative positions are dug laterally between platoons and back to company headquarters. Overhead cover is normally provided for the bunker entrances, troop shelters, individual foxholes and machinegun emplacements. Camouflage is used extensively to provide concealment.

b. *Tanks and APC's.* Tanks and APC's are normally dug in. Explosives and dozer blades, if available, are used to assist human endeavor. Camouflage is used extensively to provide concealment.

c. *Artillery.* Guns may be dug in. Camouflage is used extensively to provide concealment.

4-115. Conduct of the Battle.

a. *In the Division Security Position.*

(1) *Screening Force.* Troops from the division reconnaissance company will make contact with the enemy some 6 to 15 kilometers in front of the FEBA. They will fall back under pressure without

becoming inextricably engaged and pass through the regimental security forces into the division position in depth. Long-range artillery and air strikes will be used against reported targets.

(2) *Security Forces.* After the withdrawal of the screening force, the regimental security force, supported by air and artillery strikes, will conduct a stubborn defense. When further resistance is considered unprofitable, the division commander will order a withdrawal through the battalion and company security positions to their respective regimental PD's. As the enemy pressure increases, the battalion and company security force will be withdrawn.

b. *In the Division Main Defense Position.*

(1) *Preassault.* An intense counterbattery fire plan, assisted by combat aviation will be fired to preempt and, if possible, neutralize the enemy's preparatory bombardment. Likely enemy assembly areas and lines of departure will be targeted to disrupt his attack intentions. Troops in the defensive positions will occupy shelters to protect them against nuclear, chemical and conventional fires. Radio silence is maintained.

(2) The Assault. As soon as the enemy launches his assault on the MDP, fire from all available weapons is brought to bear on his forces. Infantry heavy weapons and supporting artillery attempt to separate hostile tanks from their accompanying infantry, so that the tanks may be destroyed more easily by infantry antitank teams, and the attack slowed down, if not halted. The first echelon battalions of the frontline regiments in the MDP, in accordance with doctrine, will not withdraw even if bypassed or surrounded. As enemy penetrations are made, the second echelon battalions of the regiments will either launch previously prepared counterattacks in an attempt to destroy the penetration and restore the integrity of the FEBA or endeavor to contain the penetration from alternate positions prepared in depth.

c. *In the Division Position in Depth.*

(1) Preplanned counterattacks are conducted at every level should the enemy succeed in breaching the defensive positions. Normally the authority of the next superior commander is required before they can be launched. Counterattacks usually consist of fire from all types of weapons followed by infantry attacking from a different direction. As with their attack tactics, the Chinese will usually try to gain surprise with a flank attack while the enemy is reorganizing or counterattack at night or when visibility is restricted.

(2) At division level two counterattack forces are normally assigned the task of destroying enemy penetrations which have survived various counterattacks delivered by the regiments in the main defensive position. The first force is the mobile combined arms group of division's second echelon which is normally deployed forward of the actual position in depth and which is under the control of the division commander. If this force is unsuccessful, the division commander will inform the army commander who will direct him to commit his entire second echelon either to:

    (a) destroy the enemy penetration and restore the FEBA, or

    (b) strengthen and defend the division PD in order to contain the penetration and cover the withdrawal of the division first echelon.

The Mobile Defense at Division Level (see figure 11)

4-116. Mobile defense is conducted when the terrain on which it is fought is not considered critical, thereby allowing the Chinese to trade space for time. At the same time, the mobile defense enables the Chinese to deploy massive forces to attack the invader. The division participates in the mobile defense usually as part of a larger force. The mobile defense is conducted as a series of defensive battles fought at previously designated lines of resistance forward of a final interception line. It is characterized by surprise, limited counterattacks, and ambushes carried out in strength aimed at inflicting maximum casualties on the enemy, not on the retention of ground.

4-117. *Division Defensive Area.*

    a. *The Security Position.*

        (1) The security force, controlled by the division commander, consists of two reinforced battalions, usually mobile, from the second echelons of the frontline regiments. It operates some 5 to 10 kilometers in front of the FEBA. Its tasks are to:

            (a) maintain contact with the army covering force;

            (b) establish and maintain contact with the enemy after the army covering force has withdrawn;

            (c) determine enemy strength and avenues of approach;

            (d) engage the enemy at long range to force him to deploy prematurely; and

            (e) conduct a delaying action while inflicting the maximum number of casualties on the enemy.

        (2) Upon completion of its tasks, the security force withdraws through the FEBA and the battalions revert to the operational control of their respective frontline regiments.

    b. *The Main Defensive Position (MDP).* The division MDP is divided into two regimental sections. Two reinforced regiments, the division's first echelon, are deployed abreast in the MDP as they are in the positional defense. The third regiment occupies the division position in depth. Any similarity to the positional defense, however, ceases at this point because within the main defense positions of regiments, battalions, and companies, usually a third of the strength constitutes the first echelon with two-thirds held back in reserve. Conversely, firepower is deployed with two-thirds of its strength forward and the remaining one-third in the rear. The regimental MDP itself is organized with a defensive belt across the FEBA with subsequent, preplanned delaying positions to the rear until regimental final interception lines are reached at the forward edge of the regimental positions in depth where a positional-type defense may be conducted. Small-scale defensive battles involving surprise attacks and/or withdrawals are fought by combined arms groups in an attempt to delay, fragment, canalize, and/or exhaust superior enemy forces until these forces are susceptible to piecemeal destruction by a major counterattack. At no stage of this operation will the Chinese become decisively engaged. When the regiments have withdrawn to the regimental final interception line, mobile defense operations by the regiments in the division MDP cease and the mobile defense by the next higher echelon is initiated.

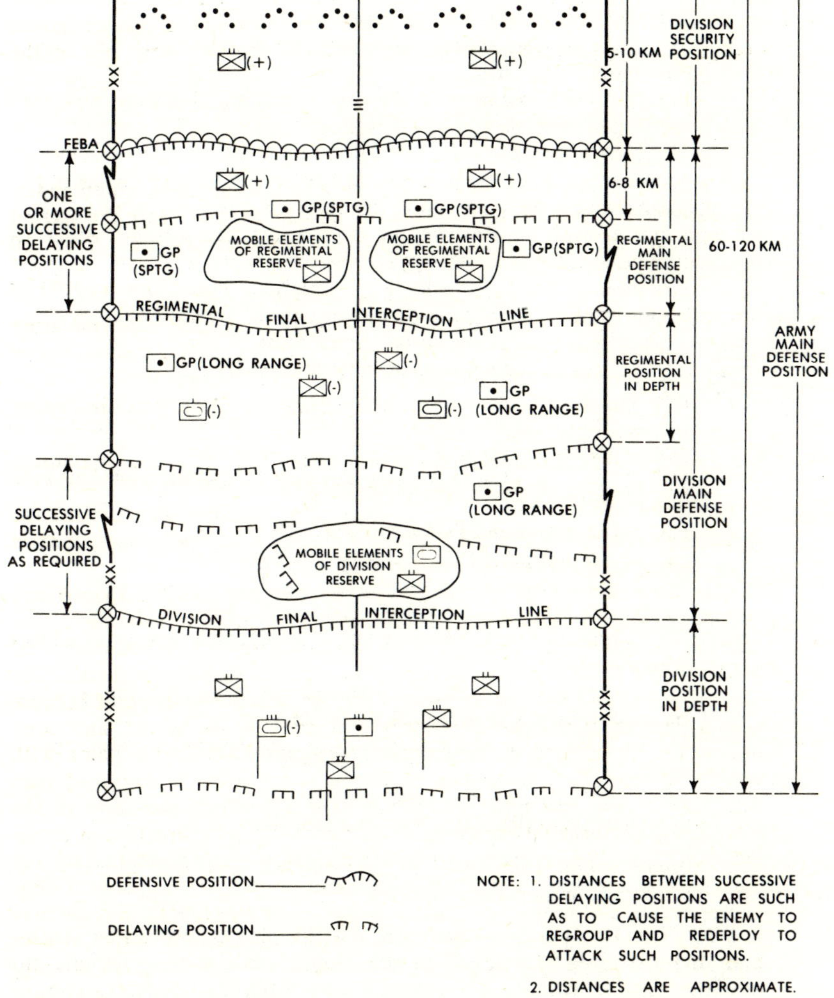

Figure 11. Mobile Defense - The Division.

(1) *Forces:*
    (a) in the division MDP—normally two reinforced regiments.
    (b) in the regiment MDP—normally one reinforced battalion.
    (c) in the battalion MDP—normally one reinforced company.
    (d) in the company MDP—normally one reinforced platoon.
    (e) in the platoon MDP—normally one reinforced squad.

(2) *Tasks:*
    (a) to inflict maximum casualties on the enemy.
    (b) to cause the enemy to deploy across the FEBA and attack the defended positions.
    (c) to effect withdrawal before becoming decisively engaged while delaying the enemy's advance.

c. *The Position in Depth (PD).* The division PD is a designated defensive zone occupied by the division's second echelon, normally consisting of the division's third regiment, the remainder of the division's organic strength and possibly reinforcements from army. The second echelon of regiments and smaller units occupying their respective PD's, on the other hand, is composed of two-thirds of the unit's strength. The purpose of the forces in the PD, depending on the situation, is either to carry out a position-type defense along final interception lines or to mount counterattacks against overextended, hostile forces.

(1) *Forces:*
    (a) in the division PD—one infantry regiment and one tank-assault gun regiment (−).
    (b) in the regiment PD—two infantry battalions and one tank company (−).
    (c) in the battalion PD—two infantry companies.
    (d) in the company PD—two infantry platoons.
    (e) in the platoon PD—two infantry squads.

(2) *Tasks:*
    (a) to mount counterattacks aimed at the destruction of enemy forces.
    (b) to conduct a position-type defense along previously designated defensive (final interception) lines.
    (c) to assist in the withdrawal of the first echelon forces from the MDP.
    (d) to provide a mobile reserve.
    (e) to provide flank and rear area security.

4-118. *Fire Support.* The principles of fire support and the allocation of artillery are described in section IV, chapter 3.

a. *Fire Plan.* In a positional defense, the fire plan is centralized at army and division levels. However, in the mobile defense the planning and employment of artillery are delegated to subordinate commanders in order that fire is responsive to the rapidly changing tactical situation.

b. *Antitank Plan.* The majority of antitank weapons are allocated to frontline units to counter potential tank threats. These units are then responsible for planning their own antitank defense within the overall defensive plan.

c. *Air Defense Plan.* Divisions and regiments plan for the deployment of their organic defense units. Priority for protection is given to:
  (1) unit headquarters,
  (2) artillery positions, and
  (3) mobile reserve.
d. *Deployment of Artillery.* Organic and attached artillery are organized into the following groups:
  (1) *Long-range Groups.* Both normally deployed some 5 to 10 kilometers behind the FEBA, providing direct support to battalions and regiments.
  (2) *Direct-support Groups.* Both normally deployed some 5 to 10 kilometers behind the FEBA, providing direct support to battalions and regiments.
  (3) *Roving Groups.* Normally deployed in the division security position or the MDP as part of a combined-arms team.

4-119. *Conduct of the Battle.*

a. *In the Division Security Position.* Following the withdrawal of the army covering force, the two reinforced battalions, which constitute the division security force and which are under the operational control of the division commander, will make contact with the enemy some 5 to 10 kilometers forward of the FEBA. This force will engage the enemy and delay him for as long as possible until he is forced to withdraw through the FEBA. The battalions then revert to the operational control of their respective regiments where they become part of the regiment's second echelon deployed in the PD.

b. *In the Main Defensive Position and the Position in Depth.* Elements of the regiment's first echelon occupying defensive positions along the FEBA will engage the enemy in an attempt to stop his advance and force him to deploy his forces for a coordinated attack. As the coordinated attack develops, the regiment commander, depending on the situation, has three courses of action:
  (1) He may order his first echelon forces to continue defending along the FEBA, without becoming decisively engaged.
  (2) He may decide to mount a counterattack employing his second echelon forces.
  (3) If enemy pressure increases to such an extent that it is considered inexpedient to continue the defense along the FEBA, he may order his first echelon forces to withdraw to defensive positions along the regimental final interception line while carrying out aggressive delaying actions, assisted by mobile elements of the regiment's reserve.
If a withdrawal is undertaken, as soon as the first echelon is deployed along the regimental final interception line, the conduct of the mobile defense is assumed by the division commander. As the enemy attack continues, the division commander is afforded the same three options as his regimental commanders: to defend, to counterattack, or to withdraw to defensive positions along the divisional final interception line while delaying the enemy's advance. Upon the division's withdrawal behind the divisional final interception line, the army commander then assumes

control of the mobile defense. This "stepping back" process continues until the purpose of the mobile defense is achieved.

4-120–4-125. *Reserved.*

SECTION IV–RETROGRADE OPERATIONS

4-126. Chinese doctrine stresses that the overall aim of retrograde operations is to create a more favorable situation for the initiation or resumption of the offensive. Retrograde operations are employed by the Chinese in both the offense and defense, either voluntarily or as a result of enemy pressure, to preserve their forces and to gain or maintain the initiative.

4-127. Retrograde operations fall into three categories:

a. *Withdrawal.* An operation, either voluntary or as a result of enemy pressure, in which a force in contact disengages from the enemy.
b. *Delaying action.* An operation in which a force under enemy pressure trades space for time. The Chinese fight a delaying action only when the enemy force has the initiative and they are unable to fall back in any other way.
c. *Retirement.* A voluntary movement to the rear by forces not in contact with the enemy.

4-128. *Purpose.* Retrograde operations are undertaken for the purpose of accomplishing one or more of the following:

a. Maintain the integrity of one's own forces.
b. Harass, exhaust, resist, delay and inflict punishment on the enemy.
c. Draw the enemy into an unfavorable situation.
d. Disengage from combat.
e. Gain time without becoming decisively engaged.
f. Permit the use of elements of a force elsewhere.
g. Avoid combat under undesirable conditions.

4-129. Whenever possible, retrograde operations take place at night. If the Chinese are forced to conduct a retrograde operation by day, they employ smoke to screen their movement. Retrograde operations are covered by intense artillery and air strikes and may be preceded by local counterattacks.

The Withdrawal (see figure 12)

4-130. The withdrawal is initiated when units in contact with the enemy are ordered to disengage and begin their movement to the rear. The division commander issues a very detailed plan which covers the following actions:

a. Small parties from all subunits are sent out to reconnoiter and plan the new defensive positions or assembly areas prior to the start of the withdrawal.
b. Field trains, nonessential supplies, equipment and personnel are sent to the rear.

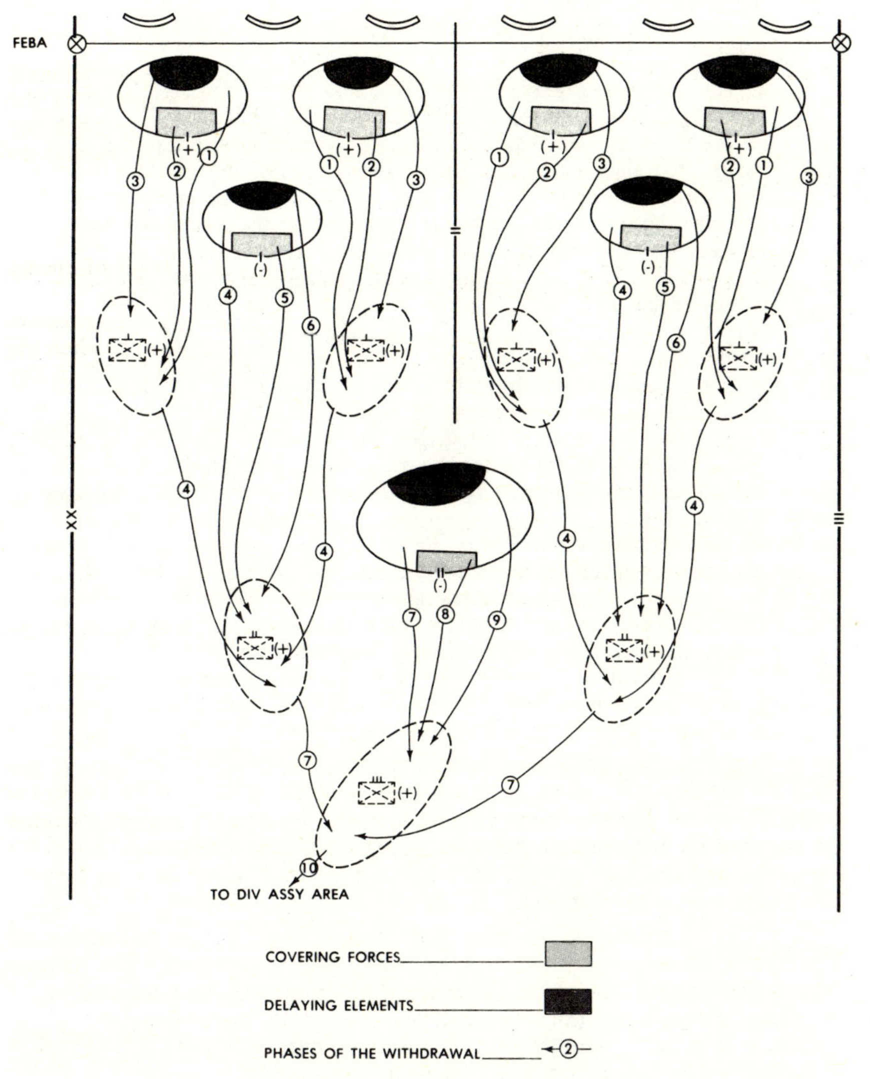

Figure 12. The Withdrawal.

c. Covering forces, normally consisting of no more than one-third of a unit's total strength, are formed from the unit's second echelon at all levels to cover the withdrawal.

d. In addition, delaying elements are left behind in their defensive positions to simulate continued defensive operations and to protect the withdrawal of their parent unit.

4-131. *Conduct of the Withdrawal.*

a. All companies along the FEBA, less their delaying elements and covering forces, move to assembly areas in the rear (phase 1). In addition to the delaying elements and covering forces, the withdrawal is covered by the battalion's second echelon; the latter also covers the subsequent withdrawal of company covering forces (phase 2) and company delaying elements (phase 3) to the assembly areas. As the assembled companies proceed to battalion assembly areas, the battalion second echelons, less delaying elements and covering forces, disengage and withdraw (phase 4). They are covered by fires of their own delaying elements and covering forces and the fires of the regimental second echelon. Disengagement and withdrawal of battalion covering forces (phase 5) and delaying elements (phase 6) complete withdrawal of the regimental first echelon. After the battalions initiate movement to regimental assembly areas, the regimental second echelon disengages and withdraws in a similar manner (phases 7, 8, 9) to its assembly area and, on division order, proceeds to the division assembly area (phase 10) under covering fires of the division second echelon.

b. Following the successful arrival of the regiment at the division assembly area, the division's covering force is withdrawn. The withdrawal is protected by rear and flank guards formed from the army's second echelon. They occupy defensive positions astride the withdrawal routes before the main body of the division begins to move.

c. The main body usually withdraws in march column as quickly as possible to its new defensive positions without occupying intermediate positions.

Delaying Action

4-132. While the Chinese carry out delaying actions similar to those of other armies, they do not consider they are fighting a delaying action *per se* unless the enemy has the initiative and is exerting such pressure that the Chinese have no other way by which to fall back.

The Retirement

4-133. The Chinese execute a retirement when they wish to avoid combat. If the forces carrying out the retirement are in contact, the initial phase of the operation is in fact a withdrawal. After contact with the enemy is broken, the retirement becomes a tactical march away from the enemy.

4-134–4-137. *Reserved.*

4-138. The PRC's airborne/air transportable forces are thought to consist of three airborne divisions located in Wuhan Military Region and are part of the PLA's strategic reserve. Airborne forces are an integral part of the PRCAF, not of the Army.

4-139. Chinese doctrine envisages the bold use of airborne troops, although the limited numbers and types of transport aircraft and helicopters available are restricting factors. Airborne operations include:

>   a. *Parachute Operations.* Carried out by paratroopers and followed, if required, by air-landed troops trained and equipped for air transportable operations.
>   b. *Air Transportable Operations.* Limited operations to quickly reinforce border areas or to maintain internal security within the PRC. In addition these specially trained air transportable troops could be used in operations to countries peripheral to China.
>   c. *Helicopter-Borne Operations.* Currently, due to lack of helicopters, only extremely limited operations can be carried out. This capability is expected to improve, however, as more helicopters become available.

Parachute Operations

4-140. *Roles.* The Chinese are expected to use their airborne forces in the following roles:

>   a. The seizure of important areas, routes and crossings in advance of major thrusts or to protect the rearward movement of Chinese forces.
>   b. Sabotage missions against nuclear delivery means, support units and guidance equipment.
>   c. The disruption of troop control, movement and logistic support by operations against headquarters, communications centers and rear area installations.
>   d. The support of amphibious landings. (This is discussed in the next section, paragraphs 4-151—4-156.)
>   e. Assistance to guerrillas.
>   f. Internal security missions.

4-141. *Size of Force.* The Chinese possess the capability to conduct up to regiment-size airborne operations against objectives within a 500-nautical-mile radius.

4-142. Organization of an airborne division is shown in appendix G.

4-143. *Equipment.* The division inventory is similar to that of a normal infantry division except that it has no tanks and only limited artillery, antitank and antiaircraft weapons.

Types of Operations

4-144. Parachute operations are divided into the following categories:

    a. *Strategic.* Operations involving the use of only one or possibly two airborne divisions in special circumstances such as:

        (1) The seizure of airbases, seaports or islands of strategic importance.

        (2) In support of deep penetrations following a breakthrough of the enemy defenses.

        (3) The holding of vital terrain features in the case of a major invasion of the PRC.

    b. *Tactical.* Operations of regiment or battalion size on the main axis in support of an army group or army offensive, timed to allow ground forces to link up with the airborne troops within 1 to 3 days.

    c. *Special Purpose.* Operations by parties of up to company strength in any area with the tasks of sabotage, disruption of control and rear service operations, and in support of guerrillas.

Conduct of Operations

4-145. Little is known about the manner in which the Chinese carry out their airborne operations but it is assumed that for the most part they will follow Soviet methods.

4-146. A division uses about four to six drop zones (DZ's) and a regiment uses one or two. Reserve DZ's are normally selected for use in an emergency or by subsequent waves. DZ's are about 3 to 4 kilometers in size and if circumstances permit may be on or outside the objective itself.

4-147. *Landing.* The fly-in is protected by fighter cover. All available fire support is used to neutralize enemy air defense weapons along the flight path. Drops will normally be made at night.

4-148–4-150. *Reserved.*

SECTION VI—WARFARE UNDER SPECIAL CONDITIONS

Amphibious Operations

4-151. The PRC conducted its first joint amphibious operation in 1955 against I Chiang Shan Island about 17 miles off the East China coast. Since that time, amphibious training has had an important place in the training of units stationed in or near China's coastal areas.[3]

4-152. At present, the PRC possesses the capability to conduct an amphibious operation involving three infantry divisions, their organic armor, artillery and those personnel and equipment that would be required during the assault phase

---

[3] The successful seizure by the PRC of the Paracel Islands in January 1974 is the most recent example of China's ability to conduct amphibious operations.

of an amphibious operation. In addition to naval amphibious ships and craft, merchant shipping and motorized junks would be used to support the effort.

4-153. *Amphibious Units.* The PRCA is believed to have a number of units which have been trained in amphibious operations. During an amphibious assault, these forces, organized into regiments, would spearhead the landing, conducting beach reconnaissance, clearing obstacles, and making the initial assault.

4-154. *Types of Operations.* Amphibious operations will necessarily take place within range of shore-based aircraft and will aim to:

> **a.** Seize and secure a beachhead on a hostile shore from which large-scale ground operations can be initiated.
> **b.** Assist the advance of ground forces by attacking the sea flanks of an opposing force.
> **c.** Seize and secure vital areas such as islands and straits.
> **d.** Conduct raids and reconnaissance.

4-155. *Scale.* A division conducting an amphibious operation is divided into two echelons: an assault echelon, consisting of two reinforced regiments, and a support echelon, consisting of the remainder of the division's forces.

4-156. *The Assault Landing.*

> **a.** *Airborne.* An amphibious landing may be preceded by, or made simultaneously with, a parachute- or helicopter-borne assault onto or near the beachheads.
> **b.** *Night.* The approach is normally made at night or under other conditions of poor visibility. Amphibious landings are normally made at night or at first light.
> **c.** *Frontages.* Frontages are similar to those for the attack described in section I of this chapter 4. Each battalion is allocated one landing point and these are at least 1 kilometer apart.
> **d.** *Control.* Chinese doctrine prescribes a unified command for amphibious operations. The commander of such an operation is usually a senior army commander who is responsible for the execution of the operation. In addition, two subordinate forces commanders are designated and charged with specific responsibilities during each phase of the operation.
>> (1) *Naval Landing Commander.* He is a senior naval officer responsible for embarkation, movement by sea, and landing ground troops on the hostile shore. During this period of the operation he is in command.
>> (2) *Landing Force Commander.* As soon as adequate communication and command facilities have been established ashore, command passes from the naval landing commander to the landing force commander. He is charged with direct command of ground force troops during the preembarkation period, coordination of ground forces during the assault, and command of tactical operations ashore to seize and secure the beachhead.
> **e.** *Tactics and Fire Support.* The tactics and fire support of an amphibious landing are similar to those employed by both Soviet and

Western armies. Coordinated air and naval gunfire provides continuous fire support aimed at neutralizing or destroying enemy defenses. Artillery on nearby land masses may also be integrated into the overall fire plan.

Cold Weather Warfare

4-157. Special attention is given to winter warfare training in the PRCA. The Chinese believe that large-scale ground operations are possible in extreme climatic conditions.

4-158. *Influence of Climatic Conditions.*

    a. Eight to twelve inches of accumulated snow will retard the mobility of infantry, armor and artillery; over 12 inches of snow will cause extreme difficulties in their movement.

    b. Heavy snowfalls require excessvie troop labor to clear essential roads and maintain fortification.

    c. Snow makes troop movement concealment difficult.

    d. Extreme cold has a direct effect on troop stamina and on their equipment.

    e. Subzero temperatures radically alter the tactical significance of certain terrain features like rivers, lakes, and swamps.

4-159. *Tactical Concepts.* Chinese tactical operations in winter do not differ greatly from those conducted under less severe conditions. Cold weather conditions increase the importance of shelters, hinder the construction of defenses, make rivers, lakes and swamps passable, and restrict air support.

4-160. Chinese doctrine emphasizes the need for more and continuous reconnaissance to locate the enemy's main strength and flanks, the direction of his movement, and the disposition of his nuclear weapons. In addition, particular attention is paid to weather reconnaissance, the depth of snow on the avenues of approach and the thickness of ice on water obstacles. The reconnaissance is conducted by small units on skis or in vehicles capable of cross-country movement.

4-161. *Organization.* No special organizations are known to exist for cold-weather warfare although some specialized equipment undoubtedly is issued to units.

4-162. *The Offensive.* In cold-weather warfare, assembly areas are located closer to the enemy than at other times to lessen approach marches and thereby minimize fatigue and the possibility of frostbite. Heated shelters are provided in assembly areas and covered shelters in attack and, if possible, in assault positions.

4-163. *Defense.* The FEBA is selected making the maximum use of natural climatic obstacles difficult to overcome in winter. All cover available to enemy in front of the FEBA is destroyed by demolition or covered with planned artillery fire. Holes are made in frozen lakes or rivers and the ice is mined. Obstacles, including minefields covered by fire, are constructed in gaps between a system of strongpoints. No more than a third of fighting personnel occupy firing positions at a time.

Fighting in Built-up Areas

4-164. *Attack*. When encountering a town that must be seized during the advance, the commander normally strives to capture it from the line of march before the enemy can establish elaborate defenses. The advance guard moves into the town, seizes important objectives and holds them until the main body arrives. When an attack from the line of march fails, the commander establishes a blockage and initiates preparations for a deliberate attack on the town. The deliberate attack is preceded by an artillery bombardment supported by air strikes. It normally consists of several converging attacks initiated in different sectors of the town to split the enemy defenses into several segments for subsequent piecemeal destruction.

4-165. *Defense*. The defense of a town or city is organized for all-round defense based on inner and outer defense zones. Inner defense zones are established throughout the entire town; their number and size are dependent on the size of the town and the overall defense plan. Each zone is based on a system of defense centers each of which consists of two or more strongpoints. The forward edge of the first inner defense zone is normally placed on the town's outskirts. Outer defense zones are established on the approaches to the town. Their number depends on the terrain and available manpower and materiel; frequently these positions are merely combat security positions.

Mountain Warfare

4-166. Chinese combat forces are trained for operations in mountainous terrain. The difficulties imposed by terrain, however, often dictate the use of special equipment. At extremely high altitudes, as along the Sino-Indian border, acclimatization is necessary.

4-167. *The Offensive*. The usual type of offensive maneuver is a frontal attack of the enemy with regiment- and/or battalion-size units operating on independent axes along roads, valleys and ridges in conjunction with enveloping movements across adjacent mountains. Enveloping forces are employed to seize commanding heights, passes and road intersections on the flanks and rear of the enemy position while the main force carries out the frontal attack. If the enveloping forces succeed in making the enemy withdraw before the main frontal attack is initiated, the main force will immediately carry out a pursuit to prevent the enemy from occupying another defensive position.

4-168. *Defense*. The defense is organized as a series of strongpoints on the commanding heights, each mutually supporting and capable of all-round defense. Gaps are covered by patrols. In the event of strongpoints being surrounded, they will continue to fight on without any thought of withdrawal. Constant observation and patrolling are carried out to prevent outflanking movement.

4-169. *Fire Support*. Fire support for Chinese forces in mountainous country does not differ greatly from the support afforded in offensive and defensive operations under normal terrain conditions.

4-170. *The Use of Armor*. Every effort is made to employ tanks in areas where the enemy will not expect them; in the defense, tanks are sometimes deployed in forward infantry strongpoints.

4-171. Combat forces assigned to areas where jungle terrain predominates receive specialized training in the conduct of jungle operations. The organization, equipment, and tactics of these forces are often tailored to offset the adverse effects of the terrain and the monsoon climate.

4-172. *Terrain.* Mountainous jungle terrain prevails in southern China, primarily in Yunnan and Kwangsi Provinces, and in Burma, Thailand, Laos, Malaysia, Cambodia, and Vietnam. These regions are characterized by rugged terrain, dense first- and second-growth jungle, small scattered villages and cultivated areas, numerous streams and marshes, few highways or rail lines, and networks of unimproved trails.

4-173. *Organization and Equipment.* Mountainous jungle terrain has a leveling effect on the relative capabilities of opposing forces since it limits sharply the employment of armor, heavy artillery, and vehicular transport, and restricts aerial observation. The standard Chinese infantry division would probably be stripped of its tank/assault gun regiment and heavy artillery so as to resemble a light infantry division. The lack of heavy vehicles and equipment in a jungle environment is a factor in the PRCA's favor. Accustomed to movement by foot, Chinese forces are capable of moving with relative ease even over areas where no trails exist. The lack of roads poses no problems for light artillery units or for logistical elements which use animal or human resources.

4-174. *Tactics.* The tactics employed by the PRCA in a jungle environment stress taking full advantage of natural cover; extensive use of infiltration, ambushes, and guerrilla warfare; secrecy and speed of movement; continuous reconnaissance; and well-coordinated planning. Maintaining control over his forces is the primary problem confronting a commander because of the restrictions on movement and communications imposed by the terrain.

4-175–4-180. *Reserved.*

Planning prior to a battle is both detailed and continuous. The use of a sand table is a common method of depicting the battlefield area.

Long experience of guerrilla warfare has made the PRCA masters of the art of infiltration.

The reconnaissance element of the antichemical warfare company of the infantry division.

A soldier and a militiaman conducting joint reconnaissance.

The Chinese are well trained in patrolling and are expected to carry out their tasks with skill and energy.

Motorized Reconnaissance.

122-mm howitzer type 54 in a night-firing exercise.

Chinese troops employing the 75-mm recoilless rifle type 56 (above) and the 40-mm antitank grenade launcher type 69.

Air defense exercise employing a 100-mm antiaircraft gun type 59.

Soldiers at rest area along the route of march.

A 37-mm antiaircraft gun type 55.

Type 59 medium tanks in the advance guard.

A Chinese soldier in winter gear attempting to clear mined area with mine detector.

Armor and infantry in the deliberate attack.

Infantry squad in the assault.

Bamboo rafts are used to carry not only weapons and equipment but injured personnel as well.

Transporting recoilless rifles on makeshift floats.

CHAPTER 5
LOGISTICS AND PERSONNEL

SECTION I–LOGISTICS

Overview

5-1. The continuing effort to modernize China's armed forces has required concurrent strengthening of logistical support at all levels. Considerable improvement is apparent when current supply and service procedures are compared with those of the Korean War era, when China entered that conflict with little in the way of a formalized system for the logistical support of its forces. Although there are inherent weaknesses in organization and equipment maintenance at the operational level, the PRCA's logistical system, especially its supply, transportation, and medical support functions, is considered well adapted, at least in theory, to the military establishment it is intended to support.

5-2. Chinese logistical doctrine has been influenced by the following:

a. Experience gained during the Korean War.
b. Influx of Soviet doctrine, training, and equipment in the 1950's.
c. Lessons learned from the North Vietnamese support of their forces and the Viet Cong in the face of enemy air supremacy.
d. Experience acquired in moving troops and supplies during breakdown of communications caused by the Cultural Revolution.
e. Redeployment of troops and equipment to the north in response to the Soviet threat.

5-3. *Strengths and Weaknesses.* The main strengths and weaknesses of the Chinese logistical system are:

a. *Strengths.*
(1) The PRC has the ability to mobilize civil resources, including mass manpower, to support a military effort.
(2) The stamina of the individual Chinese soldier and his familiarity with marginal living conditions simplify supply problems.
(3) Equipment is kept to the minimum required for efficient operation; rations are simple; and personal needs and comforts are few.
(4) The Chinese soldier is prepared to improvise necessities that the logistical system fails to provide.
b. *Weaknesses.*
(1) The vastness of the Chinese mainland, a less than adequate transportation system, and deficiencies in defense-related industries restrict the PRC's logistical capability.
(2) China's logistical system remains untested in prolonged modern warfare.
(3) A shortage of qualified, lower-echelon logistical officers, evident in the 1960's, probably still exists.

5-4. *Principles.* The following principles govern logistical activities in the PRCA:

a. *Centralized Planning.* Logistical planning is centralized in specialized staff elements at all echelons of command.

b. *Command Control.* Within each echelon, logistics is regarded as a function of command.

c. *Standardization.* Considerable effort has been made to standardize weapons and equipment in order to simplify and facilitate maintenance, repair and supply of spare parts.

d. *Distribution Forward.* The impetus of supply and service support is from higher to lower echelon, with transport and delivery responsibility resting with the higher echelon.

e. *Rail Transport.* Rail transport is used to the maximum to conserve stocks of motorized transport and POL reserves.

f. *Salvaged and Captured Material.* During combat, recovery, spot repair, reuse of equipment and the collection and processing of captured material are practiced.

g. *Priorities.* Supplies are classified into four categories and priorities are established as follows:

(1) Ammunition.

(2) POL.

(3) General (Quartermaster, Medical, Signal, Engineer, Chemical, Ordnance).

(4) Rations.

5-5. *Division of Responsibilities.* The General Rear Services Department promulgates logistical policy for China's armed forces and supervises its implementation. At each successive level down to regiment, a rear services department serves as the supply and service component of the commander's military staff. Rear services departments coordinate and control all logistic support activity including procurement and storage of supplies, medical and veterinary care, transportation, quartering, finance and salvage.

a. *Army.* Within the combat zone, the army formation is the key unit of logistic operations and management. The army rear services command is formed to carry out the logistical responsibilities. The commander of the army rear services command controls most service troops assigned or allocated to the army, except engineer and signal. He is responsible for the supply and service support of the divisions, army troops, and reinforcements allocated to the army; for planning and supervising all logistical operations in the army rear area; and for liaison with rear services departments of higher, adjacent and lower commands.

b. *Division.* The division rear services department develops all logistical plans relative to division operations and informs the army rear services command of division requirements. Bulk supplies and replacements are received from army and are broken down according to subordinate commands' requirements.

System of Supply (see figure 13)

5-6. Supply is by forward distribution. Supplies move from factories, warehouses, or arsenals directly to regional depots, then to army depots, via railway or motorized transport. From army depots, supplies reach division supply points by transportation organic to the army. Supplies are then normally distributed to regiments from division supply points—a main base and three mobile bases—by division transportation. On occasion, supplies are sent directly to regimental dumps to avoid unnecessary handling. Regimental supply points are little more than distributing points where incoming supplies are broken down for distribution to subordinate units. Regimental transport moves supplies to battalion distribution points, where they are further broken down for companies and moved forward by animal-drawn carts, pushcarts, pack animals or porters. Rear services departments at all levels from regiment upwards may provide additional motorized transport. PRCA transport resources may be further augmented by motor transport, pack animals or porters contracted or requisitioned from the civilian sector.

5-7. *Daily Resupply Requirements.* The following table lists the average daily resupply requirements (in short tons) of a PRCA standard infantry division at varying levels of combat:

Level of Combat	Ammunition	POL	Supplies	Rations	Total Requirement
Heavy Combat	450	10	20	20	500
Moderate Combat	250	10	20	20	300
Light Combat	100	10	20	20	150
Average Requirement (Protracted Period)	150	10	20	20	200

Ammunition

5-8. Army, division, and regimental rear services departments maintain ammunition supply dumps. Ammunition stocks to be maintained at each echelon are specified by higher headquarters. Resupply from army to division, from division to regiment, and from regiment to battalion is normally accomplished by organic motorized transport. Resupply of ammunition from battalion forward may be accomplished by human, animal or motor transport depending on the distances involved, the terrain, and the combat situation. During combat, resupply of ammunition is facilitated by the establishment of temporary ammunition dumps and frequent shifting of supply points. The stockpiling of ammunition in forward areas is a common procedures.

5-9. The PRCA uses the term "basic quantity" as the measure of ammunition supply. A basic quantity, similar to the Soviet "unit of fire," is the number of rounds to be maintained for each weapon within a unit. It is an arbitrary amount used for accounting and planning purposes, although it does have some relation to combat requirements. Ammunition is requisitioned by units or allocated for an operation in multiples of the basic quantity. Under normal conditions one basic quantity is maintained for all weapons with the units of the division; another one-half to one is held in reserve by the division rear services

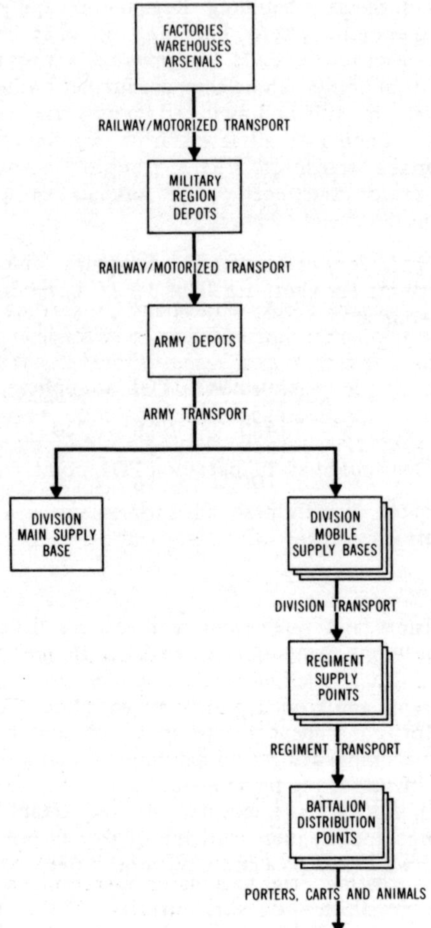

Figure 13. System of Supply.

department. In addition, a reserve of a least one, if not more, basic quantity is held at army level. Typical basic quantities for selected weapons are indicated as follows:

a. Type 59 medium tank   –   34 rounds
b. 122-mm howitzer, Type 54 –   80 rounds
c. 82-mm mortar, Type 53   – 120 rounds
d. 7.62-mm carbine, Type 56 – 100 rounds

POL

5-10. The Chinese probably follow the Soviet practice of measuring fuel in "refills." One refill is the quantity required to fill the internal and external tanks of all vehicles in a unit, plus lubricants allocated at 10 percent of the fuel required. Normally, the division carries from two-and-a-half to three refills: one in the fuel tanks of the vehicles, one-half each at battalion level and regimental level, and one-half or one at division level.

5-11. *Delivery.* Reserve POL stocks are dispersed in remote areas. These reserve sites are well hardened against air attack and are rail-serviced. Military region depots maintain peacetime stocks equivalent to wartime front or theater area stocks. Army, division, and regiment rear services departments maintain POL dumps. Most fuels and lubricants are transported and stored in 55-gallon drums and 5-gallon cans. Division vehicles haul POL forward from division POL dumps to regimental dumps. Regimental vehicles, in turn, transport POL forward to battalion supply dumps, as required. Within those battalions having organic transport, POL is distributed at the battalion POL point.

5-12. *Captured Stocks.* The Chinese will supplement normal POL with captured stocks. It is unlikely, however, that they will rely on captured stocks in their logistic planning.

Rations and Water

5-13. *Rations.* The PRCA issues three kinds of rations: the standard ration, the combat ration, and the emergency ration.

   a. The standard ration consists of rice, flour, pork, fish, eggs, soybeans, vegetables, edible oil, and salt, sugar, and other condiments. The individual soldier is issued 2 to 3 pounds of food per day. Most of the fish, pork and vegetables are produced locally by individual units for their consumption.
   b. The combat ration is spartan consisting of dried rice, dried fried wheat, or a baked mixture of soybeans, corn, millet and kaoliang to which water is added before eating. Prior to a major operation, each soldier is issued the equivalent of from 5 to 7 days' rations.
   c. The emergency ration is a compressed, rectangular biscuit made of flour, salt and oil. Each soldier carries about 12 of these biscuits in addition to his combat ration.

5-14. Under simulated or actual combat conditions, companies, battalions, and regiments each store the equivalent of 7 days' supply of rations. Divisions maintain 10 days' supply, and armies from 1/2 to 1 month's supply. Rations are delivered from division to regiment, and from regiment to battalion and company, or direct to forward positions. During troop movements in peacetime, rations are often purchased from local communes.

5-15. *Water.* The Chinese possess the equipment which enables them to supply fresh water in the field as well as the capability to test and treat contaminated local water supplies. Water supply is the responsibility of the engineer section of a given unit; water purification is the responsibility of the medical section.

Medical

5-16. Medical departments of rear services units supervise medical evacuation and designate routes and evacuation centers. Litter bearers are normally used at battalion level and below. Ambulances and/or litter bearers are used at the regiment and division levels, although supply vehicles may also be employed.

5-17. *Battalion.* Soldiers wounded in combat are attended by rifle company first aid men at company collection centers where first aid is administered and field dressings are applied. Evacuation of casualties from the company collection center to the battalion aid station is usually by litter bearers. At the battalion aid station, wounds are rebandaged, bones are set, injections are given, and the more seriously injured are prepared for evacuation to regimental field dressing stations (FDS). Battalion aid stations are usually located about 1,000 to 2,000 meters from the frontline.

5-18. *Regiment.* Regimental ambulances or litter bearers collect casualties from battalion collection centers (collocated in the battalion aid station) and transport them to regimental field dressing stations located 4 to 8 kilometers from the frontline. Emergency surgery may be performed at this level if the patient's condition makes further movement inadvisable. Otherwise, treatment at this level is limited to classifying wounds, stabilizing patients and, if required, preparing patients for evacuation to field hospitals.

5-19. *Division.* Ambulances from the division medical battalion pick up wounded at the field dressing station's collection center and evacuate them to mobile hospitals at division level and to army field hospitals. The mobile hospitals provide limited medical care, including minor surgery. The field hospitals perform major surgery and treat patients not requiring long periods of hospitalization. Serious cases requiring special care, special surgery and/or long periods of convalescence are evacuated to regional or base military hospitals found at provincial or military district level. Personnel who have recovered from wounds or injuries may be returned to duty by any medical facility in the chain of evacuation.

Recovery and Repair

5-20. General. The PRCA's current system of recovery and repair is believed to be based largely on the Soviet system. The shortage of technicians, the scarcity of spare parts, and the limited number of repair facilities were often cited in the past as indications of the PRCA's weakness in the area of recovery and repair. While simple repair is encouraged at the unit level and fabrication and cannibalization are practiced, these deficiencies are believed to have been overcome and the PRCA now can recover and repair equipment under combat conditions. Mobile field repair teams are found at many units of regiment level and above.

5-21. *Maintenance.* Appreciation for and understanding of preventive maintenance are continually stressed at all levels in an attempt to decrease the number of equipment breakdowns and to lighten repair workloads. Upgrading the technical proficiency of mechanics and operators through both special and on-the-job training is also encouraged.

5-22. *Recovery.* Battlefield recovery of both friendly and enemy material is considered of prime importance. Every unit is responsible for the collection and evacuation of all useable weapons or equipment within its area. When the collecting unit cannot handle the evacuation, specially designated recovery teams from higher headquarters will move the material to the rear where it is processed. At army and division, each service maintains a collection point for salvage material at rear area supply installations. Below division, a single collection point is established for salvage of all classes of material.

5-23. *Repair.* The Chinese have three categories of repair: minor repair, medium repair, and major repair.

> **a.** Minor repair includes periodic checks, replacement of subassemblies, and fabrication of spare parts. It is normally accomplished at regiment level.
> **b.** Medium repair includes cannibalization, salvage, and patching as well as minor repair. Medium repair is usually performed at division and army levels.
> **c.** Major repairs are normally carried out at military region level in large fixed-shops or salvage-and-rebuild installations. Here complete equipment rebuild is accomplished. Material judged not salvageable is cannibalized for parts.

5-24. Echelons of repair are determined by the capabilities of the facilities at any particular level. Repairs are made at the lowest possible echelon to reduce the time lost in evacuation. In addition, because of a lack of recovery equipment, repair is attempted at the point of disablement, although such repair is often hampered by the lack of mobile repair teams. The rear service department at both regiment and division headquarters has an ordnance repair section responsible for the maintenance and repair of all items the PRCA considers ordnance. Signal maintenance and repair are performed by the signal battalion at division level and by the signal company at regiment level.

Reinforcement

5-25. The PRCA's reinforcement doctrine is probably modeled after that of the Soviet Union. Reinforcement would likely be by complete regiments or divisions taken from the strategic reserve. Because of the PRC's limited transportation system, large-scale and rapid movement of reinforcements would most probably be accomplished by railway, although other modes of transport (e.g., motorized transport and aircraft) might conceivably be used as well.

Prisoners of War

5-26. The collection, interrogation, safeguarding, processing and utilizing of prisoners of war are functions of the army Political Department's enemy affairs section. The enemy affairs section is normally assisted by a platoon-size guard unit which operates the army POW enclosure.

5-27. The procedure for handling POW's is as follows:

a. Prisoners are evacuated from company areas to the rear immediately after their personal belongings are inventoried and weapons, documents and military equipment are confiscated. Prisoners may be retained at battalion level, but for no more than 1 day. Interrogation is not normally conducted at company or battalion level, though it may occur.

b. A prisoner receives his first formal interrogation at regiment level, where he encounters personnel from the enemy affairs section. Interrogation at regiment is brief, usually aimed at gaining information of immediate tactical importance.

c. Interrogation at division and army levels is more thorough, usually incorporating political indoctrination. Coordinated interrogation and indoctrination of POW's continue throughout the period of activity. Prisoners are evacuated from the army enclosure usually within a week of their capture.

5-28. Chinese doctrine stresses adherence to conventional rules of warfare. It may be assumed that regulations governing the treatment of POW's are similar to those of other armies. Food, clothing and medical treatment provided will be of a standard comparable to that of the Chinese themselves.

5-29—5-33. *Reserved.*

SECTION II—THE CHINESE SOLDIER

Profile of the Chinese Soldier

5-34. The Peoples Republic of China comprises diverse ethnic groups and languages which give it a multinational, multicultural character reflected, in turn, in all its institutions, including the armed forces. It is difficult, therefore, to describe the character of the average Chinese soldier.

5-35. The overwhelming majority of soldiers in China are drawn from the peasant-worker class, which constitutes over 80 percent of the population. The average soldier is a hard and willing worker and is able to survive and improvise under a wide variety of conditions. He has sufficient education to read and understand simple training manuals. While he may fall below Western standards in literacy and technical proficiency, he surpasses the average Western soldier in his ability to bear extraordinary hardships. His physical condition is considered excellent. Pervasive and continuous indoctrination from an early age has instilled in him national pride and party loyalty. He has a strong sense of obedience and under competent leadership will attempt to carry out his mission, regardless of obstacles or consequences. The Chinese soldier is considered one of the most highly motivated soldiers in the world today. The prominence and respect which the armed forces have enjoyed in recent years have enhanced the prestige and social standing of the soldier and have overcome the traditional contempt for military life of earlier eras. It is a proud family whose son or daughter is chosen for service in the PLA.

Rank

5-36. In 1965 all military ranks in the armed forces were abolished in an attempt to close the gap between officers and enlisted men. Now only one basic distinction is made in the PLA: that between "commanders" (officers) and "fighters" (enlisted men).

Morale

5-37. A standard of living well above that of the average civilian, special privileges, and an enormous gain in social status have all contributed to what is considered to be generally good morale in China's armed forces. However, morale often tends to rise and fall with fluctuations in the economy and the political climate.

5-38. How the Chinese soldier would behave under conditions of modern warfare today is unpredictable. The Chinese "volunteers" who crossed the Yalu into Korea in October 1950 were highly motivated, highly disciplined troops, instilled with the belief that their technical inferiority could be offset by pitting superior numbers against superior firepower. Constrained by fixed battle lines and confronted by growing casualties, the Chinese realized that masses and sheer determination were no match for a professionally trained, well-equipped, and technologically superior enemy. Chinese POW's confirmed that combat morale, discipline, and political control crumbled as a result of the adverse conditions of modern combat. Whether or not the "Korean experience" would repeat itself today is debatable.

Conscription

5-39. The PRC's conscription law stipulates that all male citizens who attain the age of 18, irrespective of nationality, race, occupation, social background, religious belief, or education, have the obligation to serve in the armed forces. "Counterrevolutionary" elements, landlords and bureaucratic capitalists, and those who have been deprived of political rights are not qualified to serve. The sick or disabled and "compassionate exemptees" (persons who provide sole support for a family, or a family's only son) may be exempted or deferred. Of the estimated 9 million males reaching induction age annually, some 60 percent fail the medical examination while an additional 20 percent are eliminated following an examination of their political backgrounds. Further physical and political testing results in no more than 10 percent of those initially eligible being actually inducted into the PLA. Induction normally takes place during the slack period in agriculture, generally from November to February.

Terms of Service

5-40. Since early 1974 the duration of military service for the Chinese conscript has been 3 years in the ground forces, 4 years in the air force, and 5 years in the navy.

5-41. Prior to his release, a soldier possessing certain technical skills or engaged in special duties may volunteer for extended service. Acceptance for extended duty is based on certain criteria: the need of the soldier's unit; the soldier's past performance and technical proficiency; the soldier's political thinking; and his physical condition. It is estimated that personnel on extended duty comprise about 20 to 25 percent of the PLA's total strength.

Demobilization

5-42. Upon completion of military service, the overwhelming majority of soldiers return to their homes and their civilian positions be it on a commune or in a factory. All are required to join local militia organizations. In Peking's own words: *they (militia organizations) are a great military reserve of the motherland whose members have been well-trained militarily.* Although China does not have a formal reserve system in the Western sense, it is considered to have an effective military manpower reserve pool in the militia. However, little is known of the regulations and procedures governing the mobilization of these "reserves" in the event of war.

Training

5-43. *Preconscription Training.* While the PRC has no formal preinduction training all Chinese youths receive rudimentary drilling and instruction in the communes and schools. In addition, the "everyone a soldier" movement has provided young people with an ideological orientation for future military service.

5-44. *Basic Training.* Basic training usually last 3 months and normally takes place at regimental level in temporarily formed training units. Basic training is rudimentary, consisting largely of political lectures, drill and marching, use and care of individual weapons, bayonet practice, and some tactics and fieldcraft. Following basic training the soldier is integrated into a regular unit where he receives advanced individual training. From this point, training becomes the responsibility of the service or arm to which the soldier is assigned.

5-45. *Daily Training Program.* The basic idea behind the daily training program is to keep the conscript busy from dawn to dusk. A typical daily training program might be as follows:

Activity	From	To
Reveille		0600 hours
PT/Drill	0615 hours	0700 hours
Washing/Bed Making	0700 hours	0715 hours
Morning Meal	0715 hours	0800 hours
Training	0800 hours	1200 hours
Midday Meal/Rest	1200 hours	1330 hours
Training	1330 hours	1730 hours
Evening Meal/Rest	1730 hours	1900 hours
Political Training	1900 hours	2000 hours
Individual Tasks/Study	2000 hours	2100 hours
Light Out		2100 hours

Conditions of Service

5-46. *Pay.* Officers receive a monthly salary whereas enlisted personnel are given a monthly "allowance" on the theory that soldiers are obligated to serve the state and should not be compensated for their services. This "basic pay" for both officers and enlisted men reflects the responsibility and authority of the position occupied and length of service. In addition to the "basic pay," soldiers stationed in remote areas of China (e.g., Tibet, Sinkiang), garrisoned on offshore islands, or aboard ships at sea receive an extra monthly allowance.

5-47. The following chart lists the estimated basic monthly pay for enlisted personnel in the PLA in 1973:

Years in Service	Position	Basic Monthly Pay	(U.S. $ Equivalent)
1	Conscript	6 yuan	($3.06)
2	Fighter	7 yuan	($3.57)
3	Deputy Squad Leader	8 yuan	($4.08)
4	Squad Leader	10 yuan	($5.10)
4+	Deputy Platoon Leader	Increased by 5 yuan ($2.55) each year after four years in service	

5-48. *Rations and Messing.* Rations in China's armed forces are considered superior in both quality and quantity to that of the average citizen. Most of the meats and vegetables are produced on unit farms. Following is an example of a typical daily menu in the PLA:

    a. Morning Meal. Rice, root vegetables, peppers, eggs, buns, tea.

    b. Midday Meal. Rice, soup, vegetables, fruit, noodles or bread, meat or fish, tea.

    c. Evening Meal. Rice or noodles, soup, root and green vegetables, peppers, fruit, meat or fish, tea.

5-49. *Leave.* The PLA has a very strict leave policy. Conscripts are not normally entitled to leave, except for compassionate reasons. After their initial year of service, all soldiers receive a minimum of 7 days' annual leave, with soldiers not accompanied by dependents eligible for 15 days' leave. Soldiers on extended duty are entitled to 15 days' annual leave during their first extended year; then 15 days leave every two years.

5-50. In addition to annual leave, 2-day holidays are celebrated on each of the following national holidays: Lunar New Year, Spring Festival, Armed Forces Day (1 August), and National Day (1 October).

Discipline

5-51. The *Three Main Rules of Discipline* and the *Eight Points of Attention* remain the bases for discipline within the PLA and are reiterated in chapter 3 of the *Internal Regulations*, promulgated 25 November 1975, outlining the conduct of soldiers:

    a. The Three Main Rules:

      (1) Obey all orders.

      (2) Do not take a single needle or piece of thread from the masses.

      (3) Turn in everything captured.

b. The Eight Points of Attention:
    (1) Speak politely.
    (2) Pay fairly for what you buy.
    (3) Return everything that you borrow.
    (4) Pay for anything that you damage.
    (5) Do not hit or swear at people.
    (6) Do not damage crops.
    (7) Do not take liberties with women.
    (8) Do not ill-treat captives.

5-52. *Punishments.* Following are the punishments within the PLA in ascending order of severity:

	Punishment		Authority
a.	Warning	– by –	Company Commander
b.	Admonishment	–	Company Commander
c.	Reprimand	–	Regiment Commander
d.	Expulsion from CCYL/CCP	–	Regiment Commander
e.	Expulsion from the PLA	–	Courts Martial
f.	Imprisonment	–	Courts Martial
g.	Execution	–	Courts Martial

5-53. The general principle behind punishment in the PLA is that offenders be taught the error of their ways. Minor offenses (drunkenness, failure to care for equipment) are usually dealt with at company-level criticism meetings. These meetings are attended by the accused soldier's comrades and are presided over by the deputy commander of the company or the political officer. At the meeting the soldier confesses his crime and pledges to reform. The attendees discuss the nature of the offense and then decide on an appropriate punishment.

5-54. *Courts Martial.* Major offenses (murder, robbery) are brought before military region courts martial. It is the military court which has the authority to expel a soldier from service, sentence him to prison usually at hard labor, or order him executed. The exact composition of the court is unknown. It is normally presided over by an officer whose position equates with that of a U.S. brigadier general. There is neither a prosecutor nor defender. Since there is no known manual on military law equivalent to the *U.S. Uniform Code of Military Justice*, it is believed that military courts generally follow the same legal principles and procedures as do their civilian counterparts.

Day Rooms

5-55. Each company has its own day room, sometimes referred to as a leisure or reading room. This room is used by the soldiers in their free time and usually have ping-pong equipment, newspapers and periodicals, and a selection of approved books. These rooms are similar to the "Lenin Clubs" which were established during the early revolutionary period and which served as the center of all social and cultural life in the unit. Besides serving as a library and ping-pong parlor, the early Lenin Clubs often doubled as dining halls and classrooms.

5-56–5-60. *Reserved.*

Status

5-61. In keeping with the revolutionary tradition of close relations between officers and men and in an attempt to offset Soviet-sponsored "professionalism" which was allegedly challenging Mao's "proletarian military line," all ranks and insignia were abolished in mid-1965. The PLA returned to the pre-1955 practice of referring to officers (leaders or commanders) by job title or position (e.g., Company Commander) and referring to soldiers as fighters. Although the abolition of ranks was essentially one of several steps taken by the Chinese leadership to insure the PLA's political and ideological loyalty, in addition it demonstrated, at least theoretically, the equal status of officers and enlisted men in China's armed forces. The belief that equality between officers and men makes for a more efficient fighting force is preached to this day.

Officer Selection

5-62. The overwhelming majority of officers/commanders are chosen directly from the ranks. Selection criteria are based as much on ideological orientation as on proven military ability. The soldier possessing the right qualifications, as determined by his unit's party committee, could expect to reach the position of platoon leader within 5 years after conscription. Officer training is conducted at military region schools or academies. Most officers assigned to research or technical positions are trained at military technical institutes. Only a small percentage of officers in this specialist category, which includes all doctors, are commissioned directly from among college graduates. A few technical officers are selected from graduates of senior middle schools for advanced training at military technical institutes after a short period of service in the ranks. Officer training programs in civilian colleges are not known to exist.

Military Education

5-63. As described above, the military education of the majority of Chinese officers begins with the training the individual receives while in the ranks. Upon selection to officer status, an individual's military education is likely to include:

a. Basic officer-type training at branch or service schools, or at technical institutes which are subordinate to the Military Region. Training at these schools can last up to 3 years and produces company-level officers.

b. Intermediate-level training at schools referred to as "Military and Political Schools for Cadres." Also subordinate to the military region, these schools reportedly offer instruction to middle-grade officers (battalion/regiment) in political philosophy, Maoist military thought, strategy, tactics, techniques and armaments. Length of schooling is unknown.

c. Training at national-level schools. Directly controlled by the Military Commission, these consist of all major officer schools, various technical schools and political academies. An example of a national-level school is the PLA Military and Political College in Peking. Its students represent the army, navy and air force, study politics, military affairs and culture, and engage in agricultural and industrial work. Attendance at the higher War College is considered to be the apex of the individual's military education.

The Life of the Officer

5-64. The life of the Chinese officer, particularly that of the "junior officer" (company level), is probably not unlike that of officers in other armies. He provides leadership, conducts training, supervises unit activities, and manages the affairs of both the unit and the individual soldier. Unlike other army officers, however, he maintains a rather close relationship with the ordinary soldier, having himself come up from the ranks. Despite higher pay and other benefits derived from his status, the officer, at least theoretically and politically, is an equal of the men he commands.

Conditions of Service

5-65. *Pay.* Officers (commanders and political commissars) receive a monthly salary that reflects the position occupied and total years in service. The current Chinese pay system lists 24 pay grades from student to national-level cadre. Following is a partial list of estimated pay scales in 1973:

Pay Grade	Position	Basic Monthly Pay*	(U.S. $ Equivalent)
1	Vice Chairman, MC	475 yuan	($242.25)
4	Military Region Commander	350 yuan	($178.50)
11	Army Commander	225 yuan	($114.75)
13	Division Commander	190 yuan	($ 96.90)
15	Regiment Commander	160 yuan	($ 81.60)
19	Battalion Commander	130 yuan	($ 66.30)
21	Company Commander	75 yuan	($ 38.25)
23	Platoon Leader	50 yuan	($ 25.50)
24	Student/Officer Trainee	45 yuan	($ 22.95)

*Estimated monthly basic pay including longevity increments.

5-66. *Leave.* Bachelor officers are entitled to 15 days' leave every 2 years as are married officers accompanied by their dependents. Married officers unaccompanied by dependents are granted 30 days' leave annually.

5-67. *Promotion.* Officer promotion within the PLA depends on military competency and political reliability and because there are no ranks it would be a promotion in position: for example, from deputy battalion commander to battalion commander. Career progression, however, normally remains in either the military or political command fields. Crossovers to the other field may occur at the higher levels of command, but are exceptions to the rule.

5-68. *Retirement.* An officer's age, his record and his future potential, as well as the needs of the service, are all considered when a decision is made to retain him on active duty or separate him from the military. There is no known annuity-type military pension system. At the time of separation or retirement, a one-time cash bonus is made based on the number of years served and the monthly base pay for the position held at the time of discharge.

5-69. *Work after Retirement.* Retired officers, if medically qualified, normally return to work in their local communes or industries, where they also serve in the militia.

Combat Efficiency

5-70. One of the major concerns of the Chinese military leadership today is how the present generation of junior leaders will perform in combat. Although the military training, physical conditioning, and political orientation of today's young PLA officer is considered sound, his grasp of tactics, technical proficiency and ability to lead and inspire troops remain untested in modern warfare. He is constantly reminded of the PLA's revolutionary traditions and is encouraged to emulate veterans whose military careers spanned entire decades of incessant combat against the Japanese, the Nationalists, and in Korea. However, most senior officers are experienced veterans and are considered efficient and capable in both tactics and command.

5-71–5-75. *Reserved.*

CHAPTER 6
THE CHINESE NAVY

Historical Background

6-1.   The Peoples Republic of China Navy (PRCN) grew out of units formed when the Chinese Communist ground forces gained control over large segments of the China coastline and a number of naval units and facilities fell into Communist hands. A motley assortment of abandoned and captured ships and craft was deployed against withdrawing Nationalist Chinese troops and provided the nucleus of the PRC Navy.

6-2.   The PRCN was formally established in September 1950 when the various regional naval forces were unified and placed under the direct command of the general headquarters of the Peoples Liberation Army. A naval air force (PRCNAF) was created in 1952.

6-3.   A reorganization of the navy followed the governmental reorganization of August 1954. All duties of the previously existing naval districts were relegated to fleets, the headquarters of which were subordinate to naval headquarters. The PRCNAF was expanded at that time.

6-4.   Soviet aid increased after 1953. Between 1954 and 1960 the Soviet Union supplied the PRC with a variety of combatants, and Soviet advisers and instructors assisted with the organization and training. With Soviet aid, a shipbuilding industry was developed with emphasis on the construction of medium and small units, especially submarines.

6-5.   In the 1960's the navy continued to improve the quality and increase the quantity of its ships and personnel despite the PRC's economic setbacks, the Sino-Soviet rift and the withdrawal of Soviet advisers, and the upheaval of the Cultural Revolution.

Current Status

6-6.   Influenced by the Soviet concept of coastal defense in the 1950's, China's navy has expanded to become the largest indigenous navy in Asia. In numbers of units it now ranks second only to the Soviet Navy. The surface force consists mostly of coastal patrol craft such as missile boats, motor gunboats and torpedo boats. It also includes guided-missile destroyer/frigate-type ships, mine-warfare ships, amphibious ships and craft, and support units. The PRCN fleet of diesel-powered attack submarines is the third largest in the world and continues to grow. Moreover, the Chinese have constructed one diesel-powered Soviet GOLF-class ballistic-missile submarine and a nuclear-powered submarine of indigenous design. It is possible that these are part of a ballistic-missile nuclear submarine development program.

Mission

6-7.   The PRCN is primarily a defensive force; however, it also has a limited offensive potential. Its missions include defending the coast against maritime assault, maintaining the security of territorial waters, protecting sea lines of communications, and supporting the PRC's foreign and domestic policy. Navy tasks in support of these missions include submarine warfare, antisubmarine warfare, surface warfare, amphibious warfare, mine warfare, and logistics support of the forces involved.

Capability

6-8.   The PRCN has an impressive capability for coastal defense. The expansion of naval forces has resulted in a capability to enforce the stated PRC policy of coastal defense to . . . *turn China's coastline into a great wall of iron.* It is clear that the Chinese could inflict substantial damage on the forces of would-be invaders from seaward, including those of the superpowers.

6-9.   PRC naval forces are best suited for operations in the shallow waters along China's extensive coastline where hit-and-run tactics under shore-based air cover are most effective. The current emphasis is on construction of guided-missile boats and diesel attack submarines. Motor torpedo and guided-missile boats are considered to be the most effective of the PRCN's coastal surface combatants, while submarines are the most likely units to be employed if operations outside of immediate coastal waters are to be undertaken.

6-10. The PRCN's capability to conduct extended-distance or long-duration operations at sea is very limited. The present inventory of 18 destroyers and frigates could form the nucleus for an oceangoing force, but they are limited by inadequate air and submarine defenses when operating in the open ocean beyond the range of ground-based air support.

6-11. The PRCN has a sufficient number of conventional amphibious vessels to lift a force of over 30,000 men and equipment in a regional (less than 30 hours' transit) amphibious assault. The over-the-bench lift could be augmented by over 400 merchant ships in an administrative lift of support personnel and equipment. Several thousand coastal junks could also be utilized in an amphibious lift role. Successful employment of such a prodigious force against a well-defended objective is subject to:

   a. The limitations of the size and age of the current inventory of naval amphibious vessels,
   b. The capability to obtain air and naval superiority in the objective area,
   c. Determination and defensive strength of the enemy, and
   d. The acceptable ratio of assault forces to defenders according to PLA doctrine.

Organization

6-12. As a major branch of the PLA, the PRCN is controlled through naval headquarters which is directly subordinate to the Military Commission through the General Departments (see figure 14).

6-13. The Commander in Chief of the PRCN, assisted by his deputies and staff at naval headquarters, is responsible for a variety of forces, facilities, and organizations. Some are directly subordinate to naval headquarters, while others are controlled through subsidiary headquarters. Many naval elements appear to be under dual subordination, and in some instances interservice coordination must be effected as well.

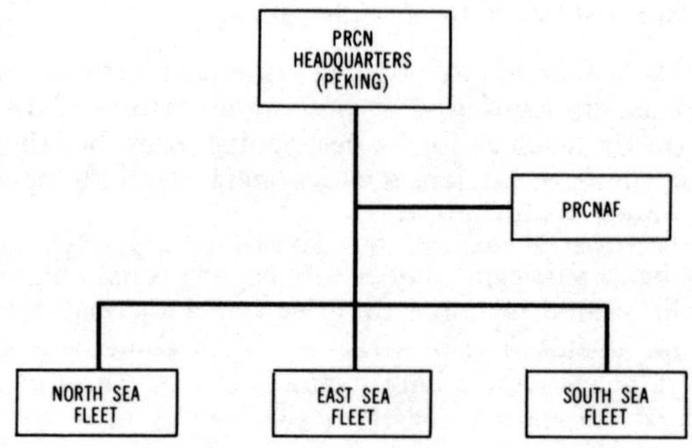

Figure 14. PRCN Organization.

6-14. PRCN Headquarters. The top command of the PRCN consists of a commander and a political commissar who are assisted by deputies and a headquarters staff to supervise the operational, political, support, training and other functions of the navy. In line with Chinese military practice, the commander and political commissar share responsibility. The naval commander serves also as a Vice Minister of National Defense.

6-15. Joint action of naval units with other elements of the armed forces, such as aircraft, coastal defense or antiaircraft artillery units, is coordinated through naval headquarters.

6-16. The PRCN is organized into three fleet commands: North Sea, East Sea, and South Sea. The headquarters of these fleets exercise operational control in their respective areas over all afloat forces, naval air units, and the ashore elements of coastal defense. The fleet commands are also believed to have administrative control over base, shipyard, repair, and training facilities located in their respective areas, although there is necessarily a degree of direct control of most of these installations by naval headquarters.

6-17. Fleets.

    a. The North Sea Fleet protects Peking and the strategically critical northeast plains from attacks through the Yellow Sea and Po Hai Gulf.
    b. The East Sea Fleet defends the industrial Shanghai area and the contested Taiwan Strait.
    c. The South Sea Fleet guards commercial Canton and China's insular flank in the South.

6-18. Chinese naval order of battle data can be found in figure 15.

6-19. *Naval Air Force.* The primary mission of the PRC Naval Air Force (PRCNAF) is air defense of naval installations and surface forces. The force is land based and can provide only close-in support. Secondary missions include maritime reconnaissance, tactical support of the PRC fleets with antishipping bombing and torpedo attacks, and support of amphibious operations.

6-20. The majority of the aircraft are air defense fighters. There are also a few intermediate-range jet bombers and a moderate number of medium-range jet bombers and attack aircraft. Order-of-battle figures in the PRCAF section of this handbook include aircraft assigned to the PRCNAF. A list of naval combat aircraft, by type, includes:

    a. Bombardment: Intermediate-range—Tu-16 BADGER
                            Medium-range—Il-28 BEAGLE
    b. Air Defense: MiG-17 FRESCO
                            MiG-19 FARMER
    c. Surface Attack: F-9 FANTAN

6-21. The close coordination required between air force and naval force defense operations probably necessitates the operational control of naval air defense units being under the PRCAF. Other naval air units are responsible directly to naval headquarters in Peking through the three fleet headquarters.

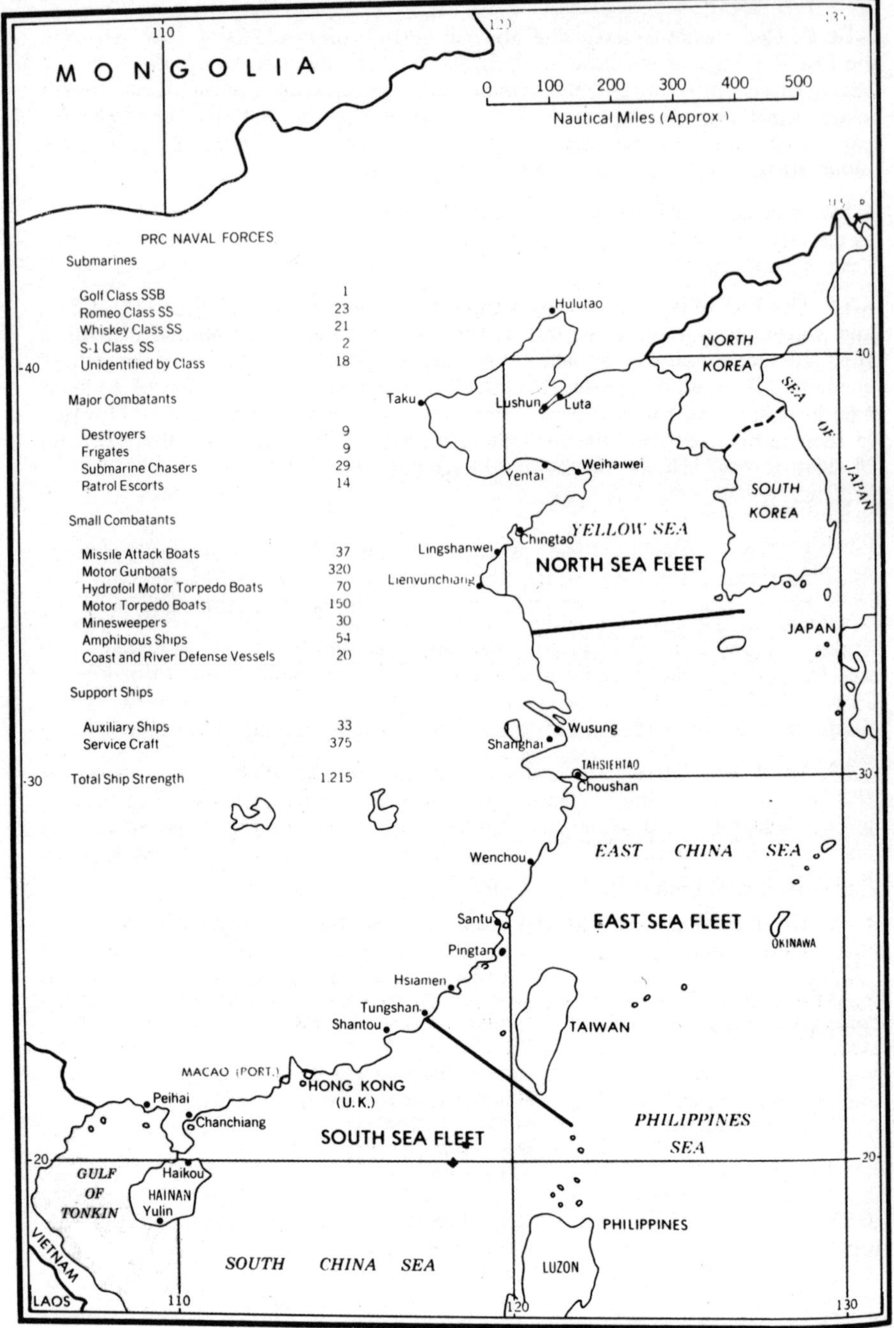

Figure 15. Naval Order Of Battle And Bases.

6-22. *Coastal Artillery.* Patterned along Soviet lines, the coastal artillery units of the PRCN support naval air and afloat forces in defensive operations. They are believed to be organized as independent regiments administratively subordinate to the naval base commander and are stationed in the vicinity of the various ports and naval bases. These naval coastal artillery units work in close cooperation with army artillery units.

Doctrine and Tactics

6-23. The primary mission of the navy—defense of the PRC coast—is accomplished through construction of ships and craft well suited to their assigned tasks, through deployment of these units in accordance with strategic priorities, and reportedly through administration of a vigorous and expanding training program.

6-24. China's navy is the seaward extension of the PLA. As such, it supports a well-coordinated national defense plan. The outer ring of defense is believed to be the growing fleet of diesel-powered attack submarines which would defend against an approaching force with torpedoes and mines. This outer perimeter is backed up by bomb- and torpedo-armed attack aircraft of the PRCNAF. Destroyer-type units provide a second defensive ring. Their firepower, sea-keeping ability, range and speed provide flexibility and mobility to the defensive plan, enabling naval headquarters to quickly fill gaps through intra/interfleet transfers. This perimeter, however, is limited in depth to the protective range of fighter aircraft. Close-in defense, also under the protective air umbrella, is the task of the large and ever-increasing number of fast missile boats, torpedo boats and gunboats, as well as patrol and mine craft. PRCN tactical doctrine allegedly emphasizes the use of surprise attacks, combat at night and during periods of poor visibility, close combat with infiltration of an enemy's rear, and destruction of an enemy with a concentration of force. In addition, it is probable that extensive protective minefields would be laid both to protect shipping and to guard against amphibious assaults.

Personnel and Training

6-25. *Personnel.* The total PRCN personnel strength is in excess of 250,000 men, including shipboard and shore-based manpower and naval air personnel.

6-26. *Recruitment and Service.* Recruits are assigned to the PRCN as necessary from those who are called up annually under the PRC military conscription system. A flawless political background and excellent health are considered to be the main prerequisites for selection. Although current information is inconclusive, normal term of service in the PRCN is thought to be 5 years.

6-27. *Training.* The PRC has developed a national program for the training of naval officers and enlisted men. Officer training is accomplished in part through naval schools. The best known of these is the permanent naval academy, the First Naval School, which was established with the founding of the PRCN in 1950. More advanced training is given at the Naval War College.

6-28. The enlisted training program has considerable operational flexibility. All military conscripts receive a few weeks of orientation and rudimentary basic military training. During this period selections are made for service in the various service arms. Those selected for the navy become naval recruits and assume, for the first time, a strictly naval identity. They are then sent to one of the naval schools or shore commands for further training. If an individual is to be assigned aboard ship, he is sent to one of the fleet schools for several months. Upon completion of this training the seaman, no longer a recruit, is assigned to an afloat unit for practical on-the-job training. The duration of this stage is flexible and is determined largely by the ability of the individual and the personnel needs of the department. Those recruits assigned ashore are absorbed directly into a naval command or activity where they commence on-the-job training without further formal naval schooling. Here again, the length of indoctrination is indefinite and phases out gradually as the need for supervision diminishes. Political training, however, is given continuously to all personnel for the duration of their service terms.

6-29. *Pay and Allowances.* PRCN personnel reportedly receive 10 percent more in pay and allowances than do army personnel in comparable positions. Allowances probably are given for sea and submarine duty and for length of service.

Naval Vessels

6-30. The PRCN inventory includes a variety of vessels of foreign (Soviet, Japanese, British, and United States) origin, as well as an increasing number and assortment of vessels from Chinese yards. Many of those supplied by the Soviet Union and almost all of those taken over from the Chinese Nationalists are World War II warships. Domestic production resulting from an ambitious shipbuilding program begun in the 1950's emphasizes submarines, missile boats, gunboats, torpedo boats, patrol boats, destroyers, frigates and auxiliary craft.

6-31. *Order of Battle.* PRC naval order of battle includes 1,215 ships and craft and continues to grow. The submarine force consists of one GOLF-class ballistic-missile submarine and 65 conventionally powered torpedo attack submarines, the majority of which are WHISKY- and ROMEO-class units. Additionally, the PRCN has a HAN-class, possibly nuclear-powered submarine of indigenous design. Major surface combatants include:

    a. Nine guided-missile destroyers.
    b. Five guided-missile frigates (one of which is possibly equipped with surface-to-air missiles).
    c. Four frigates.

Auxiliary vessels and yard and service craft round out the naval inventory.

6-32. Chinese naval vessels are depicted in annex Y.

6-33. *Logistics and Materiel.* The Rear Services Department under naval headquarters is responsible for logistic service. In general, the PRCN logistical system and practices follow those of the Soviet navy.

6-34. Navy units originally were equipped mainly with materiel of Soviet origin or design. Since the 1950's, however, the PRCN has been undergoing a modernization program aimed at acquiring the capability to build and equip various naval vessels without outside assistance. The precipitous withdrawal of Soviet aid caused a severe hardship on China's navy, but it accelerated the development of a domestic capability.

6-35–6-40. *Reserved.*

CHAPTER 7
THE CHINESE AIR FORCE

Historical Background

7-1.   The PRC Air Force (PRCAF) was formally organized in 1949. Its origins, however, can be traced to the 1930's when the Communist forces of Mao Tsetung acquired aircraft belonging to the Nationalist government. The force was further increased in 1946 with captured Japanese aircraft and in 1949 when the Communists attained control of mainland China. The Korean War heralded a period of rapid modernization with the Soviet Union supplying large numbers of jet aircraft and providing aircrew training. Deteriorating Sino-Soviet relations climaxed in 1960 when the Soviets recalled their technicians and withdrew military aid. By then, however, the PRC had aircraft production facilities in Manchuria and some experience in jet aircraft production. Chinese versions of the MiG-15 and MiG-17 were produced under Soviet license in the mid to late fifties. By 1965, Chinese technology had progressed considerably; they were able to begin series production of the MiG-19 FARMER and later the Il-28 BEAGLE, Tu-16 BADGER, and limited numbers of MiG-21 FISHBED. The first aircraft both designed and produced by the Chinese, the F-9 FANTAN fighter-bomber, entered the inventory in the early seventies.

Current Status

7-2.   In the last decade the PRC has developed the third largest air force in the world and the only Asian air force, with the exception of the Soviet Union, with a strategic nuclear capability.

Mission

7-3.   The primary mission of the PRCAF is the defense of mainland China with the preponderance of the force being air-superiority aircraft. Tactical missions include close air support and interdiction of enemy targets, military airlift, and reconnaissance. The intermediate-range and a small number of the medium-range bomber forces have a limited nuclear-strike capability but they are probably designed primarily for regional operations.

Capability

7-4.   The PRCAF can provide effective air defense against any potential Asian aggressor with the exception of the Soviet Union, and the tactical bomber force is capable of providing effective close air support and interdiction of enemy lines of communication. The nuclear bomber capability of the PRCAF is probably, by itself, not sufficient to deter any Soviet military ambitions; it adds significantly to PRC international prestige, however.

Organization

7-5.   The PRCAF organization is based on the air district system with air districts being generally analogous to the military regions. PRCAF Headquarters exercises command responsibility directly to each air district with no intervening level of command. The military region headquarters probably exerts some degree

136

of control over regional air forces for overall coordination of the military effort. Strength of individual air districts is determined by their proximity to potential threats; therefore, the comparative strength of Shenyang, Peking, Nanching, and Kuangchou is greater than that of other air districts. The largest operational unit within the PRCAF is the air division with, generally, each air division consisting of three regiments, each regiment consisting of three squadrons and each squadron consisting of three flights. Figure 16 is an estimate of the command relationships from the Military Commission to air division levels.

Doctrine and Tactics

7-6. *Fighter Tactics.* The basic fighter tactic is multilayered flights with two elements of aircraft per flight providing mutual support at as many as four different altitudes. Of the leading two aircraft, the leader is the offensive aircraft, with the other providing flight defense and massing of firepower. It is possible that the PRCAF has a limited air-to-air missile capability with ATOLL-type heat-seeking and possibly alkali-type beam-riding missiles. The majority of the force, however, is probably fitted with cannon only. Only a small percentage of the air defense force has an all-weather capability.

7-7. *Bomber Tactics.* Bomber crews are considered proficient in both low- and high-level bombing. Enemy capabilities would greatly influence tactics; for any given situation, however, tactics would probably be traditional. Mass low-level attacks against enemy targets would be multidirectional at varying speeds and altitudes and high-level bombing would be conducted in formation or trail. Ground attack missions will be predominately preplanned sorties since the PRC appears to lack a ground or airborne forward air control system; therefore, in a fluid battlefield situation, tactical bombers would be much less effective. Night operations are limited to the BEAGLE and BADGER force.

Personnel and Training

7-8. *Personnel.* Current estimates place the manning in PRCAF operational units at over 170,000 personnel. Of this total, 10,000 are pilots.

7-9. *Recruitment and Service.* Recruits are assigned to the PRCAF as necessary under the military conscription system. Selection is often limited to those recruits possessing technical training. Term of service in the PRCAF is for a period of 4 years.

7-10. *Training.* Flight training of PRCAF aircrews is divided into three phases: primary, intermediate, and advanced. Training normally lasts 2 years.

    a. Primary flight training includes a curriculum of basic theoretics, aerodynamics, theory of flight, meteorology, elementary flying, and political education. Primary flight training normally lasts approximately 6 months.

    b. Intermediate flight training encompasses daytime flying under both normal and complex weather conditions, night flying, fixed-aiming bombing, aerial gunnery, and intermediate theoretics. Duration of this phase of training is approximately 9 months.

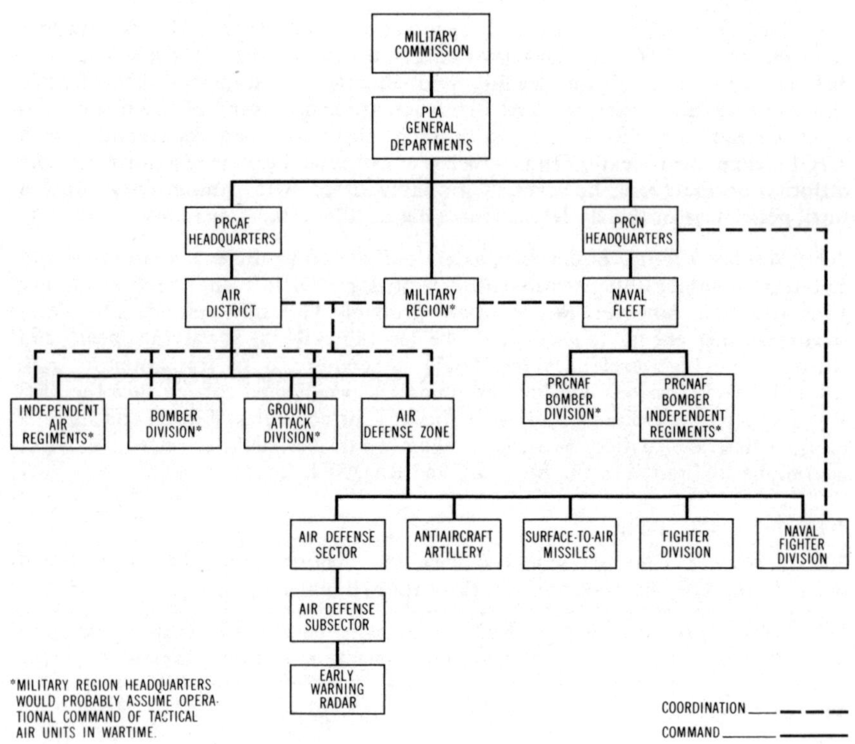

Figure 16. Organization of PRC Air Forces.

c. Advanced flight training includes flight under complex weather conditions, high-altitude flight acrobatics, instrument training, interception, and formation flying. Advanced flight training normally lasts 9 months. Upon completion of advanced flight training, aircrew members are assigned to an operational unit for transition and operational training.

Aircraft

7-11. The aircraft inventory of the PRC, although large, consists mainly of Korean War-vintage aircraft. The bomber force includes some 65 Tu-16 BADGER intermediate-range jet bombers and over 400 Il-28 BEAGLE medium-range jet bombers. The PRC air defense system includes more than 4,100 aircraft with MiG-17 FRESCO and MiG-19 FARMER jet fighters comprising the bulk of the force. Only a few relatively advanced MiG-21 FISHBED are included in the interceptor inventory. The force is mainly a clear air-mass daylight force with only a small percentage of the aircraft having an all-weather capability. The tactical bomber force has over 400 MiG-15 FAGOT and F-9 FANTAN fighter-bombers (the latter designed and produced by the Chinese based on the Soviet MiG-19 FARMER).

7-12. PRC aircraft inventory is tabulated in annex Z; silhouettes of representative aircraft are depicted in appendix 1 to annex Z.

Airfields

7-13. There are presently approximately 400 operational airfields in the PRC. The majority of these airfields are located east of the 108-degree meridian in the most populous area of China. Most of the military airfields—those used by the various air force operational units—have runways of 6,000 feet or more in length and are generally utilized in an air defense posture.

7-14. Following is a description of PRC airfields as of November 1975.

Runway Length (in feet)	Runway Surface*			Total
	P	T	N	
14,000 and over	4			4
13,000 - 13,999	1			1
12,000 - 12,999	2			2
11,000 - 11,999	5	1		6
10,000 - 10,999	9			9
9,000 - 9,999	11	2		13
8,000 - 8,999	46	2		48
7,000 - 7,999	85	7		92
6,000 - 6,999	42	10	3	55
5,000 - 5,999	10	16		26
4,000 - 4,999	13	22	1	36
under 4,000	14	52	17	83
under construction				6
seaplane stations				2
	242	112	21	383

* P = Permanent
  T = Temporary
  N = Natural

7-15—7-18. *Reserved.*

CHAPTER 8
CHINESE MISSILE SYSTEMS

Overview

8-1. In order to insure its national security by deterring an attack by a superpower and to establish its international negotiating position, the PRC has built an increasingly powerful strategic military establishment. PRC ballistic-missile capabilities are relatively modest compared to those of the United States and the USSR, but they are growing at a significant and deliberate rate. Although currently posing no strategic threat to the continental United States or to Western Europe, and only a partial threat to the Soviet Union, the PRC perceives its emerging nuclear capability as a credible and effective deterrent.

Background

8-2. China's development of a nuclear ballistic-missile force was based on the technical aid provided by the Sino-Soviet Defense Agreement signed in late 1957 or early 1958, although assistance had probably started a year or two earlier. Following the Sino-Soviet split in 1960, the PRC was able to develop native-designed surface-to-surface missiles using this Soviet technical base. Since 1966, when the PRC announced that it had fired its first nuclear-tipped ballistic missile, the Chinese have made progress in increasing the size and effectiveness of their nuclear missile force. Although their nuclear stockpile is limited compared to that of the United States or USSR, it is expected to increase fairly rapidly over the next few years as the availability of fissionable material increases.

Strategic Capability

8-3. The painstaking, methodical approach used by the Chinese in their strategic missile program has resulted in a modest but highly credible nuclear retaliatory capability against the USSR and other nations on China's periphery. While this capability does not yet extend to the continental United States, China does have the ability to conduct nuclear strikes against targets around the periphery of the PRC including U.S. and allied installations in the western Pacific.

Strategic Ballistic-Missile Systems

8-4. Currently, the PRC has a variety of operational nuclear weapons systems including a medium-range ballistic missile (MRBM) and an intermediate-range ballistic missile (IRBM). China is also actively pursuing a viable intercontinental ballistic-missile (ICBM) developmental program. (See annex AA for details.)

   a. *Medium-range Ballistic Missiles.* China's MRBM force consists of a small number of liquid-fueled, single-stage, road-transportable missiles similar to earlier Soviet systems. This 600-nautical-mile (nm) missile, which has been operational since 1966, is believed to carry a warhead of about 20 kilotons (kt). MRBM's can strike targets in all of Korea and Taiwan and in most of Thailand and Japan. They can also reach some allied and U.S. bases in the Far East and some key military/industrial targets in the Soviet Far East.

b. *Intermediate-range Ballistic Missiles.* Although China has a penchant for maintaining obsolescent hardware in its inventory, the MRBM may be replaced eventually by the IRBM. China's IRBM force, operational since 1972, is also small in number. It is a native-designed, single-stage, storable liquid system with a range of 1,500 nautical miles. Operational deployment of this system is presently underway. Although such deployment provides the PRC with the capability to apply strong political and military pressure against countries such as Japan and India, the system is probably intended for relatively large population centers in central and eastern Russia.

c. *Intercontinental Ballistic Missiles.* China's perception of its strategic nuclear role vis-a-vis the United States and the USSR has necessitated its active pursuance of a viable ICBM developmental program to complement the MRBM and IRBM force. One system, a limited-range, multistate, liquid-fueled missile capable of reaching targets in European USSR, could be operational at any time. It is expected to be the first Chinese system deployed to silos. The program, however, is a major enigma because development has been painstakingly slow, and it does not appear that deployment will be extensive. The reason for such limited deployment is difficult to ascertain, but is may be that China has decided to wait for its full-range ICBM to become operational. This full-range ICBM program is progressing at a slow but steady pace. This missile, similar to the U.S. TITAN, could carry a multimegaton warhead over a range of about 7,000 nautical miles. This would provide China, for the first time, with the capability to strike the continental United States. Deployment of this system, which will probably be to hardened silos, is not expected until the late 1970's or early 1980's.

Submarine-launched Ballistic Missiles

8-5. The Chinese have also been working for some time on the development of a submarine-launched ballistic missile (SLBM). They have one Soviet-type GOLF-class diesel-powered ballistic-missile submarine which they built in the 1960's from components supplied by the USSR. If the PRC is, in fact, developing an SLBM, it is reasonable to assume that the GOLF-class submarine will be used as the test platform. It is difficult to forecast the rate of progress of the SLBM program, but it is believed that such a system will not be operational until the 1980's. While there is no firm evidence for estimating an initial operational capability for a solid system, it is thought that the SLBM will be solid fueled when operational. China has made large investments in research, development, and production facilities for solid-propellant missile systems including possibly MRBM's, IRBM's, and a second generation ICBM. Such investments present significant implications for the future of China's ballistic-missile force.

Tactical Nuclear Missiles

8-6. The PRC does not currently possess a tactical nuclear missile capability, although it is believed that such systems are within its technical capability. From certain selected locations throughout the country, portions of China's strategic ballistic-missile force could be used in a theater support role against invading forces. Command and control of the missile resources would most likely remain under Peking's authority. It is doubtful that the use of these missiles would be delegated to the PLA ground forces.

Other Missile Systems

8-7.   Other PRC missile systems include the surface-to-air missile (SAM) and cruise missile—surface-to-surface missile (SSM).

> **a.** *Surface-to-Air Missiles (SAM).* China's basic operational SAM, the CSA-1, is the Chinese variant of the Soviet SA-2 system. Thinly deployed, numbering only a few hundred launchers, this system provides only a limited point defense of key urban and industrial areas and of advanced weapons complexes. The missile is quite effective against subsonic aircraft and would be supplemented by tactical air and antiaircraft artillery. The overall Chinese SAM force, however, would be relatively ineffective against the large modern air forces of the United States and the Soviet Union. For the next several years, the PRC is expected to increase the number of SAM launchers as they extend SAM defenses to protect other important areas not now defended. China probably will also eventually develop a low-altitude SAM system.
>
> **b.** *Cruise Missiles—Surface-to-Surface Missiles (SSM).* The majority of the PRCN's major surface combatants are equipped with a cruise SSM which is modeled after the Soviet-designed STYX. China may have also deployed a few coastal defense missiles. Although this type of missile could be used tactically in support of ground forces, like the Soviet SALISH cruise missile, the PRC probably intends to employ it primarily against enemy naval vessels.

8-8—8-10.   *Reserved.*

CHAPTER 9
THE POLITICAL STRUCTURE OF THE PEOPLES LIBERATION ARMY

Background

9-1. The importance of political leadership over the armed forces by the Chinese Communist Party (CCP) has been a constant theme throughout the history of the PLA. By the time that he had fled to Chingkang Mountain in 1928, Mao Tsetung had accepted the inevitability of armed struggle as the only means by which to achieve his revolutionary goals. This struggle was to be waged by an army which was not only militarily strong but ideologically motivated and politically loyal to the CCP and the cause it espoused. The dictum that *political power grows out of the barrel of a gun—the party commands the gun and the gun must never be allowed to command the party*, has remained the basic tenet guiding political-military relations in the PRC.

Politicization of the PLA

9-2. The theory of party leadership over the PLA consists of two distinct elements. The first is that of political control—control by the CCP over the military leadership in order to insure that its policies are implemented. The second is that of political education—the process by which support for the policies of the CCP is secured with the armed forces. Normally referred to as the process of politicization, this dual theory of political control and political education has had a direct influence on the PLA's conception of and attitude toward its role in Chinese society and its relationships with other actions in the Chinese sociopolitical system. Time and again politicization has been used to shape beliefs, implant values, and guide action, insuring the PLA's loyalty to the CCP and making the PLA always responsive to the party's will—be it foreign intervention, road construction, or involvement in domestic politics.

9-3. Politicization in the PLA is accomplished by means of a complex, political apparatus composed of two distinct and separate hierarchies, paralleling the military chain of command and corresponding roughly to the functional division between political control and political education: party committees and political departments.

9-4. *Party Committee.* The first hierarchy is composed of a series of party committees which extend downward from the Military Commission (MC) of the Chinese Communist Party to the regimental level. At the battalion level the party committee is known as the "general branch"; at the company level, the "branch"; and at platoon level, the "cell." The party committee exists independent from but parallel to the military command structure. It is responsible to the next higher party (military organization) committee and (in peacetime) to the civilian party committee of the locality where the unit is stationed. The party committee of a given unit is elected by all the members of the unit subject to the approval of the next higher party committee. Membership almost always includes the unit's military commander and political commissar whose selection must have the approval of the higher-level party organ.

PRCA troops crossing the Yangtze River on TPP heavy ponton bridge.

N2P-45 steel ponton bridge used by PRCA troops in a river-crossing exercise.

PLA troops erecting a KMM bridge.

Bridging.

145

An infantry unit conducting a river-crossing operation.

PRCA regular forces and militia organized into antitank teams.

PRCA troops and militia practicing a counterattack.

Artillery is brought in as soon after the initial landing as possible to support tactical operations ashore. These are 57-mm antitank guns, type 55.

Cold-weather warfare. In the Sino-Indian conflict of 1962, the Chinese proved themselves well adapted to cold-weather, high-altitude fighting.

Urban militia members being trained to fight in built-up areas.

Mountain warfare training.

Chinese soldiers manufacturing land mines.

Various types of PRCA transport.

Movement of supplies is by motorized transport whenever possible.

POL handling equipment.

Cooking in the field.

Litter bearers evacuating injured soldier.

Air force helicopters may be used to assist in medical evacuation.

Preventive maintenance is stressed at all levels. Howitzers are the 122-mm type 54.

An artillery unit performing minor repair.

Squad receiving instruction on repair of motor vehicles.

The Chinese soldier is a hard and willing worker with an ability to improvise under a variety of conditions. He is one of the most highly motivated soldiers in the world and can endure extraordinary
hardships.

9-5. The party committee fulfills its role of political control over the military leadership by seeing that all party decisions, directives and orders are expeditiously implemented and judiciously adhered to. In addition, the party committee is responsible for planning and policymaking within its jurisdictional spheres, for unit discipline, and for personnel matters including promotions, demotions and transfers.

9-6. *Political Commissar.* The exercise of political control by the party committee is personified in the political commissar. The political commissar serves as the official representative of the party in the military unit and as such is directly responsible for all political activities in the unit. He normally serves concurrently as the secretary of the unit's party committee. The political commissar enjoys a status that is theoretically equal to that of the military commander. Under this dual command system, the commissar shares responsibility with the commander for all military work. In principle, the commander is responsible for the unit's "military" matters: combat operations, logistics, and tactical training. The commissar, on the other hand, is responsible for purely "political" matters: security, discipline, personnel affairs, and ideological training. However, over the years the political commissar has often emerged as the key figure in the command structure by virtue of his being the spokesman for the party in all matters, whether military or political.

9-7. *Political Department.* The second hierarchy in the political apparatus is the system of political departments. An integral part of the military's formal command structure, the political department exists parallel and subordinate to the party committee at each level of command. Political departments extend from the General Political Department (GPD) of the PLA Headquarters in Peking down to the regimental level "political office." The personnel of the political offices supervise the battalion-level "political education officers" and the company-level "political instructors," who in turn oversee the political activities of "political fighters" in platoons and squads.

9-8. The primary function of the political department is to implement the decisions of the corresponding party committee and to secure the support of the rank-and-file for the party's policies through political education. At regimental level and above, the political department is subdivided into various functional sections responsible for matters relating to counterintelligence, morale, education, propaganda, welfare and recreational/cultural work.

9-9. At the lower levels of the army's organization, particularly at company level, the functions of the political commissar and of the representative of the political department merge in the person of a single political officer or "political instructor." Responsible for all political activities in the unit to which he is assigned, the company-level political officer embodies both the control and the educational functions of the political apparatus and serves as the vital link between the decisionmakers and the ordinary soldier.

Political Schools and Academies

9-10. Although political education is an essential element in the curriculum of all Chinese military schools and academies, special political schools have been established to train field grade political cadres. These include the Marx-Lenin

Political Academy and the PLA Political College, both in Peking, and four or more national-level political schools. Information on admission, length of course, and curriculum is not available.

9-11–9-15. *Reserved.*

CHAPTER 10
UNIFORMS AND INSIGNIA—AWARDS AND DECORATIONS

SECTION I—UNIFORMS AND INSIGNIA

Background

10.1 In June 1965 all insignia indicating rank and branch of service were abolished and a standard uniform for all branches of the PLA was adopted. Officers have since been distinguished from enlisted men by the number of pockets on the coat: officers' coats have four pockets; those of enlisted personnel have two pockets. There have not been any noticeable changes in the uniforms of the army and the air force since 1965. However, in 1974 changes were made in the uniforms of navy personnel, particularly those worn aboard naval vessels.

Army Uniforms

10-2. There are three types of army uniforms:

    a. Parade dress.
    b. Service dress.
    c. Field dress.

10-3. Parade and service dress are basically the same except that brown leather belts with side-arm holsters or ammunition pouches, white gloves, and black leather boots instead of shoes are worn with the parade dress. The winter parade dress uniform includes a brown fur cap and an overcoat with a brown fur collar. (Figures 17 and 18.)

10-4. The field dress uniforms for winter and summer are made of olive-green cotton material, identical in color and style, except that the winter uniform has an inner lining of quilted cotton padding which gives it a bulkier appearance. These uniforms (winter and summer) become combat types with the addition of pouches, belts and other equipment. A light-green, faded outer shell worn over the winter field dress uniform has been observed. (Figures 17 and 19.)

10-5. Female personnel wear the same type of summer and winter dress uniforms as the males. As of 1 May 1974, they were authorized a new service dress uniform, olive green in color, consisting of an open-collar coat and a below-the-knee skirt, worn with a buttoned white blouse, and a beret-type cap with red piping. The uniform is worn with single-strap black shoes and green socks. (Figure 18.)

Navy Uniforms

10-6. There are three types of naval uniforms with distinctive styles for afloat and shore-based personnel:

    a. Parade dress.
    b. Service dress.
    c. Field dress.

10-7. *Officers.* Naval officers afloat have two styles of summer service dress uniforms. The first consists of a white coat and dark blue trousers, both made of a cotton material, black leather shoes, and a service cap with a black visor and a white crown. The other uniform is identical except that the coat and the *Chieh-fang* (Liberation) cap are blue. The winter service dress uniform is of the same style and color except that the material is wool. A brown leather belt and holster, white gloves, and black boots are added to both summer and winter service dress uniforms for wear as a parade dress uniform. A blue overcoat with a brown fur collar, a fur cap, and the above-listed accessories are used with the winter parade dress uniform. (Figure 20.)

10-8. The summer and winter field dress uniforms worn by shore-based personnel are of the type introduced in 1965. (Figure 20.)

10-9. *Enlisted personnel.* The summer service dress uniform afloat consists of a traditional white jumper with a red rectangular patch on each shoulder, a blue and white striped undershirt, blue trousers, and a large, round, white-crown cap. This uniform without cap and jumper is also used as a work uniform. The same style uniform, all dark blue and made of wool material, is worn as a winter service dress uniform. Black leather shoes and boots and olive-green, canvas, rubber-soled shoes are issued to afloat personnel. A cap band with Chinese characters is worn on the new sailor cap. (Figure 21.)

10-10. In addition to the 1965-style uniform, shore-based personnel wear a service dress uniform of serge-type material consisting of dark blue coat with closed collar and dark-blue trousers, a dark-blue, *Chieh-fang* cap, and black leather shoes. The parade dress uniforms for enlisted personnel are similar to those worn by officers. (Figure 22.)

10-11. Female personnel have the same type summer and winter uniforms as the males. In addition they are authorized to wear a new uniform consisting of a white, open-collar coat with red collar tabs, a below-the-knee skirt, white bobby socks, black strap shoes or sandals, a buttoned, white blouse, and a dark-blue, beret-type cap with white piping. (Figure 22.)

Air Force Uniforms

10-12. There are four types of air force uniforms:

    a. Parade dress.
    b. Service dress.
    c. Field dress.
    d. Flight dress.

10-13. The air force parade dress uniform is believed to be similar to that of the army; however, no information is available for positive identification.

10-14. The summer service dress uniform for both officers and enlisted personnel consists of an olive-green coat with red collar tabs, blue trousers, and black leather shoes. (Figure 23.)

10-15. Officers have a summer field dress uniform consisting of an olive-green, open-collar, waist-length jacket, blue trousers, and black leather shoes. No verifiable information is available on the enlisted personnel summer field dress uniform, although a work uniform of the same style as the officer summer field dress uniform has been identified. The jacket, like the trousers, is dark blue, not olive green. (Figure 23.)

10-16. Since 1 May 1974 female personnel have been seen wearing a new uniform consisting of an olive-green, open-collar coat, a buttoned, white blouse, a below-the-knee skirt, green bobby socks, black leather shoes or tennis shoes, and a green, beret-type cap with blue piping. (Figure 23.)

10-17. Flight personnel wear sheepskin-lined, brown leather jacket, trousers and boots. This uniform with blue instead of brown leather trousers and the *Chieh-fang* cap has also been observed. (Figure 24.)

Special Uniforms

10-18. *Paratroopers.* Paratroopers wear an olive-green coat with blue trousers, green-ribbed helmet, and light-green jump boots. (Figure 24.)

10-19. *Chemical Warfare.* For this activity there is a green, one-piece protective suit, apparently made of rubberized fabric, a protective mask, gloves, and buskins or boots. (Figure 19.)

10-20. *Armored.* Armored troops wear a heavy, olive-drab, one-piece coverall over the standard uniform in both summer and winter. A ribbed crash helmet of strong canvas material is worn with the coverall. (Not shown.)

10-21. *Public Security Bureau.* As of 1 May 1974, the Peoples Police, including firefighter, border, forest, and railroad police, were authorized a new summer uniform consisting of a green, closed-collar coat, blue trousers, black shoes, and a service cap with a black visor and green crown. Traffic control police wear a white, closed-collar coat, blue trousers, black shoes, and a service cap with a blue visor and a white crown in summer and a completely blue uniform in winter. Female personnel wear a green, open-collar coat, a buttoned, white blouse, blue skirt, and a green, beret-type cap. The cap insignia for all personnel is the national emblem, *T'ien-an-men* (Heavenly gate), and the collar tabs are red. (Figure 25.)

10-22. *Militia.* Members of the militia apparently do not have an authorized uniform. They have been identified wearing several different types including:

    a. Discarded PLA uniforms without the red star or collar tabs.
    b. Factory work clothing.

Insignia

10-23. *Collar Tabs.* Red collar tabs are a mandatory item for all uniforms,[1] except for afloat enlisted personnel who wear rectangular red patches on their shoulders. Collar tabs are worn by officers and enlisted personnel, both male and female, of all services, including the public security forces.

---

[1] Not shown on the following uniform sketches (all air force): Officer Summer Field Dress, Enlisted Work, Pilot, Service, and Winter Flight Female.

10-24. *Headgear Insignia.* A red star insignia is displayed on all headgear worn by members of the PLA forces and the national emblem, *T'ien-an-men*, is worn by Public Security Bureau personnel. (Figure 25.) No headgear insignia is worn by the militia.

10-25—10-26. *Reserved.*

SECTION II—AWARDS AND DECORATIONS

Background

10-27. Since the abolition of rank and service insignia in 1965, military personnel have not been observed wearing decorations or commemorative badges on their uniforms. Although such national awards as Orders and Medals of August First, Orders and Medals of Independence and Freedom, and Orders and Medals of Liberation still exist, they are no longer awarded. Commemorative medals and badges for specific battle campaigns are no longer awarded. There is, however, a system of honors and awards for both individuals and units for efficiency, achievement and valor.

Honorary Titles

10-28. *Individual.* The present military awards are based on the "honorary title" system. In individual cases, verbal citations or presentation of a useful gift, such as a diary or a towel, is customary. Meritorious Soldier, Combat Hero, Model Soldier, and Order of Merit are among the many individual honorary titles. Some awards or citations—such as the Good Fighter Medal and the Order of Merit (four classes)—are awarded to an individual and/or a unit. The Good Fighter Medal (not shown) was instituted in late 1971 and replaced two earlier Lin Piao-inspired awards: "Good-in-Five" Soldier, an individual award, and "Good-in-Four" Company, a unit award (see below).

10-29. *Unit.* Unit honorary titles are numerous and include designations such as Red Steel and Iron 2 Company, Brave Killer Company, Tiger Company, or Sharp Sword Company. The "Good-in-Four" Company award to units for excellence in political and military training, company administration, company health, and hygiene was discontinued in late 1971 or early 1972. Unit awards may be in the form of an oral or written citation, but for an extraordinary exploit a red citation flag with the feat inscribed in gold is awarded.

Medals and Badges

10-30. Limited information is available on these medals and badges and few have been identified. Available information appears below and the illustrations (figure 26) were made from photographs.

> **a.** *"Good-in-Five"* Soldier Medal (oval design). Though no longer awarded or worn, this medal still exists; it is comparable to the Good Conduct Medal of the United States Armed Forces. It is awarded for individual achievement in the "five goods," that is, exemplary political attitude, military training and personal bearing, attitude toward discipline, physical conditioning, and the "3-8 work style." It is made of metal and with a safety-pin clasp on the back.

b. *"Good-in-Five"* Soldier Medal (pentagonal design). This medal, also no longer awarded or worn, was probably awarded under the same conditions as the one of oval design. The significance of the different designs of the "Good-in-Five" medals has not been ascertained. The illustration shown is the artist's conception as copied from a poor quality photograph.

c. *Reenlistment Badge.* Awarded to individuals who extend their period of service. Another unconfirmed reenlistment award is described as a blue felt ribbon with a suspended, red, five-pointed star with the gold inscription: *ch'ao ch'i chan shih* (long-staying warrior).

d. *Peace Medal.* Originally awarded to Communist Chinese and foreign military personnel and civilians who contributed to Chinese Communist support of North Korea during the Korean conflict. It was first awarded on 25 October 1953. Since 1956, however, the medal has become an award for cultural exchanges between Communist China and the Warsaw Pact countries. (Native North Koreans are not eligible for this award.)

e. *Mao Tsetung Badge* (round design). Issued since the early 1950's and at one time reported to have been awarded for distinguished service in combat. Probably was considered a significant award, but since the beginning of the Cultural Revolution new designs of the badge have been reported and its original significance has diminished considerably. The earlier badges had a four-digit number stamped on the reverse which may have been a manufacturer's number or a control number for a record of issue to the recipient.

f. *Mao Tsetung Badge* (pentagonal design). Believed to be the latest design. Worn beneath this badge is a rectangular badge bearing one of Mao's quotations: *Serve the People.* These badges, to be worn with the uniform, were issued to all members of the armed forces during May 1967 and signify the wearer's sworn loyalty to Mao Tsetung.

g. *Model Soldier Badge.* This badge is awarded to model soldiers; eligibility criteria are not available.

h. *Order of Merit* (design not shown). This badge is awarded in four classes and bestowed on individuals or units for exceptional combat service, devotion to duty, and bravery. The four classes are: (1) Special Merit, the highest award granted for meritorious combat service or for bravery entailing death or the loss of a limb or vital organ; (2) Class I, awarded for meritorious service resulting in a serious loss to the enemy; (3) Class II, awarded for meritorious service in which bravery beyond the call of duty was displayed; and (4) Class III, awarded for meritorious service ranging from the conscientious performance of routine duties to the performance of unusual tasks under exceptional circumstances.

10-31–10-35. *Reserved.*

MILITARY ORGANIZATION OF THE PRC

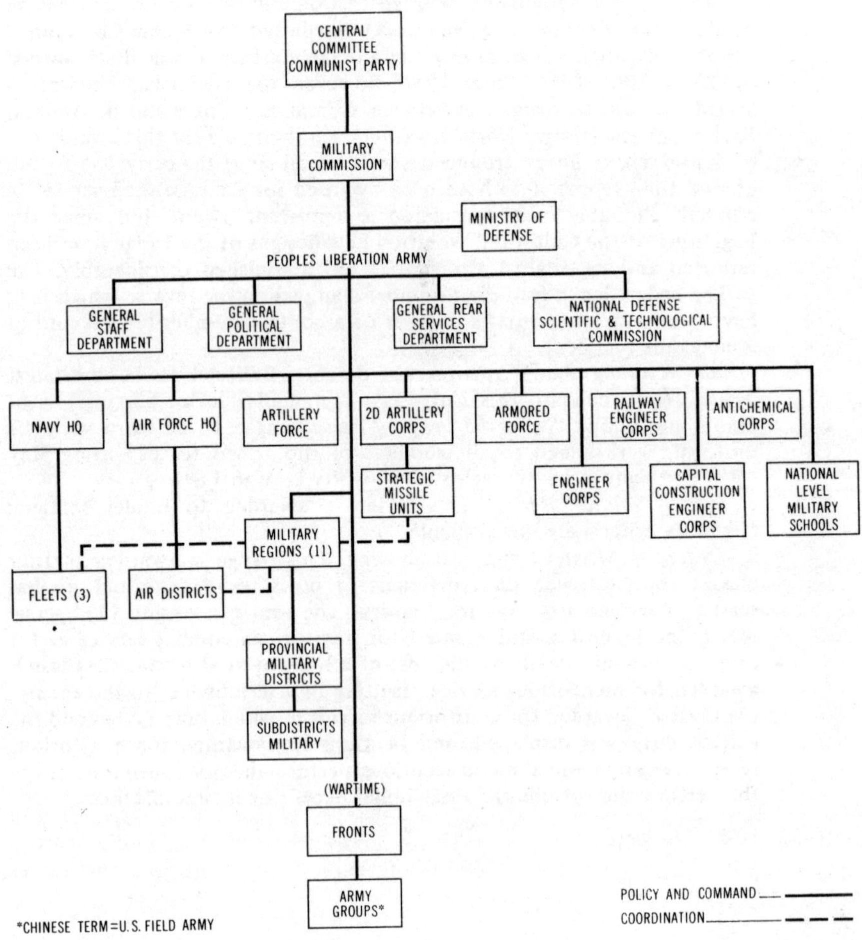

ORGANIZATION OF AN ARMY

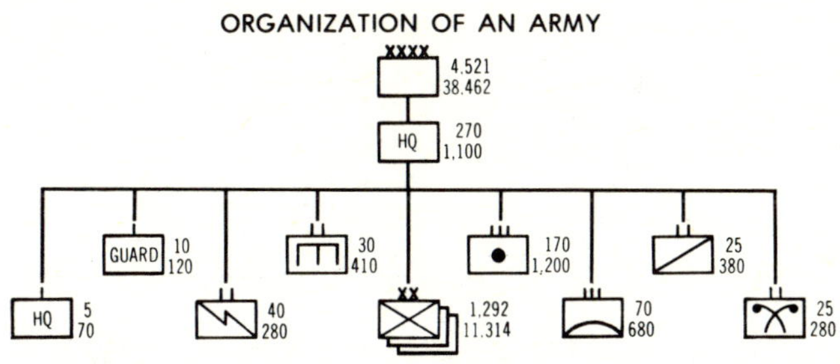

TABLE OF PERSONNEL AND MAJOR EQUIPMENT

Personnel/Equipment	Total Army	Hq Army	Hq Co	Recon Bn	Engr Bn	Sig Bn	CW Bn	Gd Co	AAA Regt	Arty Regt	Three Inf Div
Officers	4,521	270	5	25	30	40	25	10	70	170	3.876
Enlisted Personnel	38,462	1,100	70	380	410	280	280	120	680	1.200	33.942
Total Personnel	42,983	1,370	75	405	440	320	305	130	750	1.370	37.818
7.62mm LMG	1,087			30	30			10			1.017
7.62/12.7mm HMG	216										216
40mm Antitank Grenade Launcher (RPG)	1,558+			X	X			10			1.548+
57/75/82mm Recoilless Rifle	162										162
60/82/120/160mm Mortar	441										441
76/85/100mm Field Gun	54										54
122mm Howitzer	46									10	36
122/130mm Field Gun	10									10	
152mm Gun Howitzer	10									10	
140mm Rocket Launcher	18									18	
107mm Rocket Launcher	54										54
14.5mm AAHMG	46								10		36
37/57mm AA Gun	79								25		54
Tank, Medium	96										96
Assault Gun	30										30
Armored Reconnaissance Vehicle	27			9							18
Truck, Cargo/Prime Mover	1,464	120	15	2	13	3	2		90	100	1.119
Artillery Tractor/Truck, Prime Mover	24									24	
CW Equipment, Various	X						X				X
Flamethrower	81										81
Boat Inflatable, 4 - 10 man	X			X	X						X
Bridging Material	X				X						X
Radio Portable/Manpack	1,383+	X	X	20	3	25	X	X	40	80	1.215
Radio, Vehicle Mounted	248+	X	X	7	X	4	X	X	X	X	237

X - Amount of equipment not available.

ORGANIZATION OF AN INFANTRY DIVISION

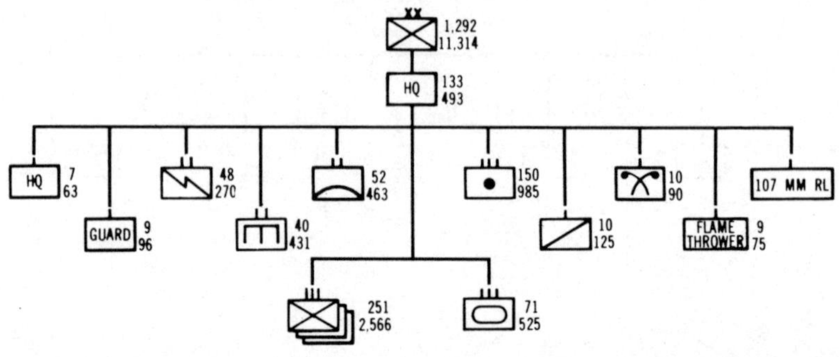

TABLE OF PERSONNEL AND MAJOR EQUIPMENT

Personnel/Equipment	Total Inf Div	Hq Inf Div	Hq Co	Recon Co	Engr Bn	Sig Bn	AAAW Bn	CW Co	FT Co	Gd Co	Tk/Aslt Gun Regt	Arty Regt	Three Inf Regts (total)
Officers	1,292	133	7	10	40	48	52	10	9	9	71	150	753
Enlisted Personnel	11,314	493	63	125	431	270	463	90	75	96	525	985	7,698
Total Personnel	12,606	626	70	135	471	318	515	100	84	105	596	1,135	8,451
7.62mm LMG	339			9	27					6			297
7.62mm HMG	54												54
12.7mm HMG	18												18
40mm Antitank Grenade Launcher (RPG)	516+	48		X	X					X			468
57/75/82mm Recoilless Rifle	54												54
60mm Mortar	54												54
82mm Mortar	81												81
120/160mm Mortar	12											12	
76/85/100mm Field Gun	18											18	
122mm Howitzer	12											12	
107mm Rocket Launcher	18?												
14.5mm AAHMG	12						12						
37/57mm AA Gun	18						18						
Tank, Medium	32										32		
Assault Gun	10										10		
Truck, Cargo/Prime Mover*	373+	67	12		15+	3	60				29	97	90
Motorcycle w/Sidecar	44+			9	4	X		5			12	5	9
CW Equipment, Various	X				X			X			X		X
Flamethrower	27								27				
Radio, Manpack/Portable	405			8	5	21	31				18	70	252

X - Amount of equipment not available.

* - Includes 6 ambulances.

ORGANIZATION OF AN INFANTRY REGIMENT, INFANTRY DIVISION

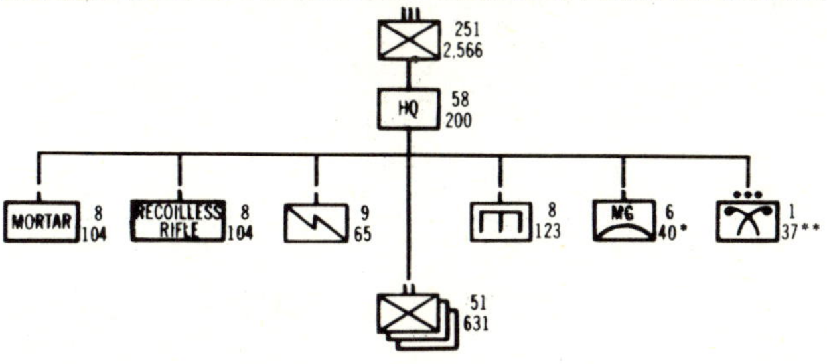

* SOME REGIMENTS MAY HAVE AN AAMG PLATOON.
** NOT ORGANIC TO EVERY REGIMENT.

TABLE OF PERSONNEL AND MAJOR EQUIPMENT

Personnel/Equipment	Hq Infantry Regiment						Mort Co	Rcl Rifle Co	Sig Co	Engr Co	AAMG Co	CW Plt	Three Inf Bns (total)
	Total Inf Regt	Ops Ofc	Polit Ofc	RSvc Hq & Staff	Tpt Co	Med Co							
Officers	251	16	14	9	9	10	8	8	9	8	6	1	153
Enlisted Personnel	2566	26	15	35	75	49	104	104	65	123	40	37	1893
Total Personnel	2817	42	29	44	84	59	112	112	74	131	46	38	2046
7.62mm Pistol	235	16	14	9	9		8	8	9	8	6	1	147
7.62mm Assault Rifle	817						48	30	16	46	10	4	663
7.62mm Carbine	1398						55	73	48	76	30	33	1083
7.62mm Assault Rifle/Carbine	151	26	15	35	75								
7.62mm LMG	99									9			90
7.62mm HMG	18												18
12.7mm HMG	6										6		
40mm Antitank Grenade Launcher (RPG)	156				6		6	6	6	12	6	6	108
60mm Mortar	18												18
82mm Mortar	27						9						18
57mm Recoilless Rifle	9												9
75/82mm Recoilless Rifle	9							9					
Mine, Antitank	X									X			
Radio, Manpack	84						1	1	7	5	4		66
CW Equipment, Various	X												X
Truck, Cargo	30				30								
Motorcycle w/Sidecar	3				3								

X - Amount of equipment not available.

ORGANIZATION OF A TANK/ASSAULT GUN REGIMENT, INFANTRY DIVISION

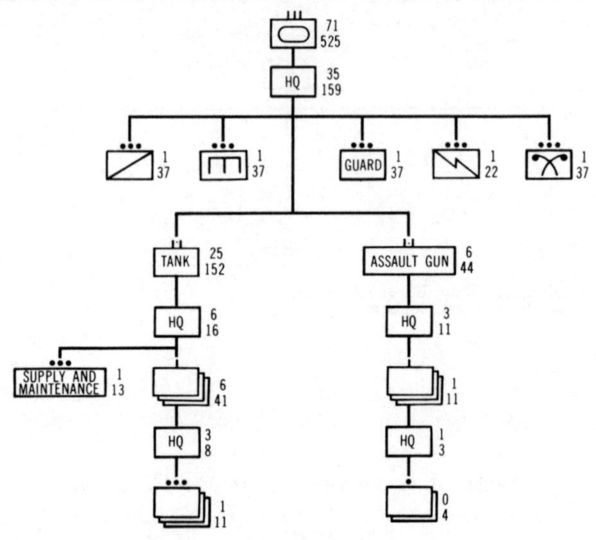

TABLE OF PERSONNEL AND MAJOR EQUIPMENT

Personnel/Equipment	Total Tk/AG Regt	Hq Tank/Assault Gun Regiment					Recon Plt	Engr Plt	Sig Plt	CW Plt	Gd Plt	Tk Bn	Aslt Gun Bn
		Ops Ofc	Pol Ofc	RSvc Hq & Staff	Trans Plt	Mnt Co							
Officers	71	12	9	9	1	4	1	1	1	1	1	25	6
Enlisted Personnel	525	17	10	19	37	76	37	37	22	37	37	152	44
Total Personnel	596	29	19	28	38	80	38	38	23	38	38	177	50
7.62mm Pistol	182	14	9	8	1	4	6	1	1	1	1	104	32
7.62mm Assault Rifle	233						32	33	19	33	33	66	17
7.62mm Carbine	15							4	3	4	4		
7.62mm Assault Rifle/Carbine	150	15	10	12	37	76							
Tank, Medium	32	1										31	
Assault Gun	10												10
Armored Reconnaissance Vehicle	3						3						
Armored Recovery Vehicle	2					2							
Truck, Cargo	29				18	2			1			6	2
Truck, ¼ - ½ ton	7	1							1		2	2	1
Motorcycle w/Sidecar	12						12						
Mines, Antitank	X							X					
Mines, Antipersonnel	X							X					
Demolition Equipment	X							X					
CW Equipment, Various	X								X				
CW Decontamination Vehicle	2								2				
Radio, Manpack	18						4	1	3	2		6	2
Radio, Vehicle Mounted	73	2				2	3		2			48	16

X - Amount of equipment not available.

ORGANIZATION OF AN INFANTRY BATTALION

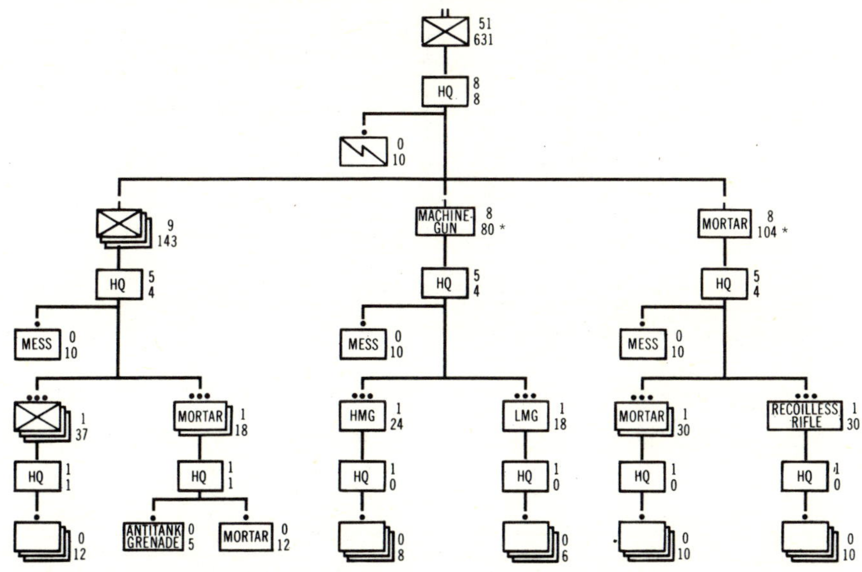

*SOME BATTALIONS DO NOT HAVE THESE COMPANIES BUT DO HAVE A MACHINEGUN AND A MORTAR COMPANY MADE UP FROM ELEMENTS OF THEM.

TABLE OF PERSONNEL AND MAJOR EQUIPMENT

Personnel/Equipment	Total Infantry Battalion	Hq and Signal Squad	Three Rifle Companies (total)	Machine-gun Company	Mortar Company
Officers	51	8	27	8	8
Enlisted Personnel	631	18	429	80	104
Total Personnel	682	26	456	88	112
7.62mm Pistol	49	6	27	8	8
7.62mm Assault Rifle	221	11	147	21	42
7.62mm Carbine	361	5	246	49	61
7.62mm LMG	30		27	3	
7.62mm HMG	6			6	
60mm Mortar	6		6		
82mm Mortar	6				6
40mm Antitank Grenade Launcher (RPG)	36	3	27	3	3
57/75 Recoilless Rifle	3				3
Radio, Manpack	22	2	18	1	1
Switchboard	X	X			
Field Telephone	X		X	X	X
Horses/Mules	14 +	2	X	X	12

X - Amount of equipment not available.

ORGANIZATION OF AN AIRBORNE DIVISION

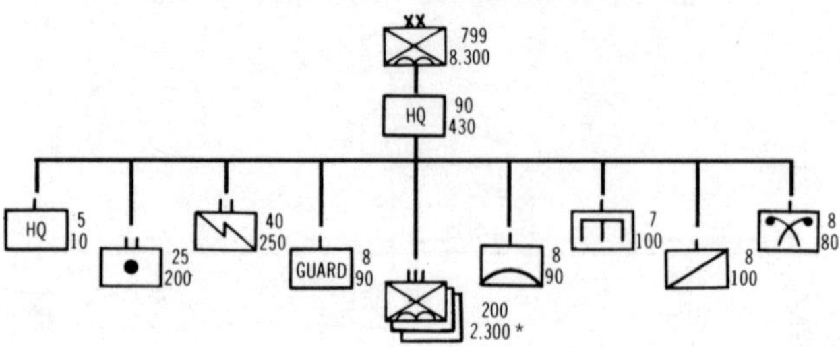

*ORGANIZATION OF AIRBORNE REGIMENTS
AND BATTALIONS IS SIMILAR TO THAT
OF INFANTRY REGIMENTS AND BATTALIONS
BUT MINUS THE HEAVY WEAPONS.

TABLE OF PERSONNEL AND MAJOR EQUIPMENT

Personnel/Equipment	Total Abn Div	Div Hq	Hq Co	Gd Co	AA Co	Eng Co	Recon Co	CW Co	Sig Bn	Arty Bn	Three Abn Regts (total)
Officers	799	90	5	8	8	7	8	8	40	25	600
Enlisted Personnel	8300	430	60	90	90	100	100	80	250	200	6900
Total Personnel	9099	520	65	98	98	107	108	88	290	225	7500
7.62mm LMG	294			5		7	7				240
7.62mm HMG	75										75
14.5mm AAMG	15				3						12
60mm Mortar	45										45
82mm Mortar	45										45
120mm Mortar	9									9	
40mm AT Grenade Launcher (RPG)	516+										516+
82mm Recoilless Rifle	75										75
37mm AA Gun	5				5						
Gas Mask/Protective Clothing	189							90			99
Radio, Manpack	307									7	300
Radio, Portable/Manpack	28				8		2		18		
Radio, Vehicle Mounted	3								3		
Truck, Cargo	105	25		5							75
Truck, Utility	2								2		
Parachute, Main	8511	110	32	98	80	90	90	70	216	225	7500
Parachute, Reserve	8511	110	32	98	80	90	90	70	216	225	7500

ORGANIZATION OF AN ARMORED DIVISION

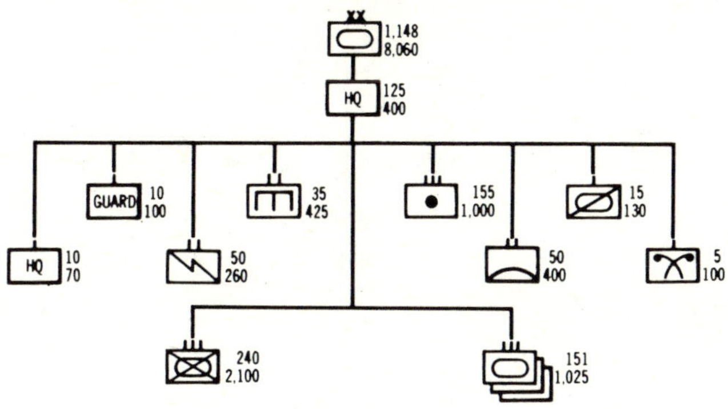

TABLE OF PERSONNEL AND MAJOR EQUIPMENT

Personnel/Equipment	Total Armd Div	Hq Armd Div	Hq Co	Recon Co	Sig Bn	Engr Bn	AAA Bn	Gd Co	CW Co	Arty Regt	Mech Inf Regt	Three Tank Regts (total)
Officers	1148	125	10	15	50	35	50	10	5	155	240	453
Enlisted Personnel	8060	400	70	130	260	425	400	100	100	1000	2100	3075
Total Personnel	9208	525	80	145	310	460	450	110	105	1155	2340	3528
7.62mm LMG	125			10		30		5			80	
12.7mm HMG	5										5	
40mm Antitank Grenade Launcher (RPG)	156 +			X		X		X			156	
57/75mm Recoilless Rifle	8										8	
75/82mm Recoilless Rifle	9										9	
60mm Mortar	15										15	
82mm Mortar	25										25	
120/160mm Mortar	10									10		
76/85/100mm Field Gun	20	X								20		
122mm Howitzer	12									12		
14.5mm AAHMG	12						12					
37/57mm AA Gun	15						15					
Tank, Medium	301	1										300
Armored Reconnaissance Vehicle	22			10								12
Armored Personnel Carrier	85										85	
Armored Recovery Vehicle	15											15
Truck, Cargo*	535	50	10		5	10	50			90	80	240
Truck, ¼ - ½ ton	72	5	10		1	1				5	20	30
Wrecker	8	1								2	5	
Motorcycle w/Sidecar	58					3			3	3	19	30
CW Equipment, Various	X					X			X	X	X	X
CW Decontamination Vehicle	5								2			3
Radio, Manpack/Portable	335			10	20	5	30			60	105	105
Radio, Vehicle Mounted	628	6		6	6						100	510

X - Amount of equipment not available.

* - Includes 7 ambulances and 3 radio trucks.

ORGANIZATION OF AN ARMORED REGIMENT, ARMORED DIVISION

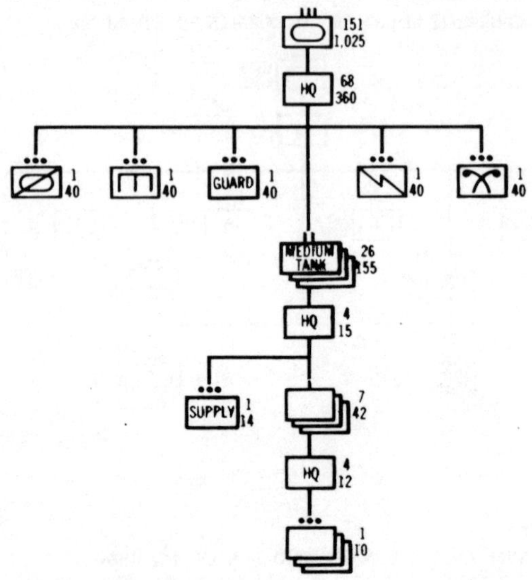

TABLE OF PERSONNEL AND MAJOR EQUIPMENT

Personnel/Equipment	Total Armd Regt	Headquarters, Tank Regiment						Recon Plt	Engr Plt	Gd Plt	Sig Plt	CW Plt	Three Med Tk Bns (total)
		Ops Ofc	Polit Ofc	RSvc Hq & Staff	Mnt Co	Trans Co	Med Co						
Officers	151	10	15	15	8	10	10	1	1	1	1	1	78
Enlisted Personnel	1025	20	20	30	140	130	20	40	40	40	40	40	465
Total Personnel	1176	30	35	45	148	140	30	41	41	41	41	41	543
Tank, Medium	100	1											99
Armored Recon Vehicle	4							4					
Armored Recovery Vehicle	5				5								
Truck, Cargo	80					59							21
Truck, ¼ - ½ ton	10	1				6				2	1		
Motorcycle w/Sidecar	10							10					
CW Equipment, Various	X											X	
CW Decontamination Vehicle	1											1	
Radio, Manpack/Portable	33							4	2		4	2	21
Radio, Vehicle Mounted	152	2				3		3			3		141

X - Amount of equipment not available.

ORGANIZATION OF A MECHANIZED INFANTRY REGIMENT, ARMORED DIVISION

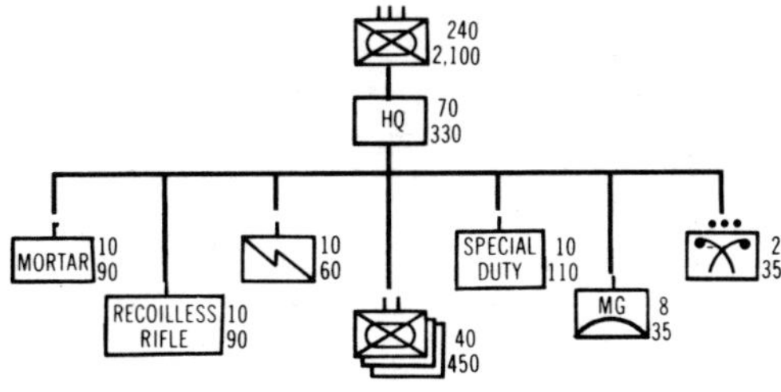

TABLE OF PERSONNEL AND MAJOR EQUIPMENT

Personnel/Equipment	Total Mech Inf Regt	Hq Mech Infantry Regiment					Mort Co	Rcl Rifle Co	Sig Co	SD Co	AAA Co	CW Plt	Three Mech Inf Bns (total)
		Ops Ofc	Pol Ofc	RSvc Hq & Staff	Trans Co	Med Co							
Officers	240	20	15	10	15	10	10	10	10	10	8	2	120
Enlisted Personnel	2100	30	10	30	220	40	90	90	60	110	35	35	1350
Total Personnel	2340	50	25	40	235	50	100	100	70	120	43	37	1470
7.62mm LMG	80									8			72
12.7mm HMG	5										5		
40mm Antitank Grenade Launcher (RPG)	156				6		6	6	6	12	6	6	108
60mm Mortar	15												15
82mm Mortar	25						4						21
57/75mm Recoilless Rifle	8												8
75/82mm Recoilless Rifle	9							9					
CW Equipment, Various	X											X	
Radio, Manpack	105						1	1	8	7	4		84
Radio, Vehicle Mounted	100				85								15
Truck, Cargo	80				80								
Truck, ¼ - ½ ton	20				8								12
Armored Personnel Carrier	85				85								
Wrecker	5				5								
Motorcycle w/Sidecar	19				5					10	4		
Ambulance	1					1							

X - Amount of equipment not available.

ORGANIZATION OF AN ARTILLERY DIVISION

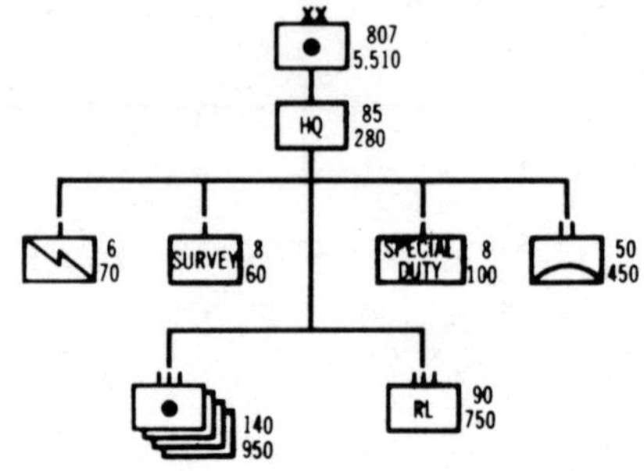

TABLE OF PERSONNEL AND MAJOR EQUIPMENT

Personnel/Equipment	Total Arty Div	Hq Arty Div	Sig Co	Survey Co	SD Co	AAAW Bn	Four Arty Regts (total)	RL Regt
Officers	807	85	6	8	8	50	560	90
Enlisted Personnel	5510	280	70	60	100	450	3800	750
Total Personnel	6317	365	76	68	108	500	4360	840
122/130mm Gun, 122mm Corps Gun, 122/152mm How, 152mm Gun How	136						136	
132/140mm RL	32							32
14.5 AAHMG	10					10		
37/57mm AA Gun	15					15		
Director, AA Fire Control	2					2		
Radar, AA Fire Control	2					2		
Generator	6					6		
Truck, Radio	2		2					
Truck, Cargo/Prime Mover	524	50	2		2	50	360	60
Truck, ¼ - ½ ton	35	2	2	1	10		16	4
Wrecker	7	1					4	2
Ambulance	7	2					4	1
Motorcycle w/Sidecar	27		8				16	3
CW Equipment, Various	X				X			
Radio, Portable/Manpack	343		6	2		25	260	50
Radio, Vehicle Mounted	4		4					
Switchboard	X		X			X	X	X
Field Telephone	X		X	X		X	X	X
Teletype	X		X					

X - Amount of equipment not available.

ORGANIZATION OF AN ANTIAIRCRAFT ARTILLERY DIVISION

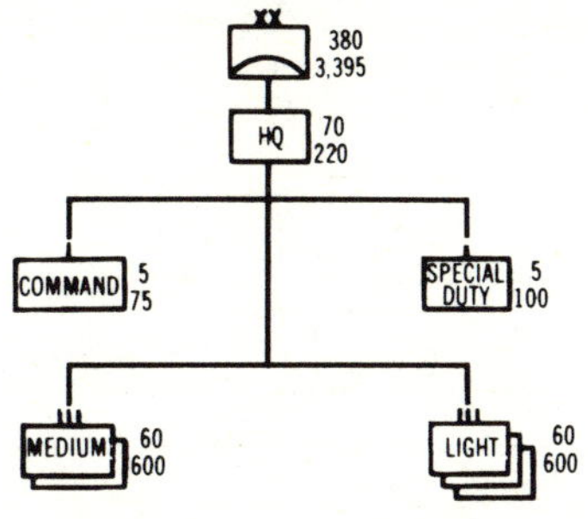

TABLE OF PERSONNEL AND MAJOR EQUIPMENT

Personnel/Equipment	Total AAA Div	Hq AAA Div	Comd Co	Special Duty Co	Two Medium Regts (total)	Three Light Regts (total)
Officers	380	70	5	5	120	180
Enlisted Personnel	3395	220	75	100	1200	1800
Total Personnel	3775	290	80	105	1320	1980
14.5mm AAMG	53				20	33
57mm AA Gun	66					66
85/100mm AA Gun	40				40	
Radar, AA Early Warning	5				2	3
Radar, AA Fire Control	15				6	9
Director, AA Fire Control	15				6	9
Range Finder, Stereoscopic	15				6	9
Generator	44				20	24
Truck, Radio	1		1			
Truck, Cargo/Prime Mover	447	30	1	1	160	255
Truck, ¼ - ½ ton	20	1	1	8	4	6
Wrecker	6	1			2	3
Ambulance	7	2			2	3
Motorcycle w/Sidecar	6		6			
CW Equipment, Various	X			X		
Radio, Portable/Manpack	179		4		70	105
Radio, Vehicle Mounted	1		1			
Switchboard	X		X			
Field Telephone	X		X			
Typetype	X		X			

X - Amount of equipment not available.

ORGANIZATION OF AN ANTIAIRCRAFT ARTILLERY DIVISION

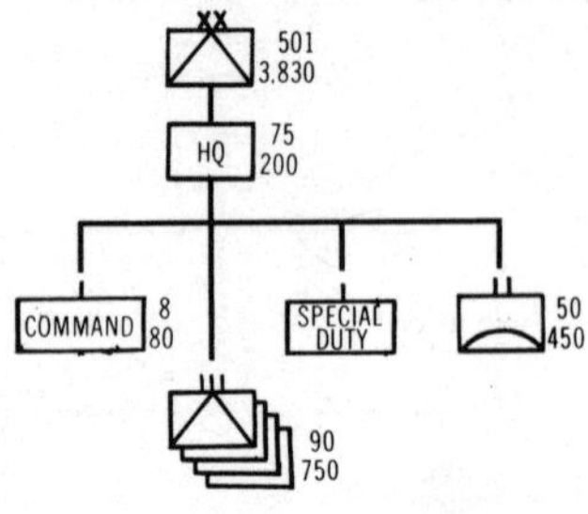

TABLE OF PERSONNEL AND MAJOR EQUIPMENT

Personnel/Equipment	Total AT Div	Hq AT Div	Comd Co	Special Duty Co	AAAW Bn	Four AT Regts (total)
Officers	501	75	8	8	50	360
Enlisted Personnel	3830	200	80	100	450	3000
Total Personnel	4331	275	88	108	500	3360
12.7mm HMG	20					20
57/76/85/100mm Antitank Gun	132					132
14.5 mm AAHMG	9				9	
37/57mm AA Gun	15				15	
Director, AA Fire Control	2				2	
Radar, AA Fire Control	2				2	
Generator	5				5	
Truck, Radio	1		1			
Truck, Cargo/Prime Mover	362	30	1	1	50	280
Truck, ¼ - ½ ton	18	1	1	8		8
Wrecker	4					4
Ambulance	10	2				8
Motorcycle w/Sidecar	22		6			16
CW Decontamination Vehicle	1			1		
Mobile Shower	1			1		
Gas Mask/Protective Clothing	32			32		
Radio, Portable/Manpack	200		3		25	172
Radio, Vehicle Mounted	2		2			

ORGANIZATION OF AN ENGINEER REGIMENT

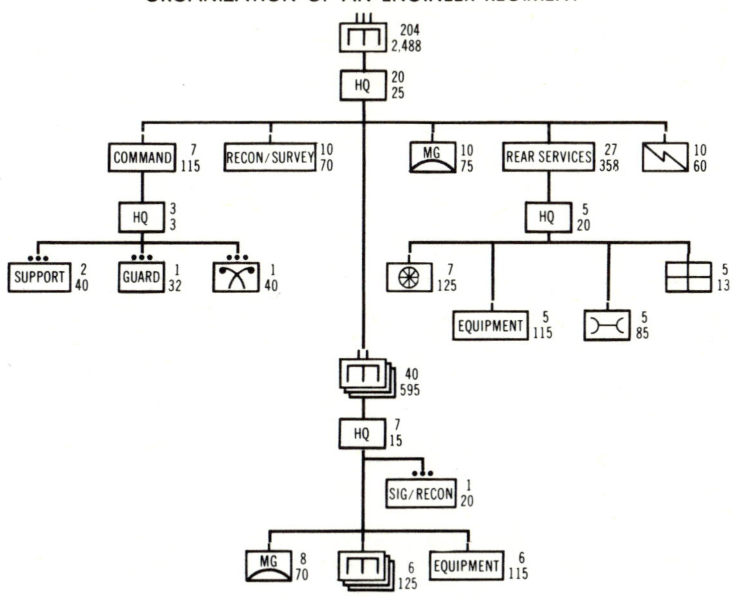

TABLE OF PERSONNEL AND MAJOR EQUIPMENT

Personnel/Equipment	Total Engr Regt	Headquarters Engineer Regiment										Three Engr Bns (total)
		Hq	Comd Co	Recon/ Survey Co	MG Co	Sig Co	RS Hq	MT Co	Equip Co	Maint Co	Med Unit	
Officers	204	20	7	10	10	10	5	7	5	5	5	120
Enlisted Personnel	2488	25	115	70	75	60	20	125	115	85	13	1785
Total Personnel	2692	45	122	80	85	70	25	132	120	90	18	1905
12.7mm HMG/14.5mm AAMG	54				15							39
40mm AT Grenade Launcher (RPG)	48		3	3	3	3						36
Truck, Cargo	85				6			48	7			24
Truck, Dump	9							9				
Truck, ¼ - ½ ton	14		1	1	1	3	1	2	1	1		3
Amphibious Armored Vehicle	8			3					2			3
Ambulance	1											
Bulldozer	3								3			
Road Grader	12								3			9
Rock Crusher	6								6			
Tractor	6								6			
Steam Roller	6								6			
Truck, Crane	9								6			3
Repair Van	6							6				
Outboard Motor Boat	8							2				6
Cement Mixer	12								9			3
Air Compressor	10								4			6
Generator	10								4			6
Truck, Radio	8		1			3	1					3
Radio, Vehicle Mounted	15		1	3	1	3		2	1	1		3
Radio, Portable/Manpack	49		1	3	4	6	1	3	3	3		24

PONTON BRIDGE REGIMENT

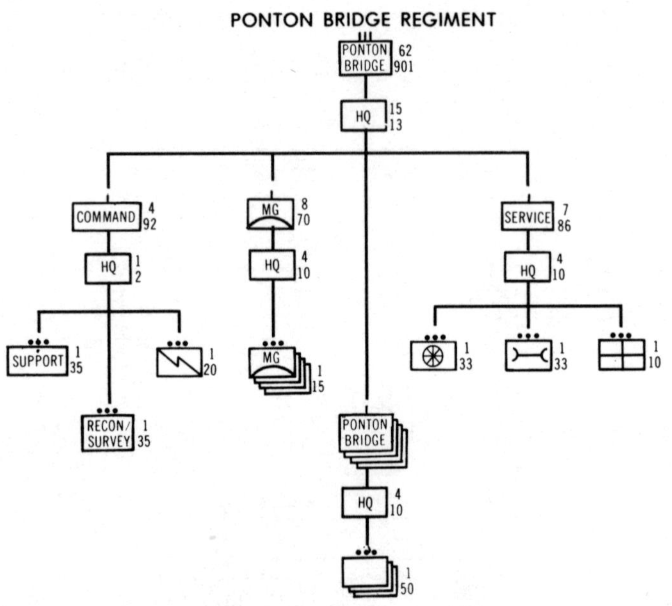

TABLE OF PERSONNEL AND MAJOR EQUIPMENT

Personnel/Equipment	Total Pont Br Regt	Hq Ponton Bridge Regiment				Four Pont Br Companies
		Headquarters	Command Company	AAMG Company	Service Company	
Officers	62	15	4	8	7	28
Enlisted Personnel	901	13	92	70	86	640
Total Personnel	963	28	96	78	93	668
7.62mm Pistol	61	15	5	8	5	28
7.62mm Assault Rifle	765		45	65	30	625
7.62mm Carbine	118	13	35		35	35
12.7mm HMG	10			10		
40mm Antitank Grenade Launcher (RPG)	21		3	4	2	12
Ponton	96/72*					96/72
Truck, Cargo	155			5	30	120
Truck, Crane	3					3
Armored Reconnaissance Vehicle	6		3			3
Motorcycle	2		2			
Bulldozer	1				1	
Ambulance	1				1	
Power Boat	13					13
Radio, Portable/Manpack	17		5	4	2	6
Truck, Radio	1		1			

*48 bow, 48 center sections/36 bow, 36 center sections

ORGANIZATION OF A SIGNAL REGIMENT

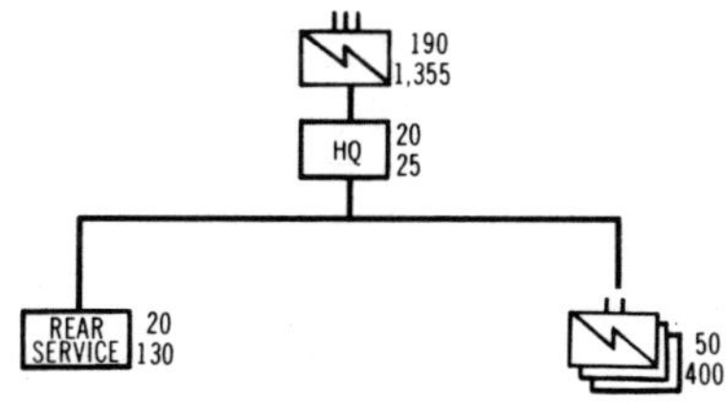

NOTE: THE SIGNAL REGIMENT PROVIDES COMMUNICATIONS FOR MILITARY REGION AND MILITARY DISTRICT HEADQUARTERS. THE STRENGTH, COMPOSITION AND EQUIPMENT WILL VARY ACCORDING TO THE NEEDS OF THE AREA THE REGIMENT SERVES.

ORGANIZATION OF A MOTOR TRANSPORT REGIMENT

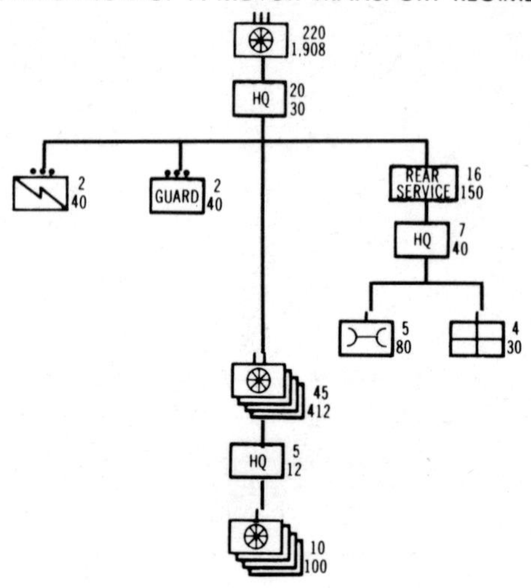

TABLE OF PERSONNEL AND MAJOR EQUIPMENT

Personnel/Equipment	Total MT Regt	Hq Regt	Sig Plt	Guard Plt	RSvc	Four MT Bns (total)
Officers	220	20	2	2	16	180
Enlisted Personnel	1908	30	40	40	150	1648
Total Personnel	2128	50	42	42	166	1828
7.62mm Pistol	172	18	1	1	12	140
7.62mm Rifle/Carbine	1800	20	30	30	120	1600
7.62mm LMG	1			1		
Truck, Cargo	702				2	700
Truck, ¼ - ½ ton	18				2	16
Wrecker	14				2	12
Ambulance	1				1	
Motorcycle	34		2			32
Radio, Portable/Manpack	25		4	1		20
Switchboard	6		2			4
Field Telephones	56		12			44

ORGANIZATION OF A RAILWAY ENGINEER DIVISION

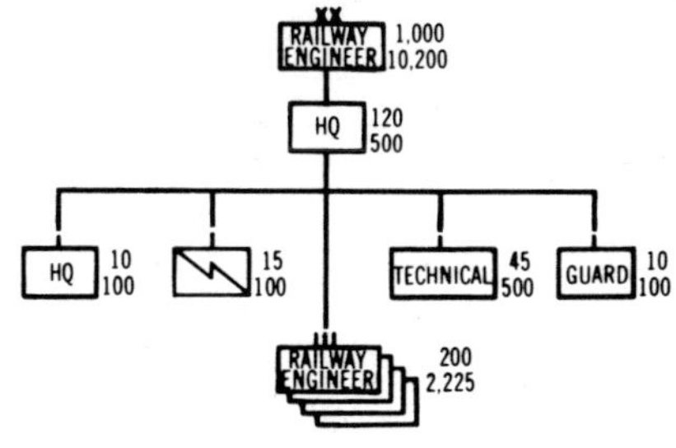

TABLE OF PERSONNEL AND MAJOR EQUIPMENT

Personnel/Equipment	Total Ry Engr Div	Hq	Hq Co	Sig Co	Tech Bn	Gd Co	Four Ry Engr Regts (total)
Officers	1,000	120	10	15	45	10	800
Enlisted Personnel	10,200	500	100	100	500	100	8,900
Total Personnel	11,200	620	110	115	545	110	9,700
Truck, Cargo	320	100			20		200
Truck, Dump	91	20			3		68
Truck, ¼ - ½ ton	63	16		2	4	1	40
Wrecker	14	4			2		8
Ambulance	7	3					4
Bulldozer	14				2		12
Repair Van	5				1		4
Road Grader	22				2		20
Rock Crusher	22				2		20
Tractor	20				4		16
Steam Roller	16				4		12
Track Laying Car	9				1		8
Truck, Crane	18				6		12
Cement Mixer	18				6		12
Air Compressor	30				10		20
Generator	30				10		20
Radio, Vehicle Mounted	18			2			16
Radio, Portable/Manpack	216	2	3	18	10	3	180

ORGANIZATION OF A BORDER DEFENSE DIVISION

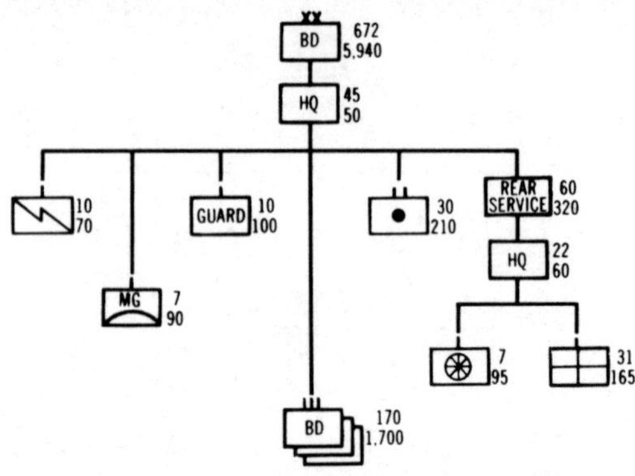

TABLE OF PERSONNEL AND MAJOR EQUIPMENT

Personnel/Equipment	Total BD Div	Div Hq	Sig Co	AAMG Co	Guard Co	Arty Bn	RSvc	Three BD Regts (total)
Officers	672	45	10	7	10	30	60	510
Enlisted Personnel	5940	50	70	90	100	210	320	5100
Total Personnel	6612	95	80	97	110	240	380	5610
7.62mm LMG	244				4			240
7.62mm HMG	24							24
12.7mm HMG	12			6				6
57/75mm Recoilless Rifle	6							6
60mm Mortar	54							54
82mm Mortar	6							6
76mm How/Gun, 85mm Gun, 122mm How	9					9		
Truck, Cargo	78					13	50	15
Truck, ¼ - ½ ton	4						1	3
Ambulance	4						1	3
Motorcycle, w/Sidecar	3		3					
Radio, Portable/Manpack	236		8			18		210
Switchboard	47		5			3		39
Field Telephone	260		20			12		228
Horses/Mules	120 +					X		120
Dogs	155				5			150

X - Amount of equipment not available.

ORGANIZATION OF AN INTERNAL DEFENSE DIVISION

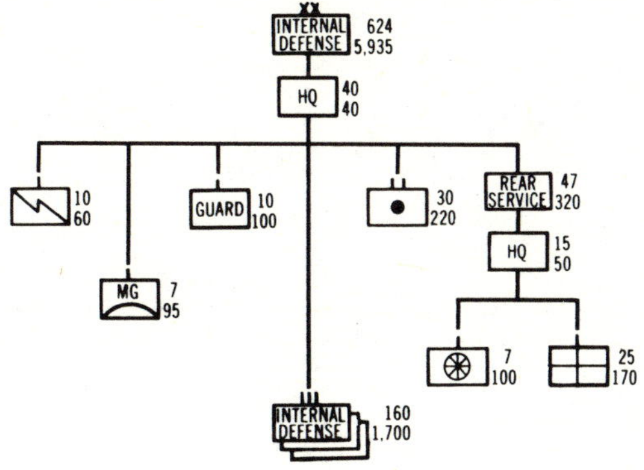

TABLE OF PERSONNEL AND MAJOR EQUIPMENT

Personnel/Equipment	Total Int Def Div	Div Hq	Sig Co	AAMG Co	Guard Co	Arty Bn	RSvc	Three Int Def Regts (total)
Officers	624	40	10	7	10	30	47	480
Enlisted Personnel	5935	40	60	95	100	220	320	5100
Total Personnel	6559	80	70	102	110	250	367	5580
7.62mm LMG	245				5			240
7.62mm HMG	24							24
12.7mm HMG	12			6				6
57/75mm Recoilless Rifle	6							6
60mm Mortar	48							48
82mm Mortar	6							6
76mm How/Gun, 85mm Gun, 122mm How	8					8		
Truck, Cargo	79					14	50	15
Truck, ¼ - ½ ton	6						3	3
Ambulance	4						1	3
Motorcycle w/Sidecar	3		3					
Radio, Portable/Manpack	125		8			18		99
Switchboard	26	5				3		18
Field Telephone	228		21			12		195
Horses/Mules	150+					X		150
Dogs	104				5			99

X - Amount of equipment not available.

ORGANIZATION OF A GARRISON DIVISION

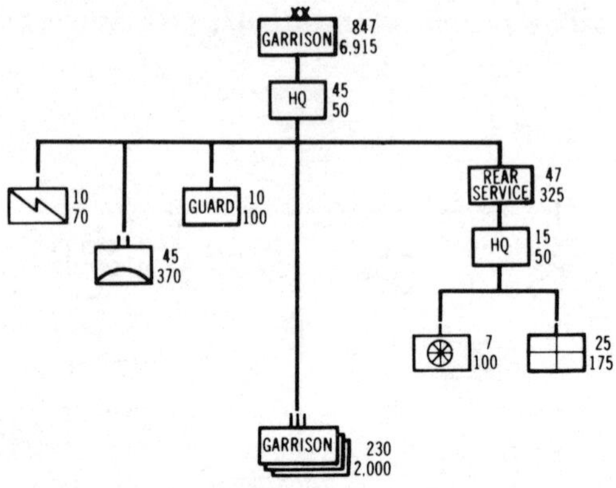

TABLE OF PERSONNEL AND MAJOR EQUIPMENT

Personnel/Equipment	Total Gar Div	Hq Div	Sig Co	AAA Bn	Gd Co	RSvc	Three Gar Regts (total)
Officers	847	45	10	45	10	47	690
Enlisted Personnel	6915	50	70	370	100	325	6000
Total Personnel	7762	95	80	415	110	372	6690
7.62mm LMG	104				5		99
7.62mm HMG	48						48
12.7mm HMG	15						15
40mm Antitank Grenade Launcher (RPG)	44				2		42
57/75mm Recoilless Rifle	48						48
60mm Mortar	15						15
82mm Mortar	24						24
57mm AT Gun	24						24
85/122/130mm Gun/ 152mm Gun How	66						66
14.5 AAMG	9			9			
37mm AA Gun	15			15			
Truck, Cargo/Prime Mover	89			5		39	45
Truck, ¼ - ½ ton	9					3	6
Ambulance	6					3	3
Motorcycle w/Sidecar	12		3				9
Boat, Transport/Patrol	38					5	33
Radio, Portable/Manpack	132		8	4			120
Field Telephone	238		21	28			189
Horses/Mules	150						150
Dogs	44				5		39

PROBABLE MILITIA ORGANIZATION

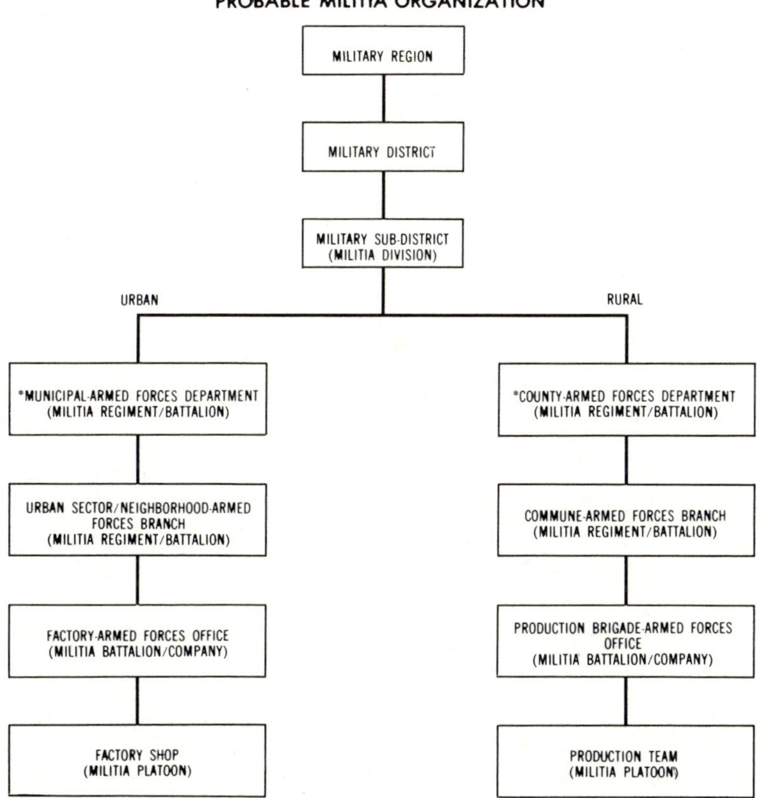

*MILITIA ACTIVITY IS SUPERVISED BY COUNTY OR MUNICIPAL "PEOPLE'S ARMED FORCES DEPARTMENTS." THESE DEPARTMENTS ARE PROBABLY SHARED BY A MIXTURE OF REGULAR PLA AND CIVILIAN PERSONNEL AND ARE SUBJECT TO DUAL CONTROL. AS MILITARY BODIES THEY ARE SUBJECT TO THE NEXT HIGHER MILITARY ECHELON, THE MILITARY SUBDISTRICT; AS POLITICAL ORGANS, THEY ARE SUBJECT TO THE COUNTY OR MUNICIPAL PARTY COMMITTEE, WHICH THEY SERVE AS A MILITARY STAFF SECTION.

NOTE: WITHIN THE VARIOUS MILITIA UNITS, ELEMENTS OF EACH OF THE THREE MILITIA CATEGORIES MAY BE FOUND, THE ARMED AND BASIC MILITIA SERVING PRIMARILY AS CADRES.

ORGANIZATION OF THE PRODUCTION CONSTRUCTION CORPS (PCC)
WITHIN A MILITARY REGION

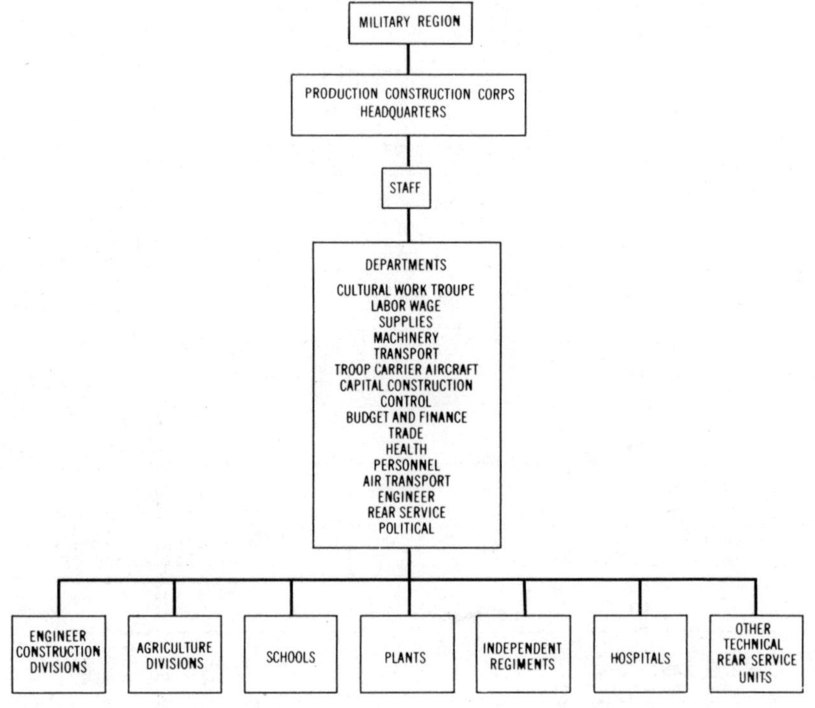

Annex X

CHINESE GROUND FORCES EQUIPMENT

1.   Chinese equipment policy is described in chapter 2, section II, and the technical characteristics are given in the appendices to this annex. In order to relate equipment to its deployment most of the appendices show the quantity (number) of equipment at the individual organizational level. Where possible, the annex pertaining to that organization is also indicated.

2.   Only the main items of Chinese equipment are included; sketches are not to scale. The Chinese possess additional equipment and some of the older or less common items in the inventory are not listed.

Appendices:	1.	Armored Vehicles
	2.	Infantry Weapons
	3.	Artillery
	4.	Engineer Equipment
	5.	Signal Equipment
	6.	Tracked Tractors
	7.	Load-Carrying, Wheeled Vehicles
	8.	Chemical Equipment

ARMORED VEHICLES

Equipment Tanks	Technical Characteristics	Role	Number by Organization	Refer to Annex	Remarks
Type 62	Crew: 4 Weight: 21 tons Main armament 85mm Ammunition: HEAT 　　　　　APHE 　　　　　AP 　　　　　HE 　　　　　SMK	Recon (light tank)			May be used as a main battle tank in especially rugged terrain, particularly in South China.
Type 63	Crew: 4 Weight: est 18 tons Main armament: 85mm Ammunition: APHE 　　　　　HEAT 　　　　　HE 　　　　　AP 　　　　　SMK	Recon (light tank)	4 Armd regt 20 Armed div		Chinese upgunned and enlarged version of Soviet PT-76 amphibious light tank. Armor thickness equivalent to APC.
T-34/85	Crew: 4-5 Weight: 32 tons Main armament: 85mm Ammunition: HE 　　　　　APHE 　　　　　HVAP 　　　　　SMK	Main battle tank (medium)			Still in armored units but being replaced by Type 59 tank.
Type 59	Crew: 4 Weight: 36 tons Main armament: 100mm Ammunition: APHE 　　　　　HEAT 　　　　　HE 　　　　　SMK	Main battle tank (medium)	3 Armd pl 11 Armd co 33 Armd bn 100 Armd regt 32 Inf div 301 Armd div	C H	Improved Soviet T54A.

191

ARMORED VEHICLES

Equipment	Technical Characteristics				Number by Organization	Refer to Annex	Remarks
Assault Guns	Maximum range (meters)	Ammo	HE proj weight (pounds)	Rate of Fire (rpm)			
SU-76	13.290	HE APHE HVAP HEAT	14	15-20	10 Tk/aslt gun regt, inf div	E	Supplied by USSR.
SU-85	15.650	HE APHE AVAP	21	15-20			Supplied by USSR.
SU-100	21,000	HE APHE HEAT	35	8-10			Supplied by USSR.

Equipment	Technical Characteristics	Role	Number by Organization	Refer to Annex	Remarks
Armored Personnel Carriers					
BTR-152	Crew: 2 Passengers: 17 Weight: 8.95 tons Armament: 7.62mm MG Wheels: 6	APC			Vehicle does not swim. Obsolete.
BTR-60	Crew: 2 Passengers: 16 Weight: 10 tons Armament: 7.62mm MG Wheels: 8 Speed in water: 10 km/hr	APC	8 In engr regt 6 In ponton bridge regt	N R	Without armored overhead cover.
M 1967	Crew: 4 Passengers: 10 Weight: 10 tons Armament: 12.7mm MG Tracked	APC	85 In trans co. mech inf regt, armd div	J	Amphibious; data not available.

Two ''fighters'' of the PRCA.

Bayonet training.

Political training in the field. M-1967 armored personnel carriers in background.

Marksmanship training.

Most PRCA units grow their food in their garrison areas.

The commander of an artillery unit assists his men in moving a heavy gun.

A commander lecturing on his unit's revolutionary traditions.

Despite extensive military training, physical conditioning, and political indoctrination, the ability of today's junior "commander" to inspire and lead troops remains untested.

WHISKEY Submarine (SS)

ROMEO Submarine (SS)

A growing fleet of diesel-powered attack submarines such as these two are expected to be the outer ring of defense against an approaching enemy naval force.

SHANGHAI II class motor gunboats (PGM) on coastal defense exercise.

Fleet of P6 motor torpedo boats (PT) anchored in an estuary. These craft are an essential part of China's close-in coastal defenses. The crews are studying the works of Mao Tsetung.

This LUTA guided-missile equipped destroyer (DD) is one of the largest surface vessels in the Chinese Navy.

P6 motor torpedo boats (PT) on a training exercise.

PRCAF pilot.

I1-28 BEAGLE medium-range jet bombers lined up at airfield during night-flying exercise.

MiG-19 FARMER jet fighters in formation.

Night-flying training in MiG-19 FARMER jet fighter aircraft.

A meeting of an armored unit's Party cells.

A company political officer instructing new recruits.

INFANTRY WEAPONS

Weapons / Small Arms	Caliber	Type of Fire	Weight (kilograms)	Feed	Effective Range (meters)	Practical Rate of Fire	Ammunition	Number by Organization	Remarks
Pistol, Type 54	7.62mm	Semi-auto	Unloaded 0.769	8 round box magazine	50	30 rpm	7.62x25mm	49 in infantry battalion	Chinese produced copy of Soviet TT-M1933.
Pistol, Type 59	9mm	Semi-auto	Unloaded 0.67	8 round box magazine	50	30 rpm	9x18mm		Chinese produced copy of Soviet PM.
Carbine, Type 56	7.62mm	Semi-auto	Unloaded 3.85	10 round box magazine	400	35-40 rpm	7.62x39mm (M-1943)	361 in infantry battalion	Copy of Soviet SKS.
Rifle, Type 68	7.62mm	Auto or semi-auto	Unloaded 3.9	15 round box magazine	400	Auto: 100 rpm Semi-auto: 40-60 rpm	7.62x39mm (M-1943)	180 in airborne battalion	Chinese developed rifle probably replacing Type 56 carbine.
Assault Rifle, Type 56	7.62mm	Auto or semi-auto	Unloaded 2.93	30 round box magazine	400	Auto: 100 rpm Semi-auto: 40 rpm	7.62x39mm (M-1943)	221 in infantry battalion	Chinese produced copy of Soviet AK-47.
Light machinegun, Type 56-1	7.62mm	Auto	Unloaded 6.6	100 round drum	100	150 rpm	7.62x39mm (M-1943)	27 in infantry battalion	Modified copy of Soviet RPD.
Light machinegun, Type 58	7.62mm	Auto	Unloaded 13.0	47 round drum magazine or 250 round belts	1,000	230-250 rpm	7.62x54mm Rimmed (M-1908)	3 in infantry battalion	Copy of Soviet RP-46.
Machinegun, Type 67	7.62mm	Auto or semi-auto	Unloaded 5.0	40 round box magazine or 75 round drum magazine	800	Auto: 150 rpm Semi-auto: 50 rpm	7.62x39mm (M-1943)		A company-level machinegun.
Submachinegun, Type 64	7.62mm								Chinese designed submachinegun. Silenced.
Heavy machinegun, Type 53/57	7.62mm	Auto	Unloaded without tripod 13.5	250 round belts	1,000	250-300 rpm	7.62x54mm Rimmed	6 in infantry battalion	Copy of Soviet Goryunov M1943 SG/SGM.

Weapons Small Arms	Caliber	Type of Fire	Weight (kilograms)	Feed	Effective Range (meters)	Practical Rate of Fire	Ammunition	Number by Organization	Remarks
Heavy machinegun, Type 54	12.7mm	Auto	Unloaded 34.0	50 round belts	Ground target: 1,500 Air target: 1,000	80 rpm	Standard 12.7mm	6 in infantry regiment	Copy of Soviet Model DShK. M1938/46.
Mortars									
Mortar, Type 63	60mm		12		Max: 1,530 Min: 200	15-20 rpm		6 in infantry battalion	Chinese designed.
Mortar, Type 53	82mm		56		Max: 3,040 Min: 100	15-25 rpm	Weight: HE: 3.05kg	6 in infantry battalion	Copy of Soviet 182mm Mortar, M-1937.
Antitank									
Grenade launcher, Type 56	Launcher: 40mm Projectile: 80mm		2.86		150	4-6 rpm	HEAT	40 Types 56/69 grenade launchers in infantry battalion	Modified copy of Soviet RPG-2.
Grenade launcher, Type 69	Launcher: 40mm Projectile: 85mm		6.3		500	4-6 rpm	HEAT		Modified copy of Soviet RPG-7.
Recoilless Rifle, Type 36	57mm		20.1		450	15 rpm	HEAT	3 in infantry battalion	Modified U.S. design.
Recoilless Rifle, Type 56	75mm		86.3		640	10 rpm	HEAT	9 in recoil-less rifle company, infantry regiment	Standard RL in PRCA units; modified U.S. design.
Recoilless Rifle, Type 65	82mm		28.2		450	6 rpm	HEAT		Chinese designed; probably replacing 75mm, Type 56. Lighter version of Soviet B-10.

ARTILLERY

Equipment	Technical Characteristics				Number by Organization	Refer to Annex	Remarks
Field Guns and Howitzers	Maximum range (meters)	Ammo	HE proj weight (pounds)	Rate of Fire (rpm)			
122mm Howitzer, Type 54	11,800	HE HEAT	48	5-6	12 In arty regt, inf div 12 In arty regt, armd div 6 In each arty regt, arty div 3 In arty bn, BD div 3 In arty bn, ID div	C H K R S	Copy of Soviet M1938.
122mm Gun, Type 60	24,000	HE APHE	55	6-7	6 In each arty regt, arty div 6 In each gar regt, gar div	K · T	Copy of Soviet D-74.
130mm Field Gun, Type 59-1	22,000	HE	73.5	5-6	6 In each arty regt, arty div 6 In each gar regt, gar div	K T	Chinese designed. On 122mm Gun Type 60 chassis.
152mm Howitzer	12,400	HE semi AP	88	3-4	6 In each arty regt, arty div	K	Copy of Soviet M1943.
152mm Gun-howitzer, Type 66	18,500	HE APHE	96	5	6 In each arty regt, arty div 6 In each gar regt, gar div	K T	Copy of Soviet D-20 On 122mm Gun Type 60 chassis.
Self-propelled Howitzer (probably 122mm)	(See 122mm Howitzer, Type 54)						China's first designed and produced self-propelled gun. Believed to be a 122mm Howitzer Type 54 mounted on an M1967 APC.

ARTILLERY

Equipment	Technical Characteristics				Number by Organization	Refer to Annex	Remarks
Antitank Guns	Point blank range at 2 m high target (m)	Types of Ammo	Armor penetration at 0° (mm)	Rate of Fire (rpm)			
57mm AT Gun, Type 55	1,100	HE APHE HVAP	140 at 500m	25			
85mm AT Gun, Type 55	1,150	HE APHE HVAP	130 at 1,000m	15-20			Copy of Soviet D-44.

Weapons Mortars	Caliber	Weight (kilograms)	Effective Range (meters)	Practical Rate of Fire	Ammunition (kilograms)	Scale of Issue	Remarks
Mortar, Type 55	120mm	275	Max: 5,700 Min: 460	12-15 rpm	Weight: HE: 15.4	Twelve 120/160mm mortars in infantry div	Copy of Soviet 120mm mortar, M1943.
Mortar, Type 56	160mm	1,300	Max: 8,040 Min: 750	2-3 rpm	Weight: HE: 41.5		Copy of Soviet 160mm mortar, M160.

Equipment	Technical Characteristics				Number by Organization	Refer to Annex	Remarks
Multiple Rocket Launchers	Number of tube	Maximum range (meters)	Warhead weight (pounds)	Reload time (minutes)			
107mm Rocket Launcher Type 63-1	12	8,050	43	3	18 In inf div	C	Has cast aluminum tubes and weighs 300 pounds less than the Type 63.
132mm Rocket Launcher, BM-13 (Soviet)	16	9,000	93.7	5-10	32 In RL regt, arty div	K	
140mm Rocket Launcher, BM-14 (Soviet)	16	9,810	90	7			

ARTILLERY

Equipment	Technical Characteristics			Number by Organization	Refer to Annex	Remarks
Antiaircraft Guns	Slant range (meters)	Cyclic rate of fire (rpm)	Fire Control			
14.5mm AAHMG, Type 56	1,400	2,400	optic	53 In AAA div 9 In AAA bn, gar div	L T	Towed, four barrels. Copy of Soviet ZPU-4.
14.5mm AAHMG, Type 58	1,400	1,200	optic	12 In AAA bn, inf div 12 In AAA bn, armd div 10 In AAA bn, arty div 9 In AAA bn, At arty div 15 In airborne div	C H K M G	Towed, two barrels. Copy of Soviet ZPU-2
37mm AA Gun, Type 55	3,000	160-180	optic	18 In AAA bn, inf div 15 In AAA bn, armd div	C H	Copy of Soviet M1939
57mm AA Gun, Type 59	6,000	120	radar/ optic	15 In AAA bn, arty div 15 In AAA bn, AT arty div	K M	Towed, single barrel. Copy of Soviet S60.
85mm AA Gun	8,382	15-20	radar	40 In AAA Division		Copy of Soviet KS-18
100 mm AA Gun Type 59	13,700	15	radar			A standard weapon of air defense units' AAA. Copy of Soviet KS-19.

ENGINEER EQUIPMENT

Equipment Vehicle Launched Bridges	Technical Characteristics	Role	Organization	Refer to Annex	Remarks
T54 MTU	Load class: 60 Span: 11 m Launch time: approx 3 min	Cantilever tank bridge			
KMM	Load class: 15 Span/unit: 7 m Span/set of 5 units: 35 m	Truck-launched treadway bridge			
TMM	Load class: 60 Span unit: 10.4 m Span set (4 units): 41.6 m	Truck-mounted scissors bridge			
Bridging **TPP**	Load class: up to 70 Length of bridge: 181 m Assembly time: 2m/min	Heavy ponton bridge	Ponton bridge regiment	R	
TMP	Load class: 70 Length of bridge: 90.8 m Assembly time: 3 hours	Heavy ponton bridge	Ponton bridge regiment	R	

SIGNAL EQUIPMENT

Nomenclature (Alternate Designation)	Frequency (Megahertz)	Type of Emission*	Power (Watts)	Transportability	Using Units	Remarks
RADIO RECEIVERS:						
A-148	1-15	Not applicable	Not applicable	Manpack Vehicle	Army Division Regiment	Copy of Soviet R-311. Receives A1, A2, and A3 emissions.
139 (XS-D14)	2-12.3 (3 bands)	Not applicable	Not applicable	Manpack	Regiment and below	Receives A1, A2, and A3 emissions.
239	Unknown	Not applicable	Not applicable			
435 (WS-430, WS-430A)	0.54-32, WS-430 0.54-25, WS-430A	Not applicable	Not applicable	Nil	Military Region	Diversity AM receiving equipment. Cabinet mounted.
7512	1.5-25 (5 bands)	Not applicable	Not applicable	Nil	Military Region	Receives A1, A2, and A3 emissions.
RADIO RELAY:						
Unknown (R-401, Soviet)	60-69.975	F2, F3, F9	2.5	Vehicle	Army Division Air defense	Provides 2 telephone and 2 telegraph signals on 1 trunk (54 fixed frequencies, 1 at a time). Used for command and administrative nets.
Unknown (R-403, Soviet)	60-69.975	F2, F3, F9	2.5	Vehicle	Army Division Air defense	Relay element of R-401.
Unknown (RVG-902, East German)	1200-1460	F9	3.0	Nil	Military Region	Provides 8 voice channels.
Unknown (RVG-903, East German)	1200-1470	F9	9.0	Nil	Military Region	Provides 8 voice channels.
Unknown	131-144	F9	5.0	Nil	Military Region	Provides 6 to 8 voice channels.
RADIO SETS: 71B (71, 71B1)	2.0-7.2. Transmitter 1.9-7.2. Receiver	A1, A3	1.9, A1 1.5, A3	Manpack Vehicle	Regiment and below	
102-E (X-D6, 55-B, 55-B1, 156)	2-12	A1, A2, A3	15.0	Manpack Vehicle	Regiment and below	Electronic copy of U.S. AN/GRC-9.
103	3.8-6	A1, A3	17.0	Manpack (2-person) Vehicle	Regiment and below	Electronic copy of U.S. SCR-694. In limited use, probably used by airborne forces.
Unkown (A-7-A, Soviet)	27-32	F3	1.0	Manpack	Regiment and below	
Unknown (2-watt station)	1.7-3.2 (2 bands) 3.2-6.0	A1, A3	3.5, A1 2.0, A3	Manpack	Company and below	Transistorized set. Chinese designed.
Unknown	40-48	F3	0.5	Vehicle	Regiment and below	

*TYPE OF EMISSION

Amplitude Modulation (AM):
    A1 - Manual Morse code, continuous wave (CW)
    A2 - On-off-keying/modulated manual Morse code (MCW)
    A3 - Telephone, double sideband, full carrier

Frequency Modulation (FM):
    F1 - Frequency shift telegraphy, single channel
    F2 - Frequency modulated Morse code
    F3 - Telephone
    F9 - Composite transmission

SIGNAL EQUIPMENT

Nomenclature (Alternate Designation)	Frequency (Megahertz)	Type of Emission*	Power (Watts)	Transportability	Using Units	Remarks
RADIO TRANSCEIVERS:						
A-130B	35.95-46.15	F3	1.3	Manpack Vehicle	Regiment and below	Infantry set. Copy of Soviet R-105D.
A-211B	28-36.5	F3	1.3	Manpack Vehicle	Regiment and below	Artillery set. Copy of Soviet R-108D.
A-220	20-22.375	F3	17.0	AFV	Regiment and below	Armor set. Copy of Soviet R-113.
A-222	2.8-4.99	A1, A3	90.0, A1 50.0, A3	AFV	Regiment and below	Armor CP set. Copy of Soviet R-112.
58	26-29	A3	0.2	Manpack	Company and below	Used where shortages of 702 transceivers exist.
63 (K63, A-131)	1.5-6 (2 bands)	A1, A3	1.3	Lightweight Manpack	Regiment and below	Chinese designed set with subminiature vacuum tubes and built-in Morse key.
71A	55-65	A1, A3	Unknown	Vehicle, fixed	Unknown	
71C	144-152	A1, A3	Unknown	Unknown	Unknown	
702 (E-459, 702D, Walkie Talkie No. 2)	26.1-37	A3	0.3	Lightweight Manpack	Company and below	Electronic copy of U.S. SCR-194 issued to U.S. Army in 1935.
883 (62)	44.8-50.2	F3	0.25	Manpack	Company and below	Transistorized set.
Unknown	45-50	F1, F3	1.0	Manpack	Company and below	Chinese designed transistorized set. Nets with A-130B and 883 transceivers.
Unknown (R-106, Soviet)	46.1-48.8	A3	0.5	Manpack	Unknown	
RADIO TRANSMITTERS: XF-D2	2-12 (3 bands)	A1, A2, A3	75.0	Vehicle	Regimental level	Similar to earlier 601 and 81 transmitters.
81 (102A, 102F)	2-12	A1, A2, A3	15.0	Vehicle	Regimental level	
91	2-16	A1, A2, A3	50.0 150.0 400.0	Vehicle	Division	
601	2-12	A1, A2, A3	75.0	Vehicle	Regimental level	High power version of 81 transmitter.

*TYPE OF EMISSION

Amplitude Modulation (AM):

    A1 - Manual Morse code, continuous wave (CW)
    A2 - On-off-keying/modulated manual Morse code (MCW)
    A3 - Telephone, double sideband, full carrier

Frequency Modulation (FM):

    F1 - Frequency shift telegraphy, single channel
    F2 - Frequency modulated Morse code
    F3 - Telephone
    F9 - Composite transmission

SIGNAL EQUIPMENT

Nomenclature (Alternate Designation)	Operation - Type	Range (Kilometers)	Remarks
TELEGRAPH SETS:			
57-1B			Chinese-character teleprinter.
Unknown. (ST-35, Soviet)		40-64 field cable, 400 open wire	TAPE PRINTER: 5-unit code plus start/stop; 382 operations per minute (OPM).
TELEPHONE SETS, FIELD:			
B-600	Magneto	8	Resembles 0743 but smaller.
CX-2	Magneto	8	Copy of Soviet TAI-43.
Q-07.1	Magneto	3.5 (est)	Similar in appearance to U.S. EE-8.
0743 (0745)	Magneto	8	Copy of Soviet TAI-43.
Unknown	Magneto	Unknown	Housed in plastic case wtih a webbed shoulder strap. Has provisions for monitoring conversations and for testing line continuity.
TELEPHONE SWITCHBOARDS:			
B-611	Local Battery	10 (est)	Portable, cordless, single position, 10-line field switchboard. Used between divisions and regiments.
JCX-1 (252B, 5421)	Local Battery	10 (est)	Exact copy of Soviet K-10. Ten-line monocord field switchboard for command posts.
Unknown	Local or Central Battery	10 (est)	Double-cord-operated 40-line switchboard. Can be used for conference calls with line or radio subscribers.
WIRE, FIELD:			
Unknown	Not applicable	10 (est)	Standard twisted pair wire; stored, dispersed, and retrieved on "H"-shaped frames with capacity of 500 meters. Wire includes 4 strands of steel and 3 strands of copper with polyvinyl sheath. Tensile strength, 200 pounds; 2 to 5 decibel loss per kilometer for voice transmission.

TRACKED TRACTORS

Vehicle Artillery	Weight (kilograms)	Maximum Payload (kilograms)	Towed Load (kilograms)	Cruising Range (kilometers)	Remarks
AT-P Armored Tractor	6,300	3 to 6 men	3,150	320	Mounts one 7.62mm tank machinegun.
Artillery Tractor, Type 59					Chinese designed and produced heavy artillery tractor.
AT-S Artillery Tractor	12,000	7 to 10 men	16,000	380	Used in arty regt, army and probably in some arty divisions.

LOAD-CARRYING, WHEELED VEHICLES

Trucks	Weight (kilograms)	Maximum Payload (kilograms)	Towed Load (kilograms)	Cruising Range (kilometers)	Remarks
BJ-212, ½-ton Utility Truck, 4x4	1,530	425		440	Chinese produced commander's jeep and reconnaissance vehicle.
GAZ-63, 2-ton Cargo Truck, 4x4 (Soviet)	3,200	2,000	2,000	780	Limited number in service. Used as prime mover for mortars and light artillery pieces.
GAZ-51- 2½-ton Cargo Truck, 4x2 (Soviet)	2,500	2,500	2,500	450	Relatively large numbers still in service. Cargo and prime mover use.
ZIL-150, 4½-ton Cargo Truck, 4x2 (Soviet)	3,900	4,000	4,500	500	Relatively large numbers still in service. Cargo and prime mover use.
ZIL-164, 4-ton Cargo Truck, 4x2 (Soviet)	4,100	4,000	6,400	405	Cargo and primer mover use.

LOAD-CARRYING, WHEELED VEHICLES

Trucks	Weight (kilograms)	Maximum Payload (kilograms)	Towed Load (kilograms)	Cruising Range (kilometers)	Remarks
CA-10, 4-ton Cargo Truck, 4x2	3,840	3,540		415	Chinese produced version of ZIL-150. Extensively used as cargo carrier.
ZIL-151, 5-ton Cargo Truck, 6x6 (Soviet)	5,580	4,500	3,600	652	Extensively used as prime mover for artillery.
ZIL-157, 2½-ton Cargo Truck, 6x6 (Soviet)	5,800	4,500	3,600	510	Cargo and prime mover.
CA-30, 2½-ton Cargo Truck, 6x6	5,450	4,500	3,600	680	Chinese produced copy of ZIL-157. Cargo and prime mover use.
NJ-230, 1½-ton Cargo Truck, 4x4	3,440	2,100	2,100	500	Chinese produced copy of the Soviet GAZ-63. Cargo and prime mover use.

CHEMICAL EQUIPMENT

Equipment	Technical Characteristics	Organization	Refer to Annex	Remarks
Flamethrowers				
ROKS-3	Flamethrower, manpack	Inf div	C	Possibly replaced by LPO type.
LPO	FLamethrower, manpack	Inf div	C	Soviet design.
TPO	Flamethrower, cart mounted	Inf div	C	
FO	Flamethrower, emplaced type	Inf div	C	Electrically controlled, usually in groups of three or five, in defensive operations.
Smoke Munitions				
DB-11	Smoke barrel	Chemical warfare bn, army. Chemical warfare co. inf div.	B C	For use in large-scale smokescreens. Soviet design.
DM-11	Smoke pot			Soviet design.
Decontaminants and Equipment				
PM-DK	Decontamination kit for mortars, machineguns, and grenade launchers. Contains liquid decontaminant.	Chemical warfare bn, army. Chemical warfare co. inf div.	B C	Soviet design.
RDP-4	Decontamination apparatus, manpack for small arms and equipment.	Chemical warfare bn, army. Chemical warfare co. inf div.	B C	Soviet design.
RDP-3	Decontamination apparatus, manpack for small arms and equipment.	Chemical warfare bn, army. Chemical warfare co. inf div.	B C	Soviet design.
ARS-12	Decontamination apparatus, truck mounted, for weapons, vehicles, other equipment, and terrain.	Chemical warfare bn, army. Chemical warfare co. inf div.	B C	Soviet design.
ADM-48	Decontamination apparatus, truck mounted, for weapons, vehicles, equipment, and terrain.	Chemical warfare bn, army. Chemical warfare co. inf div.	B C	Soviet design.

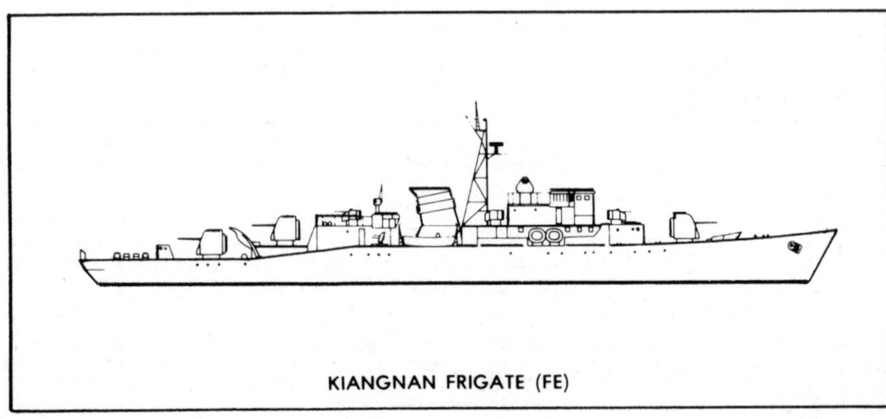

KIANGNAN FRIGATE (FE)

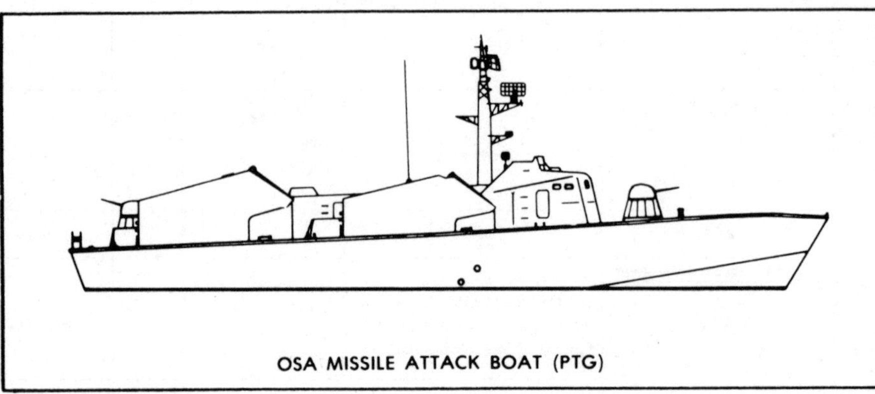

OSA MISSILE ATTACK BOAT (PTG)

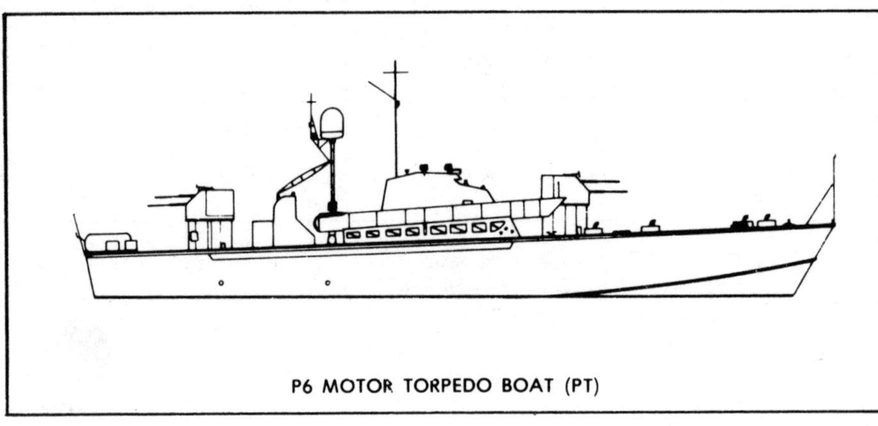

P6 MOTOR TORPEDO BOAT (PT)

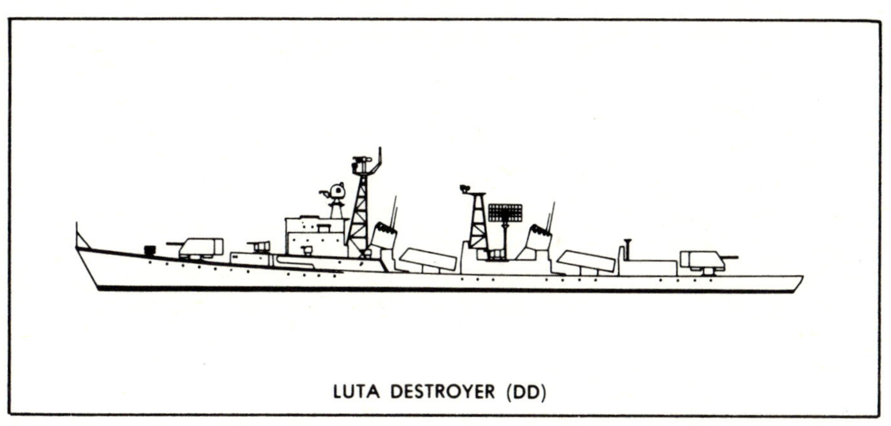

LUTA DESTROYER (DD)

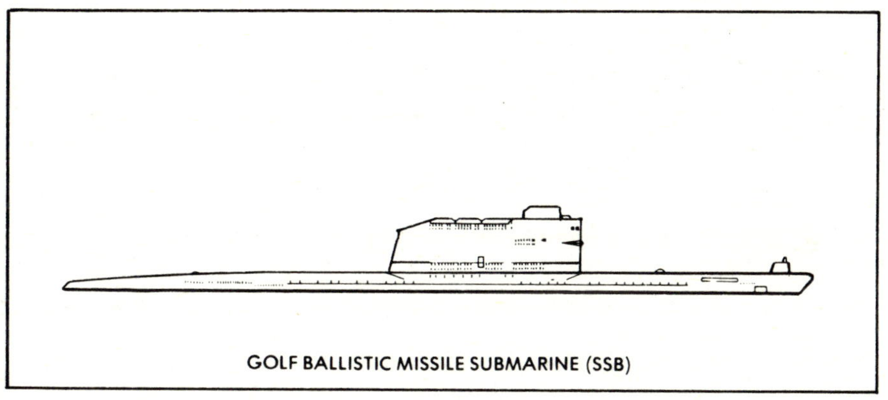

GOLF BALLISTIC MISSILE SUBMARINE (SSB)

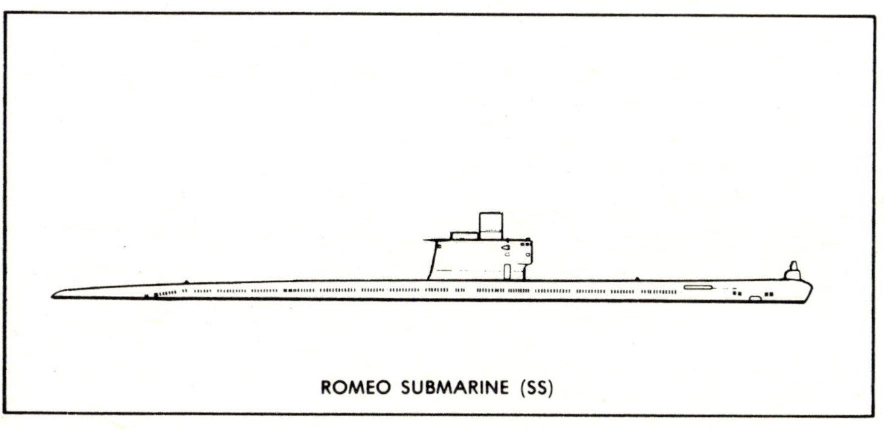

ROMEO SUBMARINE (SS)

PRCAF AIRCRAFT

AIRCRAFT	ROLE	LENGTH	WING SPAN OR ROTOR DIAMETER	ENGINES	RANGE (nautical miles)	RADIUS (nautical miles)	MAX SPEED (knots)	MISSION PAYLOAD
BOMBERS								
BADGER/TU-16	Intermediate-range bomber	116'	108'	2 turbojet	3,200	1,650	510	Normal 6,600 lbs
BULL/TU-4	Intermediate-range bomber	99'	141'	4 turboprop	3,050	1,550	225 cruise	Normal 10,000 lbs
BEAGLE/IL-28	Medium-range bomber	58'	70'6"	2 turbojet	1,000	550	504	Normal 2,200 lbs
BAT/TU-2	Medium-range bomber	45'6"	62'	2 piston	1,040		208	Normal 3,300 lbs
FIGHTERS								
FAGOT/MIG-15	Fighter-bomber	33'	33'	1 turbojet		150	585	Cannon. Two 550-lb bombs*
FRESCO/MIG-17	Interceptor	38'	31'	1 turbojet	620	280	570	Cannon. Two 550-lb bombs*
FARMER/MIG-19	Interceptor	34'	30'	2 turbojet	1,150	530	650	Cannon. Two 550-lb bombs*
FISHBED/MIG-21	Interceptor	44'	24'	1 turbojet	850	360	Mach 2	Cannon. Two 550-lb bombs*
FANTAN/F-9	Fighter-bomber	50'	33'	2 turbojet		430	Mach 2	
TRANSPORTS								
CLASSIC/IL-62	Long-range transport	160'6"	141'7"	4 turbofan	5,900		495	58,900 lbs*
BOEING 707	Long-range transport	152'11"	145'9"	4 turbofan	6,493		521	91,390 lbs*
COOKPOT/TU-124	Medium-range transport	100'	84'	2 turbofan	1,242		432 cruise	13,230 lbs
COOT/IL-18	Medium-range transport	118'	123'	4 turboprop	2,690		350 cruise	30,825 lbs
CUB/AN-12	Medium-range transport	109'	125'	4 turboprop	1,832		313 cruise	44,090 lbs
HS TRIDENT 1E	Medium-range transport	114'9"	95'	3 turbofan	2,120		520 cruise	24,000 lbs*
HS TRIDENT 2E	Medium-range transport	114'9"	98'	3 turbofan	2,120		520 cruise	26,800 lbs*
HS TRIDENT 3B	Medium-range transport	131'2"	98'	2 turbofan 1 turbojet	1,780		525	35,357 lbs*
VICKERS VISCOUNT	Medium-range transport	85'5"	94'	4 turboprop	1,500		301 cruise	14,500 lbs
CAB/LI-2	Short-range transport	64' 5"	94'6"	2 piston	1,100		145 cruise	6,600 lbs
COACH/IL-12	Short-range transport	90'	104'	2 piston	1,300		175	4,750 lbs
COKE/AN-24	Short-range transport	77'	96'	2 turboprop	1,295		243 cruise	12,566 lbs

*. Maximum payload

PRCAF AIRCRAFT

AIRCRAFT	ROLE	LENGTH	WING SPAN OR ROTOR DIAMETER	ENGINES	RANGE (nautical miles)	RADIUS (nautical miles)	MAX SPEED (knots)	MISSION PAYLOAD
TRANSPORTS								
COLT/AN-2	Short-range transport	43'	59'8''	1 piston	488		108 cruise	3.000 lbs
CRATE/IL-14	Short-range transport	70'	104'	2 piston	1.169		175 cruise	9.000 lbs
CURL/AN-26	Short-range transport	77'	96'	2 turbofan	1.348		243 cruise	11.023 lbs
CURTISS COMMANDO	Short-range transport	108'1''	76'4''	2 piston	1.000	500	160 cruise	7.500 lbs
DOUGLAS SKYTRAIN	Short-range transport	64'6''	94'6''	2 piston	1.100	700	145 cruise	6.600 lbs
HELICOPTERS								
HOOK/MI-6	Heavy	109'	115'	2 shaft turbine	335		162	24.455 lbs
HIP/MI-8	Medium	60'	70'	2 shaft turbine	229		119	8.818 lbs
HOUND/MI-4	Medium	55'	69'	1 piston	269		100	3.525 lbs
SA 321 SUPER FRELON	Medium	65'11''	62'	3 turboshaft	442		148	11.023 lbs

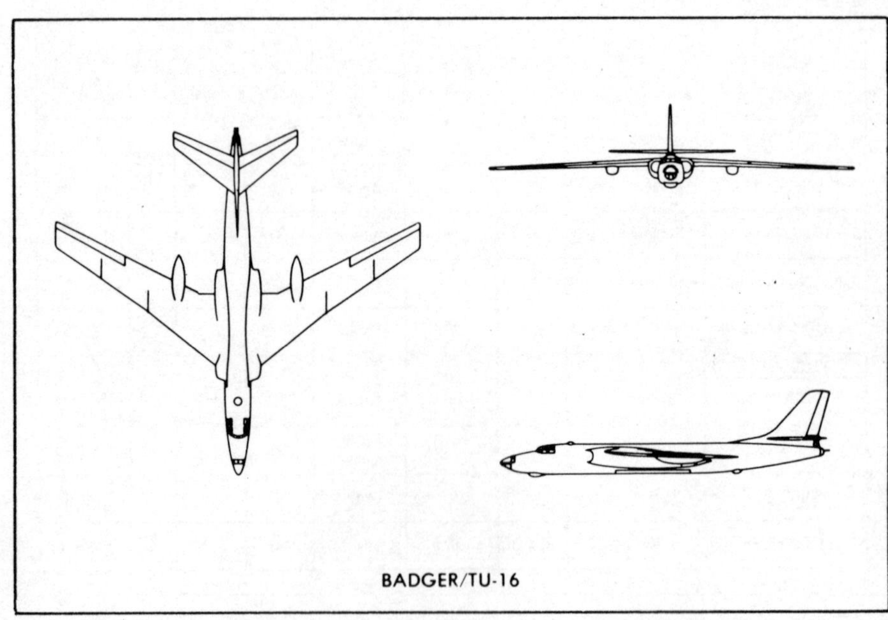

BADGER/TU-16

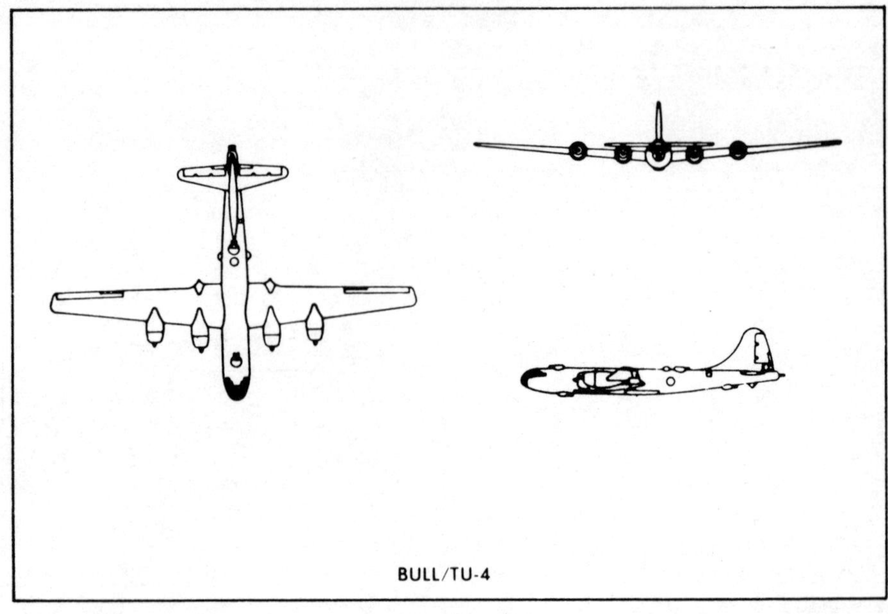

BULL/TU-4

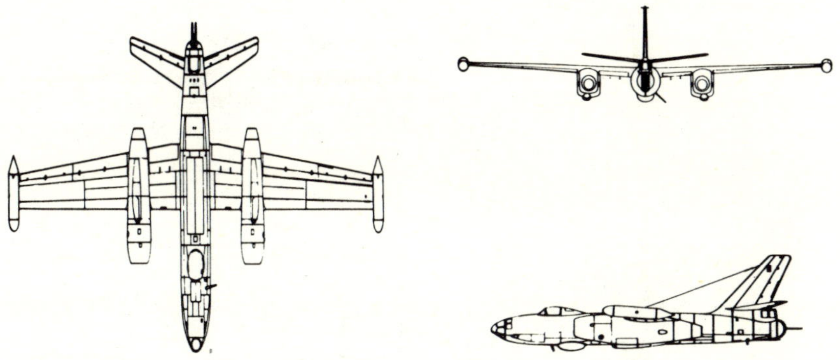

BEAGLE/IL-28

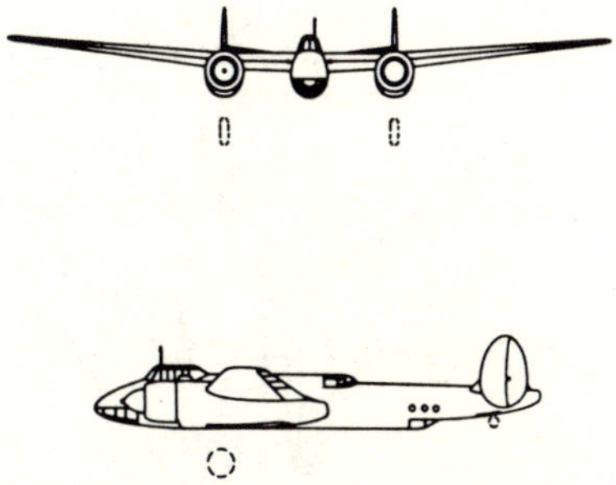

BAT/TU-2

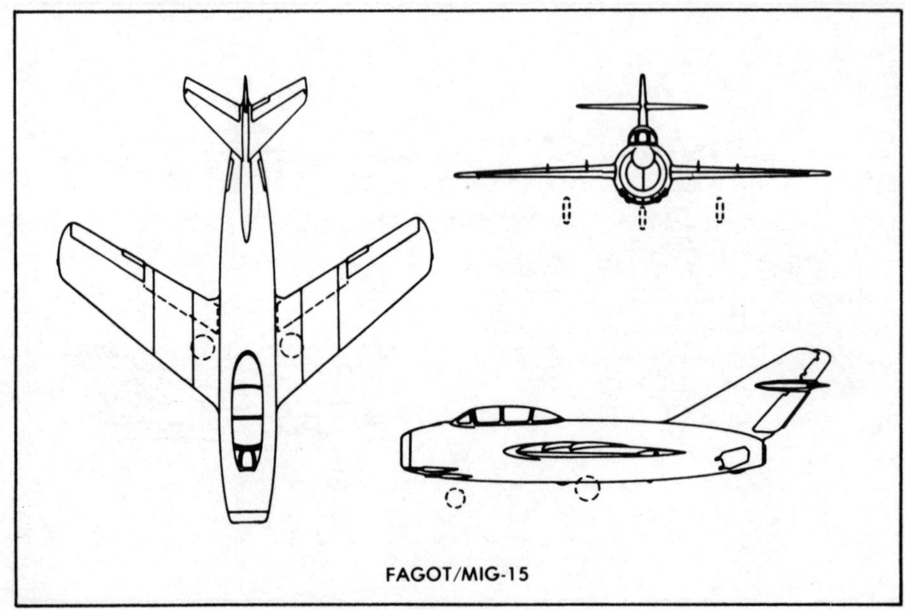

FAGOT/MIG-15
FRESCO/MIG-17

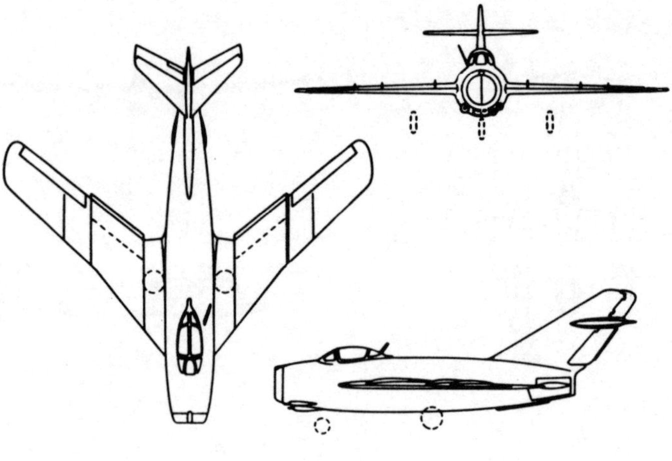

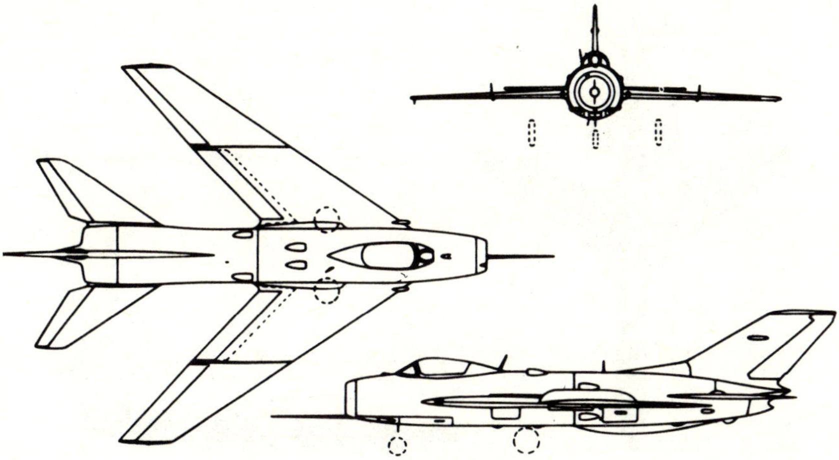

FARMER/MIG-19

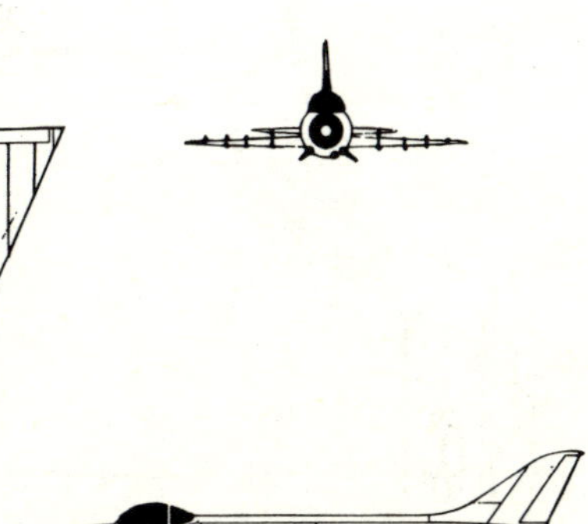

FISHBED/MIG-21

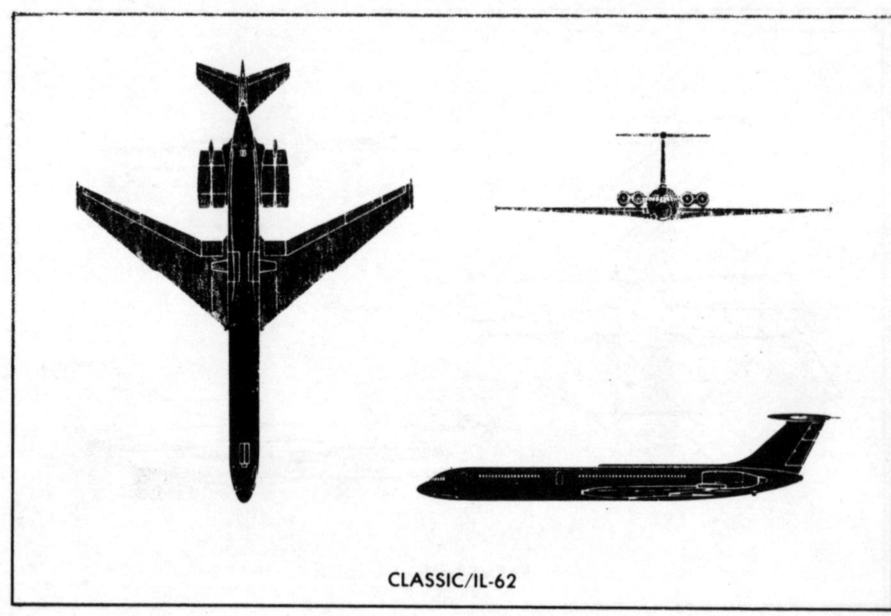

CLASSIC/IL-62

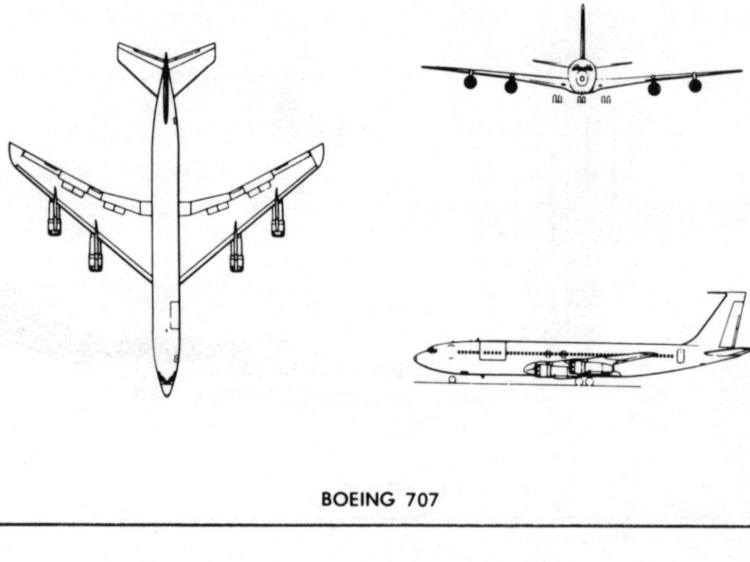

BOEING 707

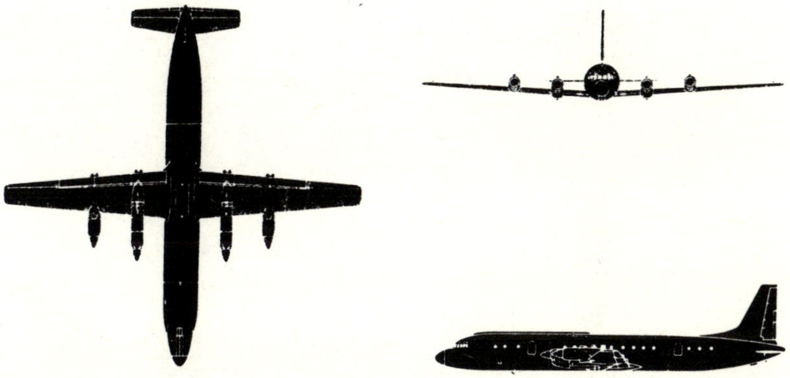

COOT/IL-18

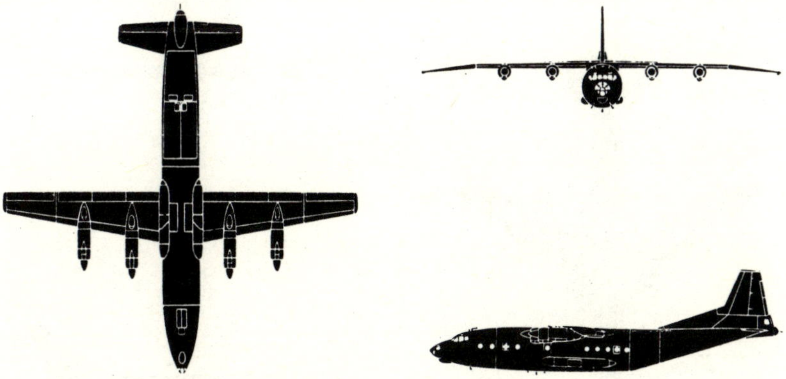

CUB/AN-12

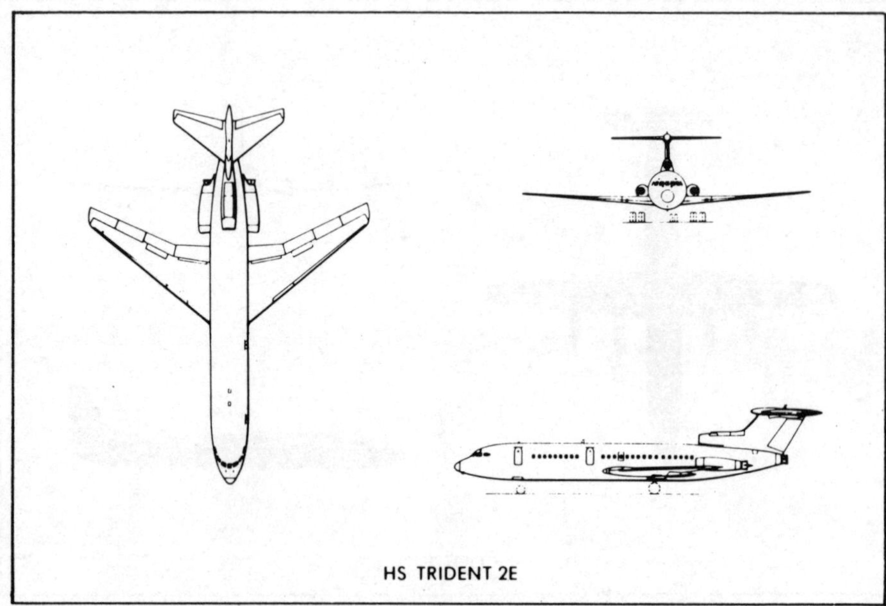

HS TRIDENT 2E

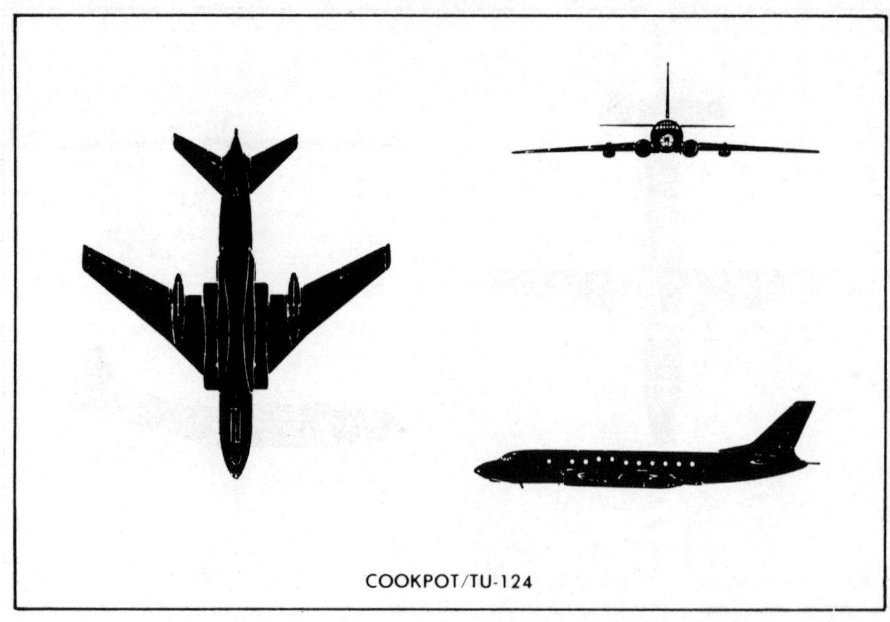

COOKPOT/TU-124

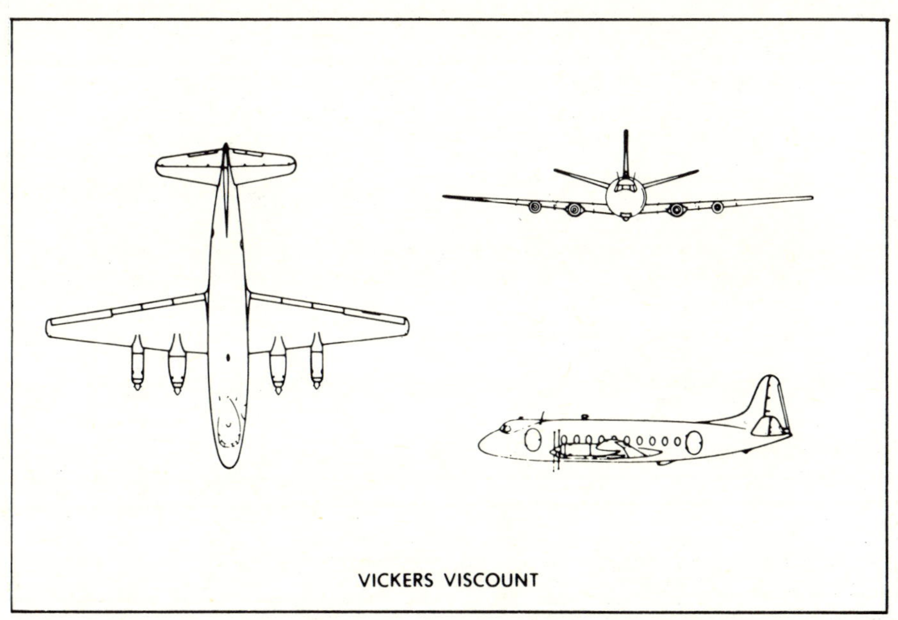

VICKERS VISCOUNT

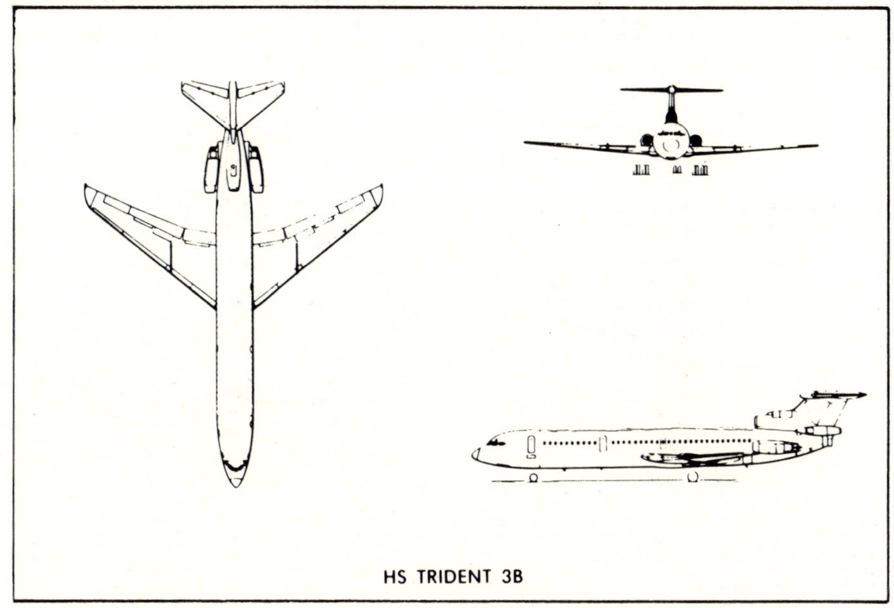

HS TRIDENT 3B

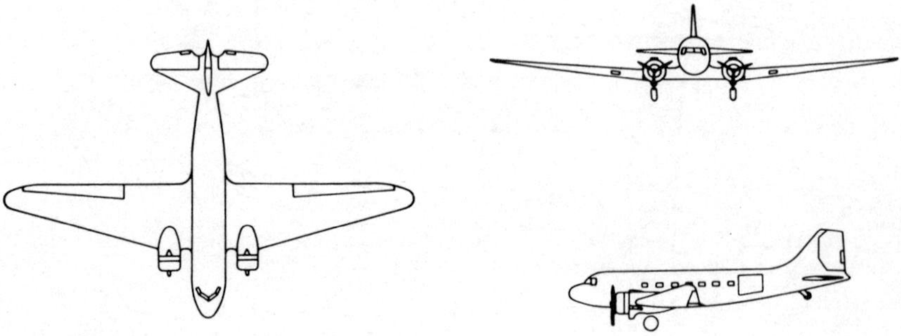

CAB/LI-2

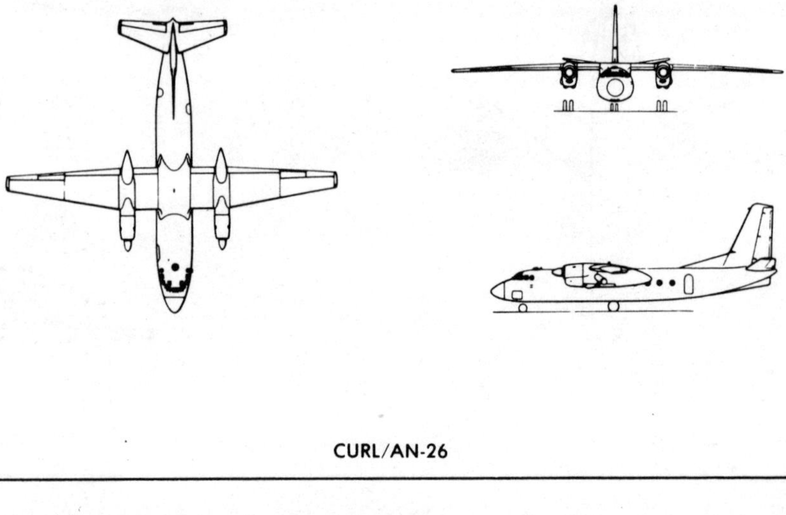

CURL/AN-26

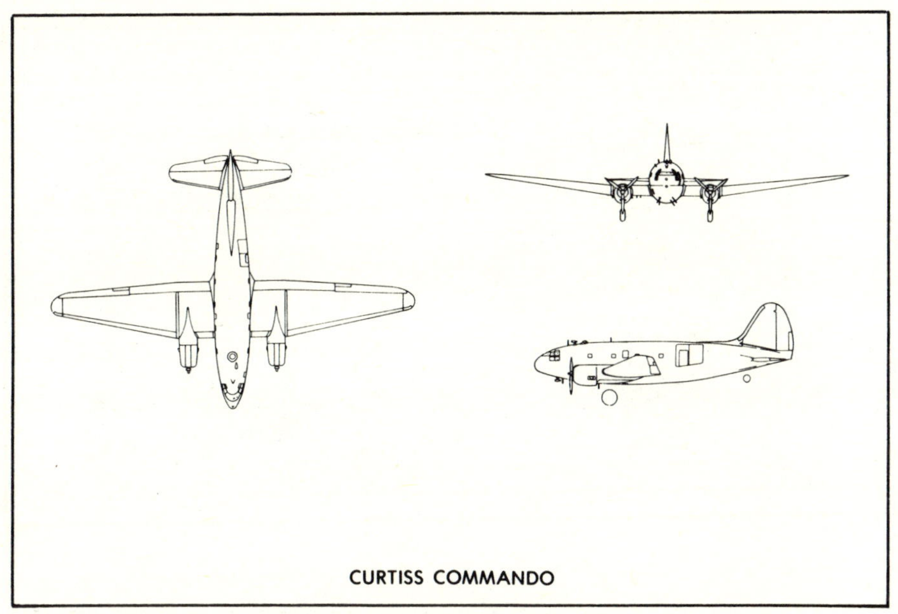

CURTISS COMMANDO

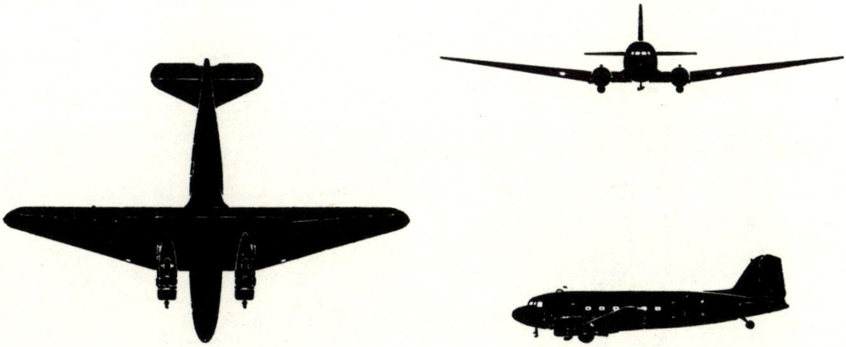

DOUGLASS SKYTRAIN

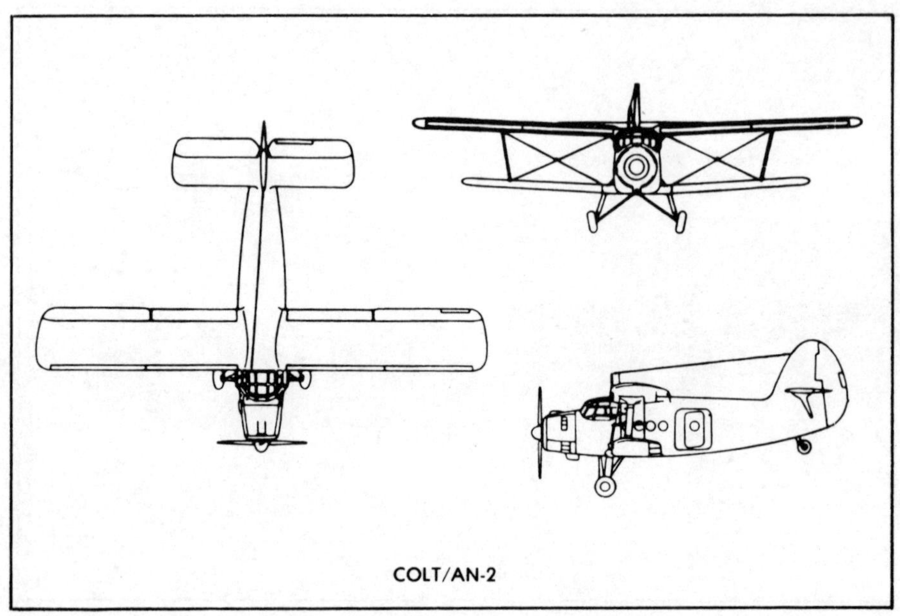

COLT/AN-2

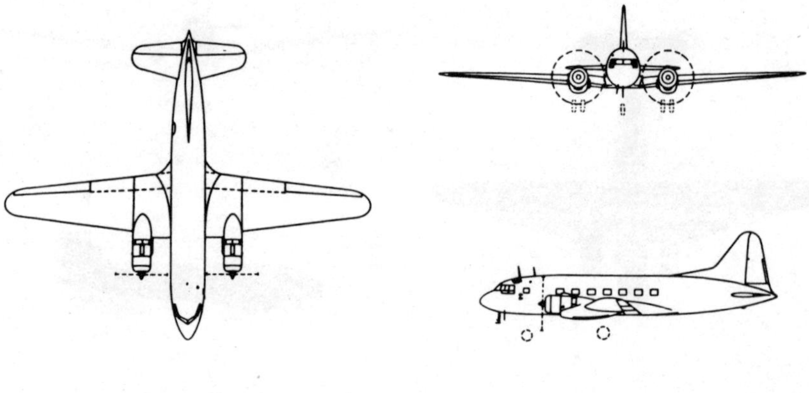

COACH/IL-12

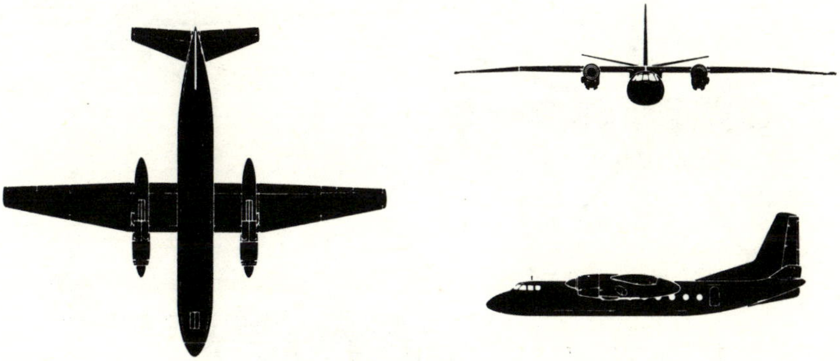

COKE/AN-24

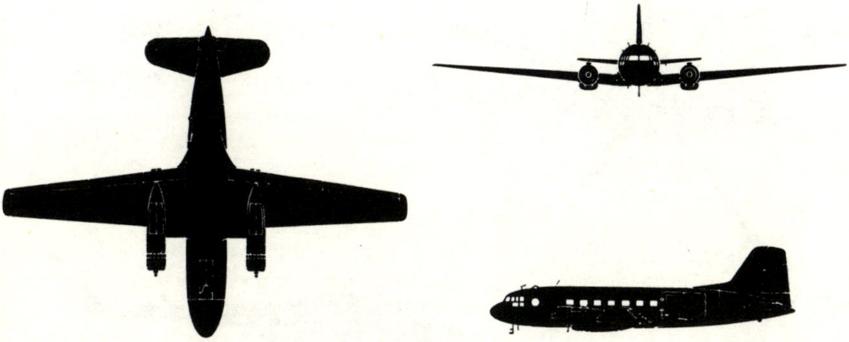

CRATE/IL-14

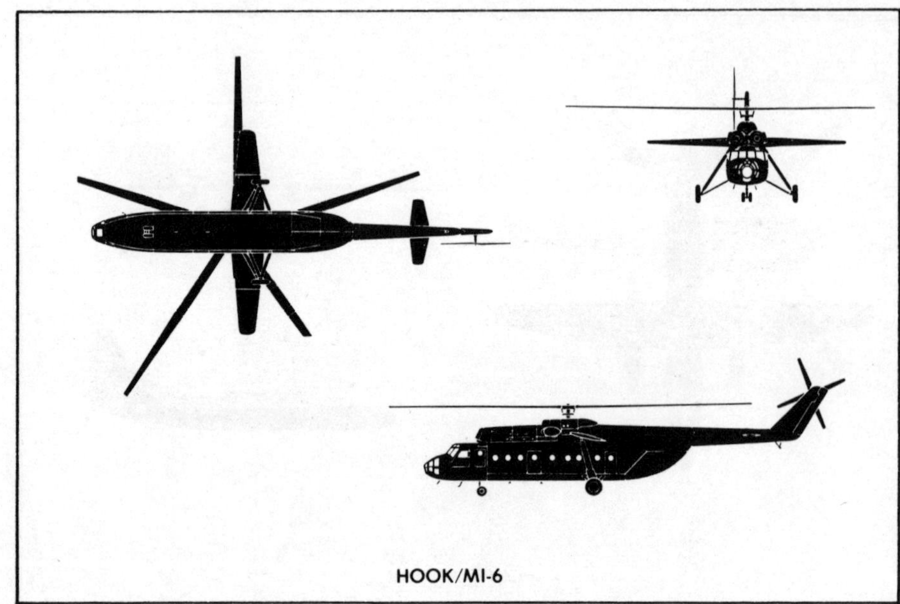

HOOK/MI-6

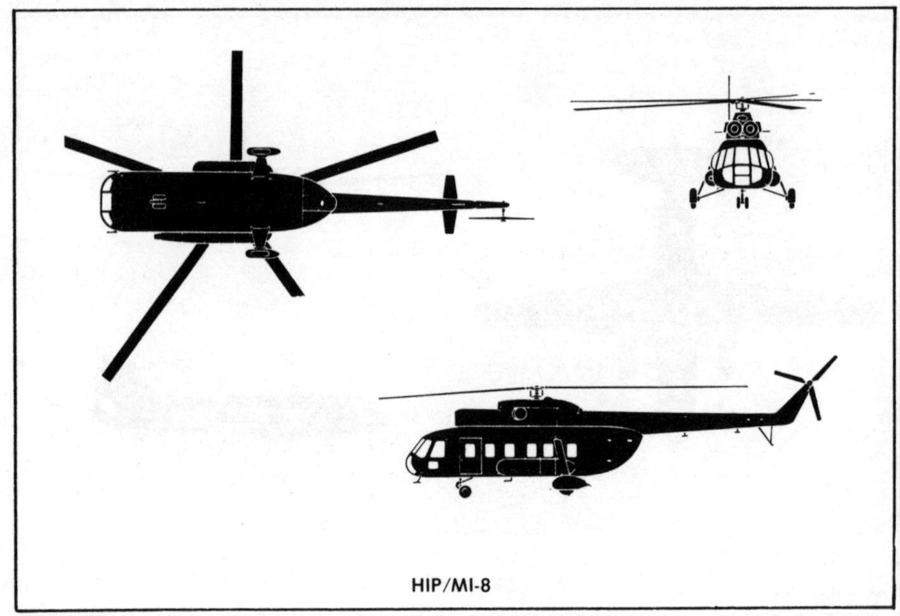

HIP/MI-8

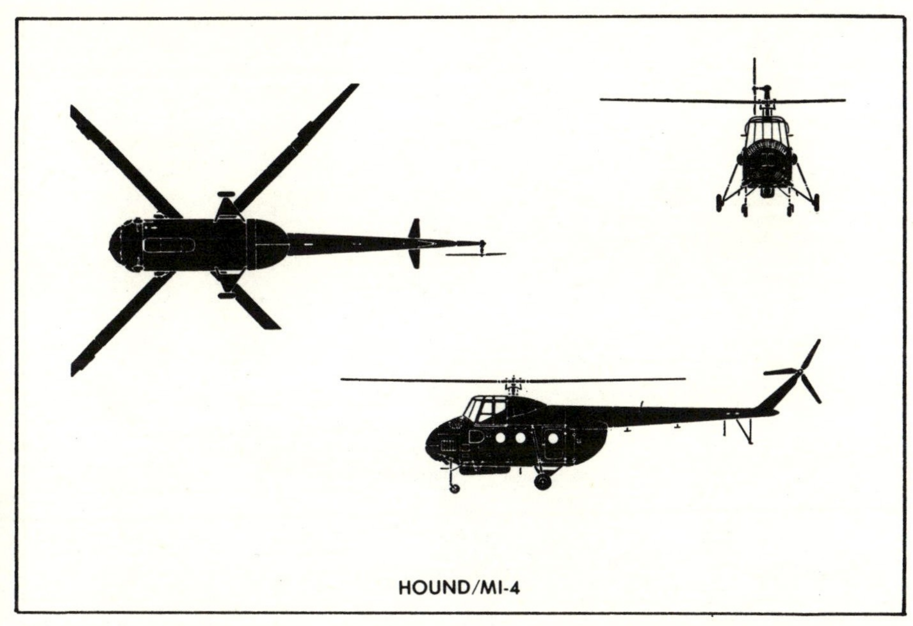

HOUND/MI-4

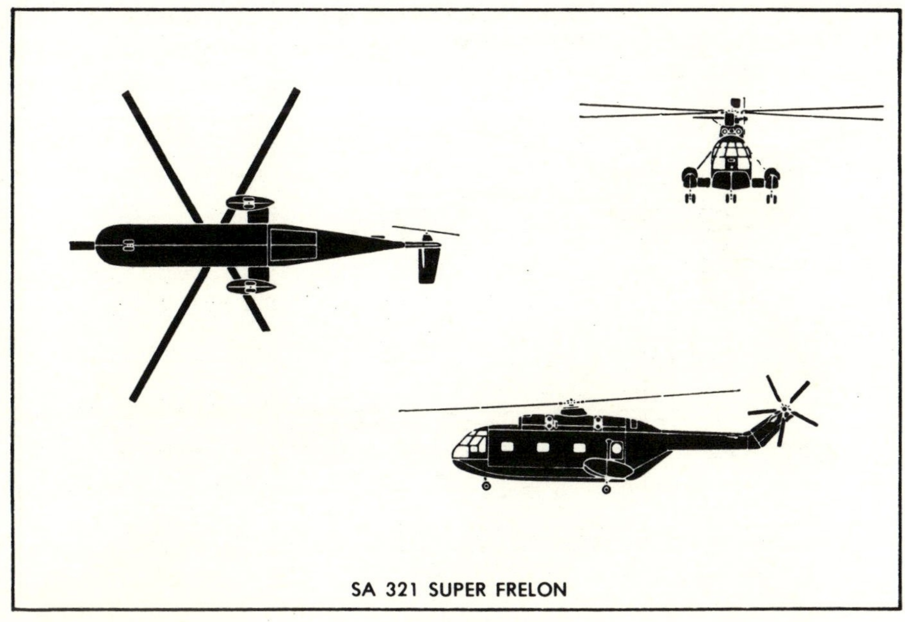

SA 321 SUPER FRELON

PRC MISSILES

System	Characteristics	Role
MRBM	IOC · 1966 Range · 600 nautical miles Yield · About 20 kilotons Configuration · Single stage Propellant · Liquid	STRATEGIC · Peripheral
IRBM	IOC · 1972 Range · 1,500 nautical miles Yield · 2-3 megatons Configuration · Single stage Propellant · Storable liquid	STRATEGIC · Peripheral
Limited-Range ICBM	IOC · Mid to late seventies Range · About 3,000 nautical miles Propellant · Liquid	STRATEGIC
ICBM	IOC · End of seventies Range · About 7,000 nautical miles Propellant · Liquid	STRATEGIC
CSA-1 SAM	Transportable medium-range SAM system. Six missile launchers per site. One missile per launcher.	AIR DEFENSE